HERE'S ED

or

How to Be a Second Banana...

by ED MC MAHON

New York

HERE'S ED

From Midway to Midnight

as told to Carroll Carroll

G. P. PUTNAM'S SONS

Contents

HERE'S ED

FOREWORD

This is not the story of my life and I'll tell you why.

Those who knew my idol, W. C. Fields, have told me that when a young writer asked for permission to write the story of his life, the great one replied, "Please do. Capital idea. Do it right away. I can't wait to see how it turns out."

I feel the same way Fields did. I'd like to know what my finish is. That's important to anyone who has ever done comedy. That's why we all live with that embarrassing feeling you get when you're in the middle of a yarn and suddenly realize that you've forgotten the finish . . . the punch line. Horrible feeling.

So, since I have no way of knowing the big, getaway finish to my life (where the ship is sinking and I tear off my life jacket and give it to Johnny Carson), this book must remain merely a collection of incidents, activities, and happenings that I still remember. Time, with a little help from an occasional toddy, could easily turn them into gross exaggerations, mammoth lies, or completely erase them from my mind.

But everything is as true as memory could re-create it and, in one way or another, is a milestone along the route that brought me to that seat on the right of Johnny Carson which I have occupied for over thirteen years, five nights a week, fifty-two weeks a year, exclusive, of course, of the nights Johnny takes off and I'm seated on the right of the highly experienced Joey Bishop or McLean Stevenson, John Davidson, Sammy Davis, Bob Klein, David Steinberg, Pearl Bailey, Joan Rivers, John Denver, Liberace, Karen Valentine, or

11

someone taking his or her first crack at the job Johnny does so well.

For that reason this book will try to give you a little background on that guy who holds up packages, demonstrates food and clothing, sells Budweiser beer, and talks to dogs while Johnny handles Raquel Welch, Ann-Margret, and other outstanding show biz personalities.

E. M.

THE GUARANTEE

It's hard to be an only child in the City of Brotherly Love or, for that matter, in Boston, New York, Detroit, San Francisco, St. Louis, and even beautiful Bayonne, New Jersey. Philadelphia's no more loving than any other city. I know. I've tried enough of them to be sure.

When I was a kid I changed towns more often than a pickpocket. I changed neighborhoods more often than a door-to-door Bible hustler. I was in and out of more schools than a chalk salesman.

They didn't know my name when I was a new boy in a New York City school so they called me Massachusetts because I had a Boston accent. So I tried to conform.

The following year, when we were again living in Lowell, Massachusetts, the kids at school didn't know my name so they called me New York.

There was a time in Philadelphia when they wouldn't send me to a local high school because of a scandal involving some of the girl students. It seems there was an epidemic of pregnancy. And this wasn't 1975! This was over thirty-five years ago when the world was young and still run by adults.

Today, I know that if you find a place dull, it's generally not the fault of the place. It's you. As the Bard almost said, "The fault, dear friend, is not in your city but in yourself." But it takes a long time to find this out when for a large part of your childhood and early youth you don't really live anywhere permanently.

As the twig is bent, so the tree will grow—which could be why traveling is such an intrinsic part of my life. Hardly a week goes by that I'm not doing something in at least one other state besides California. Many times I work in California and Nevada on the same evening.

One of the main problems when you travel a lot is how to find a good place to eat. Let me amend that. When you first start traveling, generally on a very tight budget, the problem is finding a *cheap* place to eat. As your circumstances improve, so do the places in which you dine. (Notice the switch from "eating" to "dining.") Dining is an activity very dear to my heart.

The first thing I do when I get to a city or when I'm going to spend any time in a strange place is to make the famous Ed McMahon Restaurant Survey. This is a very complicated research procedure that involves asking three people one question, "What's the best restaurant in town?"

Any three people will probably do, but the ones I ask are generally the cabdriver or chauffeur who drives me in from the airport, the bellman who takes my bags to my room, and the third is optional. It could be the manager of the theater or club where I'm playing, a cop, or some friend who, I know, has played the town.

This always results in two out of three agreeing.

Here's an example. I'm playing Kansas City and I'm on a diet which is making my life very dismal. Restaurants are out. I'm asking the bellman, "What is the best delicatessen in town?" Finally, Thursday, after three days of light eating, I felt fed up . . . or is it unfed-up? And I made my survey.

I asked my three random choices and the answer came back unanimously, Jaspers. Fine. I called Jaspers and said I'd like to come over for dinner after the show. The manager was very nice. He said they generally closed at ten but they'd stay open to welcome and feed me.

When I got there with my party the place was all but empty, naturally. But my survey had worked properly, the meal was excellent, the beer was good, the manager turned out to be a congenial companion, and we closed the place about one o'clock. I said, "I've got to go back there before the week is out."

Now, I'd called a pal who happened to be a banker in Kansas City. He was out of town but called me back on Friday morning and told me I was his guest for dinner that night at the best restaurant in town. Fine. No argument. McMahon was willing. Guess what restaurant it was.

Saturday morning an old Catholic U. pal of mine called from St. Louis to say he would be in K.C. that afternoon. He insisted on introducing me to the best restaurant in Kansas City. I thought I had an idea which one it would be. And I was right.

Now, back to my restaurant survey. The more you travel, the more you collect friends all over the country and the less you have to use the McMahon Survey. And another thing, if you *do* use the survey and you get three different answers, go on a diet.

I put this piece of information up front in this book in case anyone who is reading it happens to be on his way to a strange city. Try the Ed McMahon Restaurant Survey. See if it doesn't work.

And while on the subject of restaurants, my deep interest in such establishments brought about an awfully funny piece of business on the show one night.

I had just returned from a trip to Mexico, where the Ed McMahon Restaurant Survey had worked its magic and guided me to an excellent eating place in Acapulco. I'm ashamed to say I've forgotten the name of the spot. But I can recite the entire menu by heart.

I was telling Johnny about this gourmand's delight and happened to throw in that they had a funny little custom for encouraging informality and putting people at their ease, Mexican style.

"When you walk into the place," I explained, "if you happen to be dressed in a shirt and tie, the maître d' walks over to your table and quietly cuts off your tie."

"That's nothing," Johnny said. "There happens to be an informal little bistro in Edinburgh where, if you aren't wearing kilts, the maître d' walks over and cuts off your pants." Then he said, "You're not serious. What if you happened to be wearing one of those expensive dollar-and-a-half cravats you get at Tie City?''

"Makes no difference," I said. "It gets cut off a little below the knot. If I had a pair of scissors handy I'd show you exactly where."

"Well, I'm certainly glad you haven't," said Johnny, going into his world-famous impression of Stan Laurel.

As Johnny was saying this, I saw out of the corner of my eye that our producer, Freddie de Cordova, was at the prop man's table. He picked up a pair of shears, walked over, and handed them to me.

"This is about how far down on the tie they cut," I said, as I snipped off about half of Johnny's $22.50 Pucci tie.

By this time the studio audience that had seen the whole thing building up was in hysterics and there was nothing to do but go on with the bit. Aware what Johnny would do (you don't work with a guy for over seventeen years without getting some idea of what his reactions are), I laid the scissors on the desk and smiled as much like Ollie Hardy as I was able to.

As I sat there with a stupid grin on my fat face, Johnny picked up the shears, cut off the ends of my tie, and laid the scissors down on the desk, dusting off his hands as Stan Laurel would do.

I picked up the scissors and the studio audience went wild. They were way ahead of me. I took one end of Johnny's collar and snipped it off. He did likewise to me until neither of us had either ties or collars.

When it became my turn again my course was clear. I had to go to work on Johnny's coat and clip off a lapel. As I started to do this I saw the expression on Johnny's face. It wasn't that he couldn't get another coat (he's in the clothing business and makes a nice income), but he happened to be wearing a coat he was very fond of. There was some sentimental connection to it; and I got the message that we'd better wind up our tailoring routine.

Also, at the precise moment that we were destroying very expensive clothing, it crossed both our minds that this was a very bad thing to do at a time when there were a lot of people out of work who couldn't afford to buy clothes. And we knew if we went on to the lapels we'd have to go all the way down to the waist.

Just how Johnny communicated to me the thought he had about the bad taste of what we were doing, I can't for the life of me say. But he has often shown that consideration for others is more important than a quick and easy laugh. He's at his best when people come on the show so nervous they are almost basket cases. He brings them along and showers them with verbal bouquets of kindness until they begin to feel at home and relax.

I gather that a lot of the nervousness and tension shown by guests on the show is built up while waiting in the Green Room to go on. People have suggested to me that a lot of funny stuff must go on backstage among the guests in waiting. No way. That Green Room, I'm told, is a real compression chamber.

Each person is deeply involved in how he/she is going to look, and what he/she is going to say, and above everything else each of them is consumed with dismay that Johnny can waste so much time talking to whoever is on instead of coming directly to the "him/her" who is still sitting, fidgeting in the Green Room biting mental fingernails. . . .

I've strayed a little from the peripatetic nature of my father's business, which forced my mother and me to dwell in a lot of different places. But not for long. The result being that I always seemed to be a stranger wherever I was, even when I came back to someplace I'd been before. But not long enough. Is that clear?

In spite of all this—aggravated by a shyness I'm told I have since overcome—I might have been lonesome a lot but I was never bored. I had my fantasies. They told me where I wanted to go when I became a man. I always had enough time on my hands to keep my mind on the main chance, visualizing myself in a role I hoped would be my career.

Although my parents tried to settle down in one spot for the school year, in summer they were on the road. That was when I'd go to my grandmother Katie in Boston. Well, it wasn't exactly Boston, it was Lowell. And I didn't exactly go there. I was taken there. I was stashed there might be a better way of putting it. And nothing could have pleased me more.

My grandmother Katie was a dear, sweet lady who bore eleven children, nine of whom she raised, as the Irish say. And, as all grandpersons do, she found in her favorite son's only son—namely, me—a sort of living doll to play with . . . to spoil might be more accurate.

By and large parents are responsible for the day-to-day lives of their children as well as for shaping their character, hopes, and dreams for the future.

Grandpeople have had all that. They take the kid for a period of time—an afternoon, a day, a week, a summer—and they indulge him because it makes everyone happy. Grandparents want to be loved by the little people, having in many cases been forced out of the lives of their own children, and the little beasts respond in kind. What have they got to lose? Besides, they have no hangups about these benevolent old people, who know that after they've borrowed a grandchild for a while they can end what may have become a problem by returning the kid to its rightful owner.

But excuse me for all this cogitation on what I've seen to be the usual grandparent/grandchild relationship. Mine was different. It was something special and far less transient. I'll tell you all about it and about Katie Fitzgerald McMahon, my grandmother, later. That's not the point right here.

Our purpose at this point is to explain how you can be welcome in more than fifteen million bedrooms. First, get yourself a grandmother like Katie. Second, follow the advice given in this book, and do exactly what I did, step by step.

If after twenty-five years you haven't made it, your money—every cent you paid for this volume—will be cheerfully refunded.

THE SHOW BEGINS

Many who have in the past twelve years attended a taping of *The Tonight Show* know exactly how it goes, which is more than the cast knows.

In the sixties you stood waiting in line in the dull corridors of NBC's New York studios in Radio City. You were glad to be out of the rain, the snow, the sleet, or the heat. Pale-faced ushers kept you in line, told you when to move and where. Occasionally you saw "what's-his-name" or "who's-that-again" pass the line, smiling to be recognized en route to work. And, inevitably, you saw Bob Hope on his way to catch a plane.

When you finally reached your seat, if you ever did, you were so glad to sit down you didn't care whether you saw anything or not. Those in the coveted seats down front got a good close-up view of the cameramen's backsides. Those who were in the higher seats got a chance to see who had bald spots. And, as Johnny said, some of those in the higher seats got nosebleeds.

Now it's different.

Now you stand in line at the sprawling NBC studios on Alameda Avenue in San Fernando Valley and the one thing you don't have to worry about is snow. It sounds more romantic, right? You're standing only a scant mile from that glorious place that Dan Rowan and Dick Martin have immortalized as "Beautiful Downtown Burbank." You can see mountains if the smog is not too bad. But that doesn't keep your feet from hurting. If you've ever visited beautiful downtown

Schuyler, Nebraska, and loved it, you'll feel the same about "Beautiful Downtown Burbank."

The same ushers will keep you in line, tell you when to move and where. But now they're sunburned. Occasionally you'll see "what's-his-name" or "who's-that-again" smiling to be recognized en route to work, and occasionally you'll see Bob Hope on his way from his home a few blocks away to catch a plane.

If you finally reach your seat, if you ever do, you'll be so glad to sit down you won't care whether you can see or not. Those in the coveted seats down front will still get a nice view of cameramen's backsides, but today something new has been added: women's lib has seen to it that there are now some women camerapersons. And that's all I care to say about that except that at a recent taping, one of the camerawomen was wearing a long tight dress. This may have been because on *The Tonight Show* the crew never knows when it will wind up on camera. Or she might have been going to a party after work.

As she pulled back on the heavy camera pedestal to let me pass to the commercial area, her long dress got wound under the caster and we had to go to black while she untangled her wardrobe from the equipment. Maybe the libbers who want women to wear the pants in the family should recommend that they also wear them to work. Otherwise things are exactly the same in California as they are in New York.

Seeing accidents about to happen onstage is one of the rewards you get for standing in line to see our show. When you're in the audience and something unexpected develops you'll certainly see it before the director has a chance to put a camera on it. The night Johnny stomped on my foot—forcing me to buy five new toenails—the actual stomping was not seen by the folks at home. The mike picked up my cry of pain. All the camera picked up was Johnny's puzzled expression.

He had no idea what had happened, because I have very soft feet that squash easily and he was wearing very hard shoes.

The fact is that when things go right on an ad lib show (if

there is a right) it is never as funny as when they take a turn for the worse. Actually, things didn't go wrong when Johnny nearly crippled me. (Nothing is wrong that generates that kind of audience laughter.)

He was playing that deep, penetrating characterization for which he has become internationally famous; that deeply etched and beloved geriatric relic, Aunt Blabby.

In a fit of pique the sweet old lady stamped her little spiked golf shod foot petulantly. She prefers golf shoes to sneakers because at an early age she resolved never to become a little old lady in tennis shoes.

I only note this hilarious little incident that caused me to limp for a week, explaining that it was caused by an old war wound that acted up occasionally, because having it happen was just one of the rewards I have received for fighting my way up to being second banana. Sometimes I think I should have kept going and tried for first.

You never know the state of mind of an audience or what they came to see. My daughter Claudia told me that some friends of hers heard a young lady on line for the show in New York ask an usher if our Stump the Band routine was going to be part of that night's show.

When the usher said he was sorry but he didn't know, the lady said, "Gee, I hope so! I don't want to have to sit through Johnny's monologue for nothing." One wise guy on line in Burbank asked an usher who was the host for the evening. When the surprised usher told him, "Johnny Carson," the guy said, "Not again!"

Audiences are getting hipper and hipper. There must be many more cracks heard on line. Some enterprising usher should jot them down. It might make a funny routine. That would make a great book, *Confessions of a* Tonight Show *Usher.*

I'd stand on line myself and listen for a few cracks but I have other things to do while the audience is queued up. Also, it would be embarrassing if no one recognized me without my pancake makeup.

In reality, the show the audience sees, and which may suggest chaos in a Mixmaster, is very carefully organized confusion. Everything is thoughtfully mapped out and run through on the off chance that it will turn out right. Very few people will believe it, but I actually do rehearse the commercials. This is not because I feel any rehearsal is necessary, but because the sponsor has hired someone to rehearse me and that person has a right to make a living.

An interesting thing about rehearsing commercials is the fact that there is rarely anyone but me in the cast. Well, me and a dog.

Those dogs are very classy gentlemen and ladies and we've had every breed from mammoth St. Bernards and Russian wolfhounds to tiny Mexican Chihuahuas.

When we were in New York there was an English sheepdog we used a lot. Patrick was the hippest animal I've ever known. You've heard Johnny say to a guest, "I know you have to run," which releases the guest from the panel and gives him or her a chance to split. This is usually due to another commitment.

Well, there was a time when we had to time our show to get Patrick out of the studio because he was appearing in a Broadway show and had to be there for the opening curtain. Patrick knew his job and did it just great. He'd always be brought to the studio in plenty of time, and he'd discovered that while waiting for his turn to rehearse, the coolest place to relax was between the seats on the concrete in the cool upper part of the auditorium which, when we were in New York, was entered from the 7th floor.

When I arrived, I walked in on the studio floor, which was the 6th floor. So what I'm about to tell didn't happen because Patrick saw me. He probably didn't even smell me, although that's an idea that just crossed my mind and was suggested by the fact that Johnny makes so many cracks about my breath, which is always sweet as a baby's.

No. Patrick recognized my voice from afar. I always greeted the crew when I walked in with "Good afternoon, gentlemen." The moment Patrick heard this he jumped up from his position under the seats and trotted down to join me in the commercial area. Now that's a show biz dog.

The funny part of it is that Patrick was the only animal that ever refused the Alpo. What we do is, during rehearsal we give them just a taste of Alpo. Then when the show comes, they're ready for the full blue-plate dinner. But this day maybe Patrick had income tax problems or something. When I said, "Just wait till you see how Patrick digs into this bowl of Alpo Beef Chunks dinner," Patrick just sniffed it and walked away. There I was with egg on my face and a handful of Beef Chunks dinner.

Seeing this on the monitor, Johnny rushed around back to the commercial area, which the audience can see only on the monitor, and got down on his hands and knees and started to eat the Alpo. That's going beyond the call of duty.

Some of the things Johnny has done with animals amaze me. He'll handle snakes and reptiles that I wouldn't touch with a ten-foot pole—that's a basketball player from Warsaw. We get most of the strange beasts on the show from two sources—Actors Equity and San Diego. Almost a regular feature of our show is a gal name Joan Embry, who brings interesting animals up from the San Diego Wild Animal Farm. One night she brought three of the cutest little lion cubs you've ever seen and put them on John's desk. And right there on the desk, before millions of adoring television viewers, those little exhibitionists did what so many juveniles do, they went to the bathroom—all at once and all ways all over the desk and Johnny. But he still goes for the animals because people love them. You can tell by the "ooohs" and "ahhhhs" when Joan brings one on.

But there were none of these expressions of love and joy the time she introduced Johnny to a tarantula. She told him that if he didn't make any quick move or noise the big ugly bug wouldn't hurt him. So Johnny let her put it on the back of his hand and watched it stroll up his arm. I am telling you the gospel truth when I say there is not enough Budweiser in all of St. Louis to get me to do a thing like that.

In fact, I got good and scared by a Doberman pinscher once. It wasn't anything the dog said; it was just the mean way he looked at me. But that was nothing to the way a tiger once got me in his sights. The tiger was following a lion that looked and acted about as dangerous as Bert Lahr in *The Wizard of Oz*. So I wasn't too bothered. But the tiger had a look in his eye that told me he was out to prove how tough a tiger could be. And how tender he thought I might be. The tiger smelled me, and I smelled danger when the trainer said, "This is the first time he's ever been on television." The audience and lights and all can sometimes do strange things to animals. The boom man moves the boom, the tiger gets scared and attacks whatever is nearest to him, which happened to be me. Johnny was behind a desk but I was right out front there on the sofa looking like a tasty lunch. I knew there was no way the trainer could have held that 800-pound tiger. Fortunately, he suddenly got a whiff of the lion that had been on ahead of him. This distracted his attention. He began to sniff around the carpet in front of Johnny's desk, and I suddenly realized I had to leave the stage for a few minutes.

Another time with a ferocious animal, a jaguar, it was all set up for Johnny to give the beast ice cream because the word was that he liked this national delicacy. He came in quietly enough on a chain leash but, as in the case of the tiger, there seemed no way the trainer could hold him if he saw something on the stage he liked better than ice cream, namely Johnny or me.

Okay. Johnny's getting out the ice cream to give to the big cat. At the same time I happened to glance at the trainer and said, quickly, "Johnny. I don't think he's hungry." This surprised Johnny, who looked at me questioningly, and I pointed to the trainer's hand. There was blood pouring from three long, deep scratches. The cat had already clawed him. But the trainer's saying, "He won't hurt you, Johnny."

Johnny just looked at the blood and said, "Yeah, you may be right. He's probably not hungry. Anyway it's too late for ice cream." That ended that jaguar's appearance on *The To-night Show.*

I've strayed quite a long way from rehearsing commercials. The only other thing we rehearse is the music. Of course, Doc has to spend some time rehearsing his wardrobe. I asked him once where he bought that stuff he wears. "Are you kidding?" he said. "What makes you think I'd tell you and maybe some night we'd both show up in the same outfit?"

When Doc isn't there, Tommy Newsom conducts the band. He's just the opposite from Doc, very quiet, very conservative but, like Doc, a very good musician. He does a lot of the great charts Doc plays and he did my nightclub act. But just as we take off on Doc's clothes, we call Tommy Mr. Bland, the man who brought new meaning to the word "mundane." And that's our little family.

There are also a few personalities who have been on so often they, too, are like family. Occasionally they take over the whole show for Johnny. Sammy Davis is one of these. Which brings us to the show for which Sammy Davis walked in fifteen minutes before taping time and handed Doc the charts for a piece he'd recorded just that afternoon and wanted to introduce on the show.

Before anybody really thought about it, Sammy, Doc, and the band were rehearsing. But that rehearsal was what was being taped, before an audience, for the show that was going on that night. Of course it turned out great because there's no better bunch of musicians in the business than the men on *The Tonight Show.*

When we were in New York we started taping at seven thirty which took us to about nine P.M. This gave the boys upstairs in program acceptance enough time to bleep out whatever they thought was offensive before the show hit the air at eleven thirty. Sometimes I thought they bleeped right. Occasionally I thought their bleeps were offensive. I can actually remember when we couldn't say "pregnant" on TV. Now girls come on and talk about breast-feeding and all but reveal the source. Since we've been in California we start taping at five thirty in the afternoon and nobody worries much. The language of the seventies has become so permissive. It's astounding! Jack Benny once told me of his right to say the word "lousy" back in the days when he was the biggest star on radio.

Now I think some of the words I hear on prime time are lousy. Not that I'm a prude. It's just that I think there's a place for everything, so I think the words I'm talking about should be confined to school playgrounds and girls' slumber parties where they're most frequently heard.

The truth is that the promiscuous use of the really heavy words has seriously lightened them. It makes them worthless for use in those moments of stress when the fury of the moment might make you want to say something that's really hairy. But I rarely use such words. I did once. I'll tell you why later in this little catalogue of confessions. And also why I stopped.

About ten minutes before show time, Johnny and I meet in his dressing room and sort of psych ourselves up. And its very casual. After over fifteen years together on two different shows (the other was *Who Do You Trust?*) we understand each other's moves pretty well, so there's not much need for serious planning.

It's as if Johnny's the quarterback and when a line is snapped he takes the options. And right at this point I'd like to scotch a rumor. I could have said "put-down" or "deny" a rumor. But I prefer Scotch.

More people have asked me this than seems sensible: Does Johnny purposely put bad jokes in his monologue to get sympathy and bigger laughs because of his discomfort? No! No comedian ever did a bad joke on purpose.

He picks out the gags he thinks will go and tries them. Occasionally there'll be three on the same subject and Johnny tries a fourth. When it doesn't go, he admits this was in violation of the old comedy rule: Never do four jokes on the same subject. Sometimes he violates the old comedy rule of never doing *one* joke on the same subject. But never on purpose.

Personally, I think he has a pretty good record. Doc and I put him down when things go sour. But if you go back over the some 4,000 monologues he's done on *The Tonight Show* you'll find more than one great gag in every monologue that's worthy of a place in anybody's anthology of the 10,000,000 best jokes.

It might be very revealing to do a sort of *That's Entertainment* type of anthology of Johnny monologues, using the best gags of each. It would be an interesting picture of the way times, dress, morals, and Johnny's point of view have changed over the years. Imagine if someone had recorded all those monologues. What a great chronicle of the sixties and seventies. But could anybody handle all those monologues? It might get a little blurred.

All right. The audience is all seated and ready for the show. The warm-up is about to begin. I look at the audience. I welcome a few people who are still being seated and make some cracks about traffic. Then I look at them intently and say, "I can see by looking at you. I'm experienced in such matters. You are a drinking crowd." This generally draws applause. I don't know why it is that everyone likes to be thought of as a drunk.

A couple of more drinking jokes follow which I won't include here because I want you to laugh when you come to the show. Then follows a crack or two about Doc and his wardrobe and some praise for his band. Then I walk over to a hand mike on the side of the stage and as I pick it up to say the familiar, "And *now* . . . heeeere's Johnny. . . ." Across my mind's eye flashes a picture of a kid about six or seven holding a flashlight in front of his face, pretending it's a microphone.

He tries to be the entire cast of a radio show he's ad libbing as he stands beside the family Victrola that's supplying the music. Remember those big old mahogany things with a lid that lifted like the mouth of a rhinoceros and a needle you had to change every two or three records? That was the period.

And the kid was me.

I could have written, "the kid was I," but I've never been a show-off. I didn't go to Harvard. The closest I got was Boston College and Catholic University in Washington. And the utensil I used for a mike simulated the kind of equipment that didn't show up for years. I don't know how I knew what a hand mike would look like when invented, but I did.

I was the kid. To a certain extent, I think, practicing with that flashlight mike (it wouldn't even light) in my grandmother's parlor beside her treasured Victrola shaped my whole future, and, coupled with my father's carnival background, led me directly to the day I met Johnny Carson and my whole life lit up and went Bingo!

Most kids aren't too crazy about following in their father's footsteps. If he was very good at what he did the competition was too tough. If he wasn't, he set a fine example of what not to do. My father really set a fine example of what not to do, but he did it with such class, was such a strong character, that I guess I'd have tried to follow in his footsteps if he'd been Jack the Ripper.

Fortunately, he wasn't! More fortunately, the growth of radio as an entertainment and advertising medium paralleled the various types of work he did. So from my start as a carnival bingo caller, I slowly became deeply involved in the show business of selling—or do I mean the selling of show business?

Just let's say that with the help of my grandfather, who introduced me to radio, my father, who introduced me to his friends who were interested in the same thing he was—making a buck—I was able to put myself through college and into the spot that I enjoy so much five nights a week. It has led into so many other spots that I feel like a leopard.

As Johnny said one night, kidding me about the various activities I get mixed up in, "It isn't fair for the second banana to make so much money; he makes the first banana look like a pickle." May I say that is not true. Johnny does not look like a pickle. I have seen him in the locker room and there isn't a wart on his body.

GALENA CRYSTAL TIME

When Katie Fitzgerald McMahon climbed aboard a horse-car in Lowell, Massachusetts, to take all her kids, their lunches, and their sporting gear for an outing in the country, it was highly probable that the conductor of the car gave her a big smile and said to her cutely, "Are these kids all yours, now, or is it a picnic?"

It was a joke of the period and Katie Fitzgerald McMahon, who never let a straight line go by without swinging at it, must certainly have replied, "Sure, they're all mine and it's no picnic!" which was the required answer. And she did so without a flicker of the long lashes that shaded her beautiful, dark, deep-set eyes that were, as the Irish like to say, "put in with sooty fingers."

Katie was my grandmother and my friend. If it hadn't been for the summers I spent with her in Lowell, Massachusetts, I probably would have had no friends at all as a child. As it is, some of the kids I ran around with in Lowell, I still see. And still others, I'm sure, see me.

The Fitzgeralds of Massachusetts were a proud clan and they considered it sort of a scar on their escutcheon when their Katie married a man named McMahon, a master plumber. To them plumbing was something you used, not something you did for a living.

But Grandfather McMahon was no ordinary run-of-the-pipe, have-to-go-back-for-my-tools type of plumber. He was a plumbing engineer who could glance at a blueprint and tell you how many BTU's it would take to heat your building, and how much money it would cost. He must have done very well.

29

He had to. His house in Lowell was the size of a small hotel. For a while it got a new guest every year.

Katie was a large, capable, beautiful woman and I was a little hurt at fate, that Grandfather got to marry her before I had a chance.

It was he who got me interested in radio. He built them and was doing it long before every kid in the country was making a cat's whisker galena crystal set.

To make one of these the first thing you had to do was hook up with some guy who was a heavy cigar smoker. Father, uncle, or some friend of the family. He had to be rich enough to buy them by the box because that's what you needed to start with, a cigar box. It was the cabinet. One of my pals in Lowell swiped a cigar box from his old man and then found it still had three stogies in it. He didn't know how to get them back to his father and he was too thrifty to throw them away. So another kid and I helped him empty the box by smoking the contents in a haunted house on the outskirts of town. That day it really did house three moaning green ghosts. I can tell you this. I found out what was the sickest way to start making a radio set.

If my grandfather's wasn't the very first radio set in Lowell, it was certainly the first one that really worked well. Everybody in town who could possibly qualify for a "hello" from any McMahon, dropped in to listen to what was coming from a place called KDKA in Pittsburgh. It was actually the same feeling of being in on an incredible accomplishment that we later got from sitting in our homes and watching a man walking on the moon. Today nothing is too wild to predict. Donald Douglas once said, while his company was making some of the world's finest airplanes, that man might fly in space by 1980. Two years after he made that prophetic crack our astronauts were circling the world in equipment made by his company. It proved one thing to me. He didn't get into the office enough.

Always a little ahead of his time, my grandfather did things the way he thought best, not the way everyone else did them.

To make KDKA come true in Lowell, he had to have a very long aerial. My grandfather solved this problem not by having a mile-high rod of steel or a spiderweb of wire on the roof, but by winding aerial wire around the house like an armature.

It wasn't until the sixties that automobile manufacturers applied that idea to auto radios, thus eliminating those whips of wire so coveted by street punks in need of a weapon for a rumble.

For a while the mystery of how radio worked fascinated me. But I have the mind and the instincts of a hustler, as you will soon come to recognize. So it wasn't long before it dawned on me that there must be thousands and thousands of men like my grandfather who could make radios and keep them working. What would make people want to keep them working were people like that guy in Pittsburgh with a voice you could almost eat with a spoon. When he said, "And now KDKA is proud to bring you the dulcet strains of Danny Ditherow and his Dandies of Dansapation direct from the Dungeon Room of the luxurious new Triangle Hotel in the very heart of Pittsburgh, Pa.," he made you want to go there immediately. His was the voice of class. And he made "Pa." sound like an abbreviation for paradise. That is what I wanted to be able to do. He was what I wanted to be. And look at me now.

Do I have the dignity of an anonymous DJ in Pittsburgh, Pa.? No. But I do have the distinction, however dubious, of being the first nongolfer ever to head up his own Celebrity Golf Tournament. Those things have been slowly proliferating ever since Bing Crosby held the first one in Pebble Beach. Then, about two years ago, the action blew wide open and there were hardly enough golf-playing actors to fill the demand. So when they started to scratch the bottom of the barrel, they came down to me.

I was invited to be the host of the First Annual Ed McMahon Golf Classic in Moline, Illinois, and, as such, received a handsome compliment from a fine golfer, a great gentleman, and my friend—Sam Snead. When the tournament was over,

Sam said to me, "Ed, you may not know a bogie from a birdie but you're one hell of a host." My father would have been proud to hear that said of his son.

For a long time I wondered how guys like Glen Campbell and Andy Williams and some even lesser-known names suddenly were heading up their own golf tournaments. Now I know.

The people in Moline, Illinois, had been running a regular annual golf tournament that was attracting less and less attention every year. By 1975 they felt they needed some sort of PR stimulus and began looking around for a name to host their event.

This may now nail down how many celebrity tourneys there really are. I was the best name they could come up with. True, I didn't play golf, but I was on *The Tonight Show* more or less regularly and I had some reputation for hostmanship.

I was glad to help out. The fact that I didn't play forced me to figure some angle that would make my presence at the event meaningful, as we say in the business world.

In all the other celebrity tournaments, the celeb gets to go around the course with a few of the contestants because he's playing with, or against, them according to his game. With me it was different. The PGA has very strict rules about nonplaying "names" wandering around the course. They might create conditions antagonistic to the reflective calm needed for playing a proper game of golf.

Well, anyway, I figured out how to meet the players without playing to the gallery. When they came off the 18th green there was a tent called Ed's Place. Eighteen holes of tournament golf is a lot of work. That's one reason why I don't play the game. Games that are work I consider silly. But I do believe that God created alcoholic spirits to reward man for his hard labors, an old saying that I think I made up.

Adhering to my code, I stocked Ed's Place with some snacks, a lot of Budweiser Beer (some Budweiser Champagne and Budweiser Scotch) and when the players holed out I was there to greet them, shake their hand, and offer them a libation either for congratulations or condolence. After a couple it really doesn't matter.

Of course Ed's Place was a hit. No place with free booze has ever bombed. So next year we're continuing Ed's Place with a lot of fancy trimmings. But the thing that tickled me most was something one of the young players on the tour said to me. "Ed," he said, "I've been playing the PGA golf circuit now for over two years and the thing that made this celebrity event different from all the others is that for the first time I actually got to meet and talk to the guy whose name was up front."

The reason I had the guts to call this first shot "an annual event" is that we're going to do it again. And for that one I have another idea. It'll be a Disaster Wagon which follows the play. Of course, we can only do this the day we have the pro-am playoffs, and the whole thing is more for fun than money. So that's when the PGA has given me permission to have the Disaster Wagon.

I found a golf cart with a Rolls-Royce radiator and red, white, and blue awning. This will follow the play and when anyone gets into any bad trouble the Disaster Wagon will come to his assistance. It will bring succor to the suckers who drop their tee shots into water holes, to divot diggers who bury their balls in sandtraps, and to the slicers and hookers who go hunting for little Red Riding Hood among the trees.

The Disaster Wagon will offer them whatever assistance they need from booze to spirits of ammonia. It will be there when a golfer arrives, as many do, at that state of mind where he feels that if he's not going to win he might as well blame it on being drunk.

KATIE AND THE MARINE FIGHTER PILOT

Somebody once said the proudest person in the world must be a Texan who graduated from Harvard and became a fighter pilot in the Marine Corps. I blew Texas and Harvard. But I can tell you that being a Marine fighter pilot can make you walk mighty tall.

I missed the exaltation of seeing the light of day in Texas only by those few miles that lie between Detroit and Galveston. As for Harvard, I did go to college in Boston, which is near Cambridge, where Harvard boys turn into men.

There was a time when all male matriculants at Harvard, no matter how immature, automatically became "Harvard *men.*" If the same guy happened to go to Yale he was called a "Yale student." If he'd gone to the one in New Jersey they'd have called him a "Princeton boy."

But times change. You could hardly call the Harvard postgrad I saw not long ago sitting in the Yard discreetly nursing her baby while reading for her master's (why not "mistress"?) in electrical engineering, a "Harvard man." I don't know why it is that as many years as I spent in and around Boston in the days of Harvard's athletic eminence, I never felt the urge to wear the Crimson. But as I entered those years when a boy's head isn't the only place he's growing hair, I often had strange fantasies about stroking the crew at Radcliffe.

Those were the days when an international catastrophe that was later catalogued as World War Two was on the horizon. By the time I approached eighteen, men were beginning to answer the draft.

34

Every young man my age had to decide whether to be drafted and take his chances or volunteer and get to select the military service he'd feel good about dying in. That was when we knew and hated our potential enemy for crimes against humanity. It was also a time when war still suggested glamor.

Our elders who had fought in "the big war," as Fibber McGee used to call "the war to end war," still romanticized their carefree days in the mud of Flanders Fields.

But trench warfare didn't look like fun to me, so I set my sights on something a little more glamorous. I decided to take to the sky, to visit the Halls of Montezuma and the shores of Tripoli by plane as a Marine Corps fighter pilot. It was a high goal for a kid who up to that point had shown a very low profile to society.

There were a lot of steps to be taken; a lot of forms to be filled out, including my own. First I had to be eligible to join the Corps. Then I had to have enough schooling to become a fighter pilot. Then I had to pass all the *tests*, physical and mental. Then I had to prove I was fighter pilot material, intellectually and emotionally. Then I had to learn how to be a fighter pilot. All those were the easy things I had to do.

The hard part was convincing Katie that it was a perfectly safe way to sit out a war. I did this by a process of elimination. I pointed out that a man who was just in the Navy could get drowned. I cited films showing what terrible things happened because of Germany's undersea warfare. Again I pointed to the movies to show that all the Army held was a chance to get tired, get dirty, get confused, and get shot. They drilled you so much you figure to end up with a hernia operation.

The Marines, on the other hand, wore swell uniforms and were "the first to land." This meant that you had to jump out of an open boat into the surf, get your feet wet, and storm onto a beach full of unfriendly people firing at you at point-blank range. If you didn't catch your death of cold you could get shot.

A Marine fighter pilot, I pointed out, was above all this. When Katie pointed out that a Marine fighter pilot had another pilot shooting at him and if he happened to get in the way of one of those bullets there was no one to help him and no down staircase, I put it to her straight. I asked if she didn't think a Marine fighter pilot named McMahon could outfight any German alive?

Naturally she knew this to be true, so she grudgingly added her blessing to my parents', hoping, I'm sure, that I wouldn't make fighter pilot. But to be on the safe side she told me not to let them hurt me. I promised I wouldn't and I'm proud to say I kept that promise. To seal the deal, I proudly pointed to the windows that gave out onto the great wide porch that surrounded Katie's house in Lowell and said, "One of these days I'm going to walk through those French doors in my Marine uniform and I'm going to pin a pair of gold wings on your dress." She smiled, wondering, I guess, which of us would survive the other. I had no such misgivings. I knew I wasn't going to let a little thing like death abort my projected career as the golden voice of radio.

When I was twenty-one years and thirty-one days old on April 4, 1944, I received my wings and came home on leave to see Katie and pin them on her dress. We were both very happy, she to see me, me to see her, although she'd become very frail. She was addedly proud that she'd lived to see me accomplish my mission, and particularly happy that I was still very much alive.

Three months later Katie died. I wasn't able to get back to her funeral because of the intense training program I was involved in at the time. No one was allowed to leave base. And a grandmother's funeral was still looked upon as an office boy's excuse to go to a ball game.

I was told it was very impressive, and that Katie was buried in a plain black dress with only one decoration, my gold wings. My eyes mist up a bit just thinking about Katie. She was very dear to me.

THE SOUND OF A DISTANT SPEAKER

It was either Art Linkletter, Sam Levenson, the late Chaim Ginott, or Buddy Hackett who claimed one evening on *The Tonight Show* that he had actually seen a letter written by a little boy that said, "Good-bye forever. Am running away. You won't ever see me again. Can we have apple pie for dinner?" There was no signature because the kid probably figured his parents would recognize the handwriting.

I'm sure countless letters like that have been left for parents to puzzle over. Maybe they didn't all have exactly that same apple pie finish. Kids are different. Some prefer blueberry.

There's a classic story about a lady who sat rocking on her front porch one Indian summer afternoon in a small Midwestern town and watched the little boy who lived down the block go kicking his way through the leaves, waving to her as he passed. She returned his greeting and watched him move down the block, continuing to kick the leaves as if he had a personal grudge against each one of them. A few minutes later the lad passed the house again going the same way. Again he waved. Again she responded.

After his passing was repeated ten or twelve times, the lady finally gave in to her curiosity and asked the boy why he was doing what he obviously seemed to be doing, which was walking around the block. Without breaking his stride, and punctuating his words with added kicks at the leaves, he said, "I'm running away from home and I'm not allowed to cross the street."

37

I'm sure there are hundreds of similar stories about generations of boys who have felt the first stirring of the urge to seek adventure. In my father's day and his father's day they mostly ran away to join the circus. Most never ventured far enough to find a circus. A few did, and many of them became bums.

By that I don't mean to imply that circus folk are a bunch of nogoodniks. Some guys would have become bums no matter what they did. I'd rather cut my throat than cast the slightest aspersion on those who follow the big tops. I grew up in their shadows. With a mike in my hand.

I discovered circus folks to be generally happy-go-lucky, often extremely talented, fiercely loyal men and women who found a life-style just right for them. When you do that, you've got it made. The one thing they are not is "*home folks*."

They found that among the many lusts that lurk in the human heart and body, the one predominant in them was wanderlust. This is what lures kids away from their warm beds and Mom's apple pie. The train whistle in the night, the creak and rumble of wagons, the cry of animals, the thump of sledges on spikes, and the cursing of powerful men as they strain to raise tents in the dark before dawn, these are all part of the glamorous, picturesque life that filled a youngster's dreams. Luckily most of the kids never crossed the street. And the men and women of the circus, those who did, really never outgrew the magnetic pull the tan bark held for them as children.

But by the time I was edging into the running-away-from-home-to-join-the-circus age, I felt the call of something less tangible but more powerful—rádio. Some little show biz germ in my genes sensed its great potential. The stock market had deep-sixed and thousands of paper millionaires became bona fide paupers overnight. Nothing was left but radio to bring song and laughter, music and information, into the homes of millions who could no longer afford to buy tickets. The vaudeville acts people could no longer afford to see were finding their way into radio studios, and the phonograph records that cost a big 75 cents for a 2½ minute, double-faced 78 could be heard on the air for nothing.

It was no longer the call of a distant train whistle that inspired my young heart. Like all the other kids my head was clamped between earphones or my face was jammed into a loudspeaker. But I wanted something more than just to *hear* radio. I wanted to be the one who was *heard*. Other kids could be firemen, policemen, or cowboys. I saw only one future beckoning on the horizon. Radio was that beckoner. I was the beckonee.

WHY I DON'T LIKE PRUNES

I was born in Detroit, Michigan, but I could hardly call it my old hometown. Some of my more waggish friends have told people that six weeks after I hit Motown I had a fight with my Old Man about money and split, just up and crawled out of the house.

I deny this. I did not have any money problems during the first six weeks of my life. But I think my father did. He was always in search of some citizen who had money, or on the run from someone who wanted it. To give the fanciest name possible to the work my father did, I'd have to say he was a promoter, a fund raiser involved in midway-type carnival operations. He ran wheels of fortune or bingo games geared to help fraternal organizations raise a little scratch for their favorite charities. My dad's life may give some clue to why I'm so hooked on W. C. Fields.

My parents led a rather nomadic life, traveling on business and sometimes on advice of counsel or the local fuzz. I am told I arrived with great reluctance, threatening my mother's life.

The family Bible notes that I broadcast my first sound on a Friday afternoon at exactly two twenty-three. I weighed in at nine pounds fourteen ounces, which my father thought was heavy enough to carry the name Edward Leo Peter McMahon Junior. That's a lot of moniker to hang on a kid.

Ultimately, being a simple man, I clung to the short, sharp, Ed. Just plain Ed, that's me.

Nobody ever called me Junior because I simply would not

answer. I wanted a name, not a classification. I didn't like Eddie because that's what my mother and my father's pals called my dad. Naturally, I hated Edward. That was what everybody, my mother, my father, my teachers, everybody but my drill sergeants called me when I was in trouble.

The drill sergeants, as you must have divined, called me Mac. That's what they called everybody. Nevertheless, I have stuck staunchly to the name I chose as a little boy, even though it gave me trouble around 1961 when Alan Young, the Canadian comedian, began to pal around on television with a horse named Ed. Why I chose it I don't know. It must have struck me as a good strong name. At least it was one I owned. No one else in the family was using it.

It's interesting trying to remember deep into your childhood. Once, when George Maharis was on *The Tonight Show*, he claimed he could actually recall his infancy, the early days in hospital, even the actual birth. I happen to think this is a lot of malarkey . . . if not Maharis. But I can remember when I was five years old and played a return engagement in a hospital.

Oddly enough, it was again in Detroit. And, oddly enough, to use the old Smith and Dale joke, that was my ailment—a pain in Detroit. I was in to have my tonsils out.

Inspired perhaps by subconscious memories of my being in a hospital when I was born, I was frightened stiff.

I lay there, a pale, skinny little kid, hardly noticeable against the white walls of the corridor. I was parked outside the operating room, waiting for my turn. I've always wondered why they don't leave the operatee in his room until the operator is ready for him. Why stack them up outside the operating room like cars at a car wash?

Finally, I distinctly remember a guy in a white outfit including head covering and mask pushing me and my cart through a wide doorway and another all-white figure placing a cone of what I now know to be gauze over my nose and mouth and telling me to breathe deeply. As I did so the white figure became a sort of free-form ghost.

When I awoke the ghost was gone and so were my tonsils. They asked me what I wanted to eat and like a small idiot I ordered, of all things, prunes. I don't know why. I never particularly liked prunes. I've never ordered prunes since. This is possibly because the skin of a prune, as it always seems to do, stuck to the roof of my mouth.

If you've ever had a sore throat and a piece of prune skin stuck to the top of your mouth, you know it's no way to spend even a small part of your fifth year on earth.

I mention all this because that tonsilectomy at age five taught me a good lesson. Stay out of hospitals. I did so for about forty-four years when, one evening down in Florida, I fell getting off a boat. As Bill Fields might have said, "I was keelhauled while debarking!"

I can almost feel the concussion of your thoughts rushing to conclusions. It has been definitely established that that was *not* why I fell. I fell because while I was working my way through Catholic University I repeatedly flunked the course on how to get off a yacht. It was a very tough course for a kid like me who had to hustle to make tuition payments and lab charges. I had no place to practice.

FROM PARLOR TO TRUCK

Katie, like the man she married, was a worshiper of anything new that promised to become tomorrow's commonplace. So the radio was always "on" in her enormous house in Lowell where I spent my summers and enjoyed the goodies that were constantly available in the queen-sized kitchen, which was so big and important it had its own bathroom. So I grew up hearing a lot of radio and gaining a knowledge of what made it work. Thus was planted a strong longing to become a broadcaster.

If you find the idea of a kitchen with its own bathroom an interesting idea, remember my grandfather was a master plumber. And his plumbing office was right off the kitchen because that's where all the action was. Katie's parlor and huge formal dining room were used only twice a year, Thanksgiving and Christmas. And for wakes.

So, from the kid in the kitchen, I became the kid in Katie's parlor talking into a hand-held flashlight, announcing a program of music that was issuing from the Vic.

It made me feel pretty special to know that Katie loved me enough to allow me to put on my "radio shows" in that large, ornate, generally dark room that nobody was allowed to enter. From this sanctum sanctorum issued forth *The Ed McMahon Show*. Generally this consisted of selected readings from *Time* magazine, interspersed by Rudy Vallee and his Connecticut Yankees, Guy Lombardo and his Royal Canadians, and God only knows who else with his who knows whats. Then I'd repeat something like I'd heard the night before, such as,

"And now, ladies and gentlemen, from the beautiful sea-green ocean-view room high atop The Breakers Hotel in Omaha, Nebraska, we bring you the rustling rhythm of Rusty Ranger and his Colorado Rustlers." It didn't make any difference what I said because I never had an audience. Even Katie didn't take the time to hear me broadcast.

I take that back. There *was* an audience. Always. My dog. His name was—I know you're not going to believe this, but it's true—his name was Valiant Prince. We made a fine couple walking along the street together, Edward Leo Peter McMahon and Valiant Prince. Just a boy and his dog. Valiant Prince was very faithful. He attended all my broadcasts, never bothered me, never barked. I think this proves how valiant he was.

I was fascinated by the voices of men like Graham McNamee and Milton Cross, Norman Brokenshire, Jimmy Wallington, and Frank Gallup. But Paul Douglas, whom I used to hear on WCAU in Philadelphia, had the personality I liked best. He sold Chesterfield cigarettes and he sold them right to the people who bought them. His voice wasn't aimed at English teachers or elocutionists. He said "ya" for "you" and made other departures from the overcultured tones of most radio announcers.

"Ya gonna like the taste of Chesterfield. It's got ABC . . . A, always milder . . . B, better tasting . . . C, cooler smoking. ABC . . . Always Buy Chesterfield. They're milder." And when Paul said "they're milder" you knew that nothing, not even the smile of your firstborn baby daughter, had ever been so mild.

I still haven't gotten over being angry that when they made the film of *Born Yesterday* they gave Paul's part to Broderick Crawford. Not that he wasn't fine. He just wasn't Paul Douglas.

The most important thing about my trying to sound like Douglas and other important men on the air was that as I imitated my idol I began to realize that I, too, had "some kinduva" voice. You know how you can look in the mirror and see that you're perhaps a little better-looking than a lot of people. Well, you can also listen to your own delivery and make the same kind of a fair judgment. At least you *think* it's fair.

But play is play and fun is fun and my make-believe in Katie's parlor became as pointless as sighting an empty rifle. I wanted to get my hands on a real microphone, to hear what my voice sounded like when it came out of a speaker. I wanted to know what reaction I might get from those who heard me. It was an urge that grew stronger and stronger.

It came from the same source that made my father turn from the plumbing business to what was—let's face it, no matter what I choose to call it—the carny business.

Finally, when I was about fifteen, my father was running a big fund-raising thing for the Kiwanis Club in Lowell and had rigged up a sound truck to roam the streets plugging the affair. No one will ever know how I bugged him to let me ride the truck and talk into the mike.

Ultimately he gave in. That was my debut into the field of communication, riding in the back of a truck urging the people of Lowell (who couldn't see me) to partake of the pleasures of the swings and round-abouts, the cotton candy, games, rides, and the whirling wheels of fortune. To say nothing of the sideshows featuring girls "dancing as you have never seen them dance before."

As I was never allowed to see them dancing, it might have been true.

OLD BOY COMES HOME

I have a recurring fantasy.

I become Pope or President of the United States or Governor of Oklahoma or Mayor of Newark, something really important; so important that I, as "an old boy," am invited to speak at the graduation ceremonies of a certain institution of lower learning that we shall call Southwood Academy, to protect the guilty.

I shall open my remarks with the first and only verse of a song I wrote about the school.

> O Southwood, Old southwood,
> To you I raise my lid!
> Southwood, I would die for you . . .
> And damn near did!!

Southwood is a Catholic boarding school outside of Philadelphia. It was there that my parents once decided to stash me while they went caravaning about the country in pursuit of the elusive buck. I am convinced that my sojourn at Southwood affected my life more than any time I did in any other service or institution . . . and all for the worse. Would you believe that as a result of having lived at Southwood, I was thirty-seven before I could even look at a scrambled egg?

Students were banned from the kitchen for good reason, but from what came to the table, I imagined that instead of adding a little milk before they scrambled the eggs, they added Portland cement and moistened the mixture with Philadelphia Harbor water. This was then mixed vigorously and put into a pie plate, placed in a 400° oven, and baked for six hours. Or perhaps it was fried at high heat with a minimum of grease for seventy-five minutes. Possibly they just placed it over actively boiling water and let it stand for a day and a half. Or it might have merely been vulcanized.

When it came to table, it was still in the pie pan and ice cold, and served to the students in wedges like Mom's apple pie. It even had a crust. This was simply a topping of carbonized eggs. If you survived breakfast you were allowed to go to chapel and give thanks. If you survived chapel you went to classes.

Sunday was always a banner day at Southwood, particularly for us lonesome kids whose parents never came to see them because they were never anywhere in the area.

Creamed chicken with dumplings and mashed potatoes was the standard Sunday meal. The only thing wrong with this weekly treat was that the mashed potatoes tasted like dumplings and the dumplings tasted like modeling clay. The creamed chicken had no taste at all.

The only thing worse than Sunday dinner was the rest of the day. Some lucky kids had parents who came and took them for a day's outing. For the rest of us there was only the prospect of a rousing afternoon in Germantown, which has yet to capture the title of "entertainment capital of the world."

When Sunday night rolled round, parents heading for home left their kids sadder than the ones who hadn't been visited. And as night shadows fell, everyone looked out through a pall of gloom toward the coming week.

But the coming week looked like a barrel of laughs compared to the prospect of Sunday-night supper. This was cheese, baloney, and potato salad. The very thought could have made the late Adelle Davis give up in despair and put in with Angela Davis.

I love baloney today. The business I'm in proves that. But, as with the scrambled eggs, it took me a long time to get back into the company of men who really enjoy that succulent sausage. The potato salad was oily, with little pools of some sort of light motor oil that had seeped out of the potato mess lying stagnant around the edge of the plate. The cheese had been sliced so long before that it had begun to curl up and harden around the edges to match the baloney.

If all this sounds exaggerated, please believe me it is essentially the truth.

They didn't dare show us any of those old Warner Brothers prison movies with Pat O'Brien and Frank McHugh banging their cups for better victuals. It would have inspired us to do the same. So we just lived on in our little blue uniforms, going to classes and "playing" in the yard or being punished.

Each day of happy, carefree rollicking inevitably ended in some kind of fight. Not that we disliked one another or had anything substantial to fight about. It was just our only way to work off our aggressions. I remember what I think was my first important and only fight. It left me so terrified that from then on I tried not to get involved with anyone. That way nothing could lead to a fight. But it led to a lot of loneliness.

I don't remember what started the battle. It wasn't with fists. It was with rocks, a sort of snowball fight but with good, big, genuine stones. And it didn't last long. I happened to hurl a big hunk of granite at the moment the other kid—I think his name was Charlie—was leaning over to pick up some ammunition and my rock landed right on Charlie's thumb. The war stopped immediately and everyone gathered around to watch Charlie's thumb swell up and become a rainbow of glorious colors. I didn't know that the world is full of people who have survived crushed thumbs. This is the sort of thing they should teach kids in schools like Southwood. No boy should ever be allowed to get as frightened as I was because of my ignorance.

Like most boarding school parents, mine sent me elaborate presents but no money. Some of the things I received were embarrassing. There was the sled. You not only could steer it, but it had, of all things, a brake. In those days, while some kids had Flexible Flyers that could be steered, no kid's sled had a brake. You just dragged your foot.

One day I saw one of the nuns pushing a little kid on my fancy sled. Before I could protest, she accidentally pushed him a little too hard and he started down a steep hill with all sorts of obstacles like a schoolyard and a playground in his path. I took off down the hill after him, not worried about the kid, but about my sled.

With horror I watched it follow a slalomlike course through the playground, missing the swings and things as if the kid were steering it. The law about God protecting children and drunks had apparently been invoked. I kept hollering, "Use the brake!" But that kid knew nothing about brakes. He probably had his eyes closed. I would have closed mine. He was yelling, screaming is a better word. And while all this was happening, instead of going to call an ambulance or something, the nun was standing stock still, praying. She must have been pretty good. She prayed him right into a soft snowdrift entirely unhurt.

Seeing that really made me believe in God. How could I doubt the presence of a force that had saved my sled? Then I got to thinking about it and wondered if she were really praying for my sled, or for the kid, or for forgiveness for taking my equipment without permission. Perhaps she was afraid that if this were found out, some higher power would punish her as she and the other sisters punished us kids.

One of the most exotic ways they had of reminding us that we had transgressed was a slashing wielding of a yardstick, normally used as a pointer. I have been told by others who attended Catholic schools in the thirties, and even later, that this was in no way unique to Southwood.

There was one wiry little nun. She was only about four feet tall and she probably hated me because, skinny as I was, I towered over her. Most of the kids she'd grab by the ear and twist. That smarts. She had to stand on tiptoes to grab my ear and it must have embarrassed her. She'd haul me up in front of the class, the yardstick in one hand and, standing on tiptoes twisting my ear, she'd let me have it right behind the knees. It's a very tender spot, probably first discovered by Torquemada.

Well, one day when the class was about to be given the privilege of seeing Edward Leo Peter McMahon get caned, I decided to stop taking it like a little soldier and to make as much fuss as possible and try to shame her. As she swung at the back of my knees I yelled bloody murder. I collapsed in pain. I limped and pretended to be crippled. And the whole class laughed like the bunch of little demons we were. But the reason was she hadn't hit me. She had stopped her stroke about two inches from its mark, just as I began my preplanned reaction.

Angry, red-faced, made to look foolish before my peers, I remembered the sled incident and made up my mind to one thing. Some nuns you can't trust.

I write this hoping that it will save some boy from going through what I did at Southwood, where I was constantly ill or on detention for deeds inspired by unhappiness and frustration. I had to be kept out of school a whole semester to recuperate from Southwood.

DEAR OLD GOLDEN RULE DAYS

When people ask me where I went to school, my answer has to be, "Where didn't I?"

Mine wasn't much of an education, but it was different. Possibly it *was* an education, more effective because more challenging than the conventional way of going to one elementary school, one junior high, one high school, one college, and then on to whatever. I went to so many schools that I find when I try to think back the only ones I'm positive of are the colleges—Boston College and Catholic University.

As part of my educational experience I became a commuter long before most men get into that generally unsatisfactory way of life. We had moved back to Bayonne, New Jersey, from New York City while I was attending P.S. 23. So, naturally, I finished out the term in New York.

We'd lived in Bayonne before moving to Manhattan, but I hadn't gone to school there because, as I mentioned, I got very sick at Southwood and had to stay home to recuperate. That year in Bayonne when I was kept out of school was one of the happiest of my childhood. I'd stroll along the Kill van Kull, which ran right through town and also through the Standard Oil of New Jersey refinery. This gave the stream a fragrance not unlike that enjoyed while picnicking on a warm afternoon in Lincoln Tunnel.

I'd climb around the oil barges that were waiting to be loaded or unloaded and kill time till my less lucky friends got out of school. I don't know why I never ran afoul a truant officer

but I never did. Maybe Dad made some kind of a deal. I was—
or should have been—in the fourth grade.

When my buddies got sprung from school we'd do smart
things like swimming in the oily waters of the Kill. This was
dangerous not only because the water was so polluted, but because the channel had been dredged very deep to allow the oil
barges to come in. This created a vicious current. It eddied
and boiled and dragged you way under sometimes. A couple
of kids were drowned.

To add to the charm of this lunatic swimming hole there
was the ferry that plied between Bayonne and Staten Island.
It cost a nickel a ride. But who had a nickel? What kid would
blow that kind of dough on a trip he could make for free merely by risking his life?

If it weren't that my soul is deeply akin to anything aquatic,
I probably wouldn't be alive today. Get this. We used to climb
out to the end of the ferry slip and wait on those twenty-foot
pilings for the ferry to come slamming in. The pilot reverses
the props to slow the boat. This churns up the water at the
stern of the boat. It was into this roiling, boiling mini-mael-
strom that we dived from the top of the piling.

Why we didn't wind up in the propellers, only God knows.
But we were all very good swimmers. Once in the water we'd
swim across the Kill van Kull to Staten Island. There was a
pretty nice beach there, South Beach, and compared to
Bayonne, Staten Island was a swinging place. But that's not
why we made the swim. We swam there for only one reason.
To swim back. Later, when the Bayonne Bridge was finally
completed and we could no longer hitchhike on the currents
created by the ferries, we hitchhiked across the bridge on
trucks.

Besides risking my life foolishly in Bayonne, it was where I
started my first business enterprise. I was the first of many
lads to open a lemonade stand only to learn that if it cost you
eleven cents to make your product and you sell it for ten
cents, the volume will not make up for the loss.

Then I went into the shoeshine profession. I made myself a

box, bought some polish and brushes, stole some old towels from the linen closet, and scrammed over to an amusement park near where we lived in Bayonne. My dad had a couple of concessions on the midway there, and also a gambling casino, which was legal at the time. It was a great place. There was cotton candy, games of chance, barkers, rides, music, and circus acts.

These distractions made me lose interest in shining shoes. But I learned one thing in that park and from living in Bayonne, something I'm glad I've never forgotten: The color of a man's skin has nothing to do with the kind of man he is. So today there isn't a prejudiced bone in my head.

There was a large Japanese colony in Bayonne. Most of them were acrobats, tumblers, or jugglers in the circus acts. I got very chummy with the sons of these people in spite of the fact that their lives were very different from mine. They were very disciplined. Maybe that's what I found attractive, feeling the need for a little more discipline in my life. Possibly it was the example set me by those Japanese boys that inspired me to be as disciplined as I am today.

Whatever it was, I know why I used to like to go home with them after school. There would always be cookies and milk waiting, and there was always some for me. But what I liked more than the waiting snacks was the waiting mother. There was seldom anyone waiting at my house. Their homes were immaculately clean and calm. There wasn't a lot of that at my place.

This early association with the Japanese taught me to judge people by their merits, not by the color of their skin or the shape of their eyes. And when I wound up a member of World War Two, I spent many long evenings defending the people we were fighting. I was called "Jap lover" and "nigger lover" a lot. I felt I had to stand up for people against all man's inhumanity to man. I think I suspected there was a "family of man" before that ringing phrase was invented. Now I wonder if the women's movement will ever try to change it to the "family of persons."

I used to argue that the Japanese had been forced into an economic war that they didn't want, just as we were. They were fighting for their country, just as we were. And today, look at Japan and America, deeply involved with each other economically and industrially.

Looking back on my wartime attitude, as well as how I felt about the race riots and civil rights marches that came later, I guess I was a little ahead of my time.

Of course, like every other kid I sold *The Saturday Evening Post*, which netted me prizes like a pair of roller skates and a bicycle. With all that mobility I added the Bayonne *Times* to my *SEP* route. The paper cost a penny and I sold it for two cents. I wish I could find something today on which I could make 100 percent profit on every sale. But the competition was fierce. You had to sell your papers on the basis of the news. So every one of us became a newscaster. I wouldn't say we lied about the news. I'd rather say we bent the truth in a way that modern advertising pros call "idle puffery."

One boy would be hollering, "Fire levels Bayonne bank!" Another with the same paper might be featuring "Auto thieves threaten downtown area!" A third would be featuring, "Police nab millionaire in tax fraud!"

These were all based on some story in the paper, just blown up a little. "Fire levels Bayonne bank!" might have been a grass fire along the bank of the Kill van Kull. You sold your papers on the interests of the people. The financial people bought from the kid with the bank story, merchants in the downtown area bought the car thieves story. The car thieves also bought it. And the man who had cheated on his income tax bought the tax fraud spiel.

I'd buy fifty papers an afternoon and sometimes I'd sell out. Sometimes not. After all, I only had to sell twenty-five to split even. Which reminds me of a crack Georgie Jessel made to me one afternoon at Santa Anita. "I sure hope," said Georgie, "that I break even today. I need the money."

A WILD TIME IN THE TUNNEL OF LOVE

Those schoolless months on my own in Bayonne helped me overcome the shyness I had inherited from my mother and brought out all the aggressiveness I got from my father. I resolved never again to let anybody—parents, teachers, priests, or nuns push me around or humiliate me. I became my own little boy.

When they opened the Bayonne-Staten Island Bridge, Staten Island offered a medal to the first boy who ran across it. I resolved to win that medal. And I did. I later traded it for a Swiss Army knife. Who wouldn't rather have a tool like that than a medal with the gold wearing off? I did a lot of training to win that knife. And winning taught me that if you want something badly enough you have to think about how to get it, prepare yourself for the job, and then try harder than everyone else.

With this new "go" power, I began to get into almost everything that came along. I became the leader. I organized trips and planned adventures. One of these almost cost me my young life. We were exploring the old amusement park on the other side of town. I was considered thoroughly qualified to lead our small group into that closed and shuttered place because my father knew all about such layouts. My pals knew this because I told them. It was like a surgeon's son convincing his chums that he could take out tonsils.

Like every other amusement park in the world, the one we invaded had a concession called the Tunnel of Love. Since all of us were approaching that age when we began to realize that

55

there was something called love, and that it wasn't exactly the same as what you felt for your mother and father, we decided to explore the tunnel and discover what was this thing called love. Breaking in was the first step in the research process.

The park had not merely been closed for the season, it had been shutdown for several years. The buildings were really unsafe. And the whole place smelled strange, kind of like a zoo. But does a kid pay any attention to such matters? We were all concentrating on not being too scared if something suddenly popped out at us the way things did in the Old Mill, a less erotic name for the same ride. The Old Mill became the Tunnel of Love when some concessionaire realized that the scary objects that popped out at people gave girls an excuse to throw themselves, overcome with fear, into the arms of their escorts.

As we groped our way along the tunnel we could just barely make out objects by the little light that crept through the cracks in the roof and walls of the building. We walked slowly along the track that guided the cars around the tunnel until we came to a large space where a lot of these cars were parked. Riding is always easier than walking so we decided to get one of the cars moving, push it to a little incline, and when it got rolling, jump in.

The car wheels were stiff and rusty and the axles started to squeak and before we could climb into the car to start our ride, dogs began to bark and growl viciously.

It was not until later that we learned they were dogs. We thought they were wolves. You never heard such ferocious animal sounds, as they echoed back and forth in that tunnel. Being the leader of this intrepid little band of adventurers, I immediately gave the order to execute that classic military maneuver known as getting the hell out of here. The order was, "Follow me!" (I was the leader, wasn't I?) This was followed by a silent prayer that God would show me which way to go. We went this way and that, up this corridor and down that, until we finally came to a dead end. The barking and growling grew louder and more ominous. The echoes made it seem to come from every direction. Some love.

One kid said, "Hey, maybe it's a recording!" This we knew was the voice of desperation. Who was there to start a recording? We probably would have had a very bad time with those dogs if it hadn't been for the way the building was constructed. There were two-by-fours helping to support the roof and slanting up through a space that had been left between the eaves and the top of the outside wall to admit air. We started to shinny up these two-by-fours with strength we didn't know we had as the dogs came yammering at our heels.

These weren't guard dogs put in the building to protect it from juvenile vandals and explorers like us. They were pet dogs that had been abandoned by their owners, had found warmth and shelter in the empty building, and had bonded together in a pack, succumbing to the primal canine instinct.

Today, this abandoning of pets goes on all over America more than it ever did before because Americans move around more than they ever did. Disasters, too, add to the wild dog population. When the 1972 earthquake hit the Los Angeles area hundreds of dogs, frightened by the phenomenon, ran away from home and became disoriented. They lost the veneer of civilization and started roaming wooded areas of Southern California in search of prey. Occasionally one of them becomes an agent.

DEBUT AS A PUBLIC SPEAKER

I don't suppose it's strange that I should remember the very first time I stood up and spoke before an audience. I even remember the name of the teacher who let me do it. I remember what I said. But I can't for the life of me recall what school it was in.

The teacher's name was Miss Pine, and she was the first person to think, as I did, that I should become a broadcaster. So, at the close of the school term—I must have been graduating into junior high—Miss Pine named me class poet. This did not mean that I had to write the poem. It just meant that I got to recite something selected by Miss Pine.

The day came. Clad in my best shiny dark blue suit, I walked to the middle of the stage on cue and said:

Work
by Anonymous
Let me do but my work from day to day
In field or forest, at my desk or loom,
In roaring market place
Or tranquil room.

As I finished these magic words, I said my name and bowed, thinking then as I do now that Anonymous might have tried harder or Miss Pine might have picked a better piece.

I completed my bow, removed my hand from my stomach, turned, and, tripping over my own foot, walked off to mild applause from the parents and titering from my classmates.

Thank you, Miss Pine, wherever you are, for giving me this auspicious start on a career of talking.

WHY I NEVER RAN FOR MAYOR

As I grew older the constant matriculation into a new school every year left me feeling more and more out of it. As young people get into high school, they have already formed lasting friendships from their grade school days. And if they were cliqueish in elementary schools, as most kids are, when they get to high school they become positively masonic.

It's tough to be attending classes for several months and not have anybody know your name because they don't care what it is. This is what happened to me when the rumor began to spread that the boys and girls in a Germantown high school that I was supposed to attend showed an alarming tendency to engage in the reproductive process with remarkable success.

"Our Edward's *not* going to a school like *that!*" said my mother with finality. And for once in her life, as far as family matters were concerned, she made a decision. So I was sent to nearby Olney High School.

I attended dear old Olney from September to March of my freshman year without anybody ever saying hello to me. No one ever spoke to me except the teachers, and they frequently addressed me merely as "young man."

It got so I had a warm feeling of belonging when some kid would run into me in the hall and say, "Ooop! Sorry!" or "Whyncha look where ya goin'?" When I got home to my own neighborhood, all the kids went to that immoral school I wasn't allowed to attend.

In spite of all this, in an effort to meet a growing inner need to prove myself, I went out for football. I was tall. I weighed enough. I was football material. Above all it would give me a chance to bang into people. That was something I needed to do.

So, on the day of the football call, I headed for the gymnasium along with what seemed to be every other boy in school who was over five feet tall. When I reached the gym there was a lot of "Hey, Butch!" and "Hi, Charlie!" and greetings like that. Guys were throwing their arms around other guys and saying, "Well, ya ol' son of a gun" and all manner of locker room talk. I wanted to say to someone, "Hello, I'm Ed McMahon." But I didn't because I was sure the answer would come back, "So what?" I just sat there waiting and kept my mouth shut. But when it came time to go down to the football field, I couldn't take it any longer. I chickened out and went home. On the way to the house I made a big decision. I resolved to take a firm stand regarding my schooling. I demanded that I be allowed to spend the last years of high school in one school and that that one must be Lowell High School in Lowell, Massachussetts. Lowell was where I felt most at home because of the summers I'd spent there with Katie. I loved her. I loved her big house. I loved the permanence of it. It was where I felt wanted and special.

The kid next door was the nearest thing I had to a best friend, Francis (Frank) Fawcett, and if I saw him tomorrow, I'd recognize him immediately. This is because I recently saw him in Lowell at my cousin's wedding.

Once at Lowell, I began to make friends, and once I learned how, it became easy. I made a lot of them. I made the school magazine, *The Review*. I went out for football and, above all, I learned not to let anyone put me down.

People sometimes call me a "glad-hander." They say I'm too friendly. I don't think you can be too friendly. I remember that there are people, like I was as a boy, who are lonely because they never had any way of learning how to make friends.

When strangers grab my hand and say hello to me now, I don't feel exposed and vulnerable as some of my colleagues say they do. I see people groping for friendship, people who feel free to talk to me because I've spent a lot of time in their homes with them. They see themselves as part of a group—Johnny, his guests, Doc, and me. They feel a kinship, a right to say hello, and they have a right to be answered in kind.

Most kids don't have to wait to get into their third year of high school to connect with that one teacher who really empathizes with his pupils and makes learning a rewarding and absorbing experience. But I did. It was Ken Coward (I hope that is the right name) who taught me that learning could be easy on the mind, not just, as in Southwood, painful on the knuckles.

Mr. Coward taught physics, and instead of making the course a lot of what the kids called "dumb experiments," he'd do magic tricks and mix them in with physics experiments. We'd have to figure out which ones were physical realities and which were just legerdemain. We were seldom right.

Ken made friends of us, invited us to his home, and taught us a great many things we didn't even know we were learning. That's my idea of how education should work, how teachers should teach.

On the other side of the coin from Ken Coward there was our homeroom teacher, Mrs. Keyes. She was a large woman, so large she almost filled the room. And through the mysterious maneuvers that confuse every educational system, this enormous woman taught dancing. It was back in the days when schools tried to teach the social graces. Correction! It was back in the days when there *were* social graces. Mrs. Keyes, who moved with the grace of a bulldozer, taught what was called "ballroom" dancing. But I don't think it was prescience on her part, her ability to foresee the kind of dancing that would be popular twenty years later that made her insist that all couples remain twelve inches apart while dancing. There was little body contact in her dancing class. She had obviously decided that all teen-age boys were dirty old men. Come to think of it, maybe she was right.

I think Mrs. Keyes' main problem was her lack of any sense

of humor. I say this because of what happened around that time of year at Lowell High when they were about to hold elections to select student officials to run the city for a day. It's a good way—lots of schools do it—of indoctrinating young people into the political process and teaching them something about their local government.

Various teachers made the nominations. From these the student body elected Lowell's mayor for a day, its chief of police, and a lot of aldermen and so forth. It was a good idea and made school more interesting.

One of the guys in the class had found a little kitten wandering, lost, on the sidewalk near school. So that it wouldn't wander into the street and get killed, he decided to bring it home to his Aunt Mary, who would love it. But he didn't have time to take it all the way back home to her. So he picked it up and put it in his pocket and took it to school with him, carrying it from class to class, hoping against hope that nothing unpleasant would happen in his pocket.

When he got to his homeroom he took the little cat out and slipped it into the space under his desk so it would have some room and air to breathe. Remember those desks with an open shelf under the top where you could store books? In the upper-right-hand corner there was always a hole in which to put an inkwell.

Immediately the kitten began to play with the inkwell protruding into its living space, hitting it with its paw and threatening to spill the ink. To avoid this, the smart kid took the inkwell out of the hole. The next thing that happened was that the kitten's tail shot up through the hole and waved quietly to and fro. The class was immediately dissolved in hysterical laughter. Mrs. Keyes came to investigate, and it became immediately evident that she was no aelurophile. That's a word I learned one evening when James Mason was on *The Tonight Show*. It means a lover of cats, which Mason happens to be.

Mrs. Keyes viewed the cat's presence and the class's hilarity as one of the major disasters of the semester. The kid was ordered to remove the animal and himself at once. This he did by stashing the cat in his locker. When he returned, Mrs. Keyes said, "Class, you may not believe this but the boy I was about to name as mayor for a day was Edward McMahon. Edward will not be named."

I guess that's politics. The experience has kept me from trying to become mayor of anywhere. I figured if one simple act of kindness could keep me out of office, who needed it?

MUTH AND DAD

Muth. What a wonderful name for a dog. Any kid in the world would be proud to have a pooch named Muthsie.

But that wasn't the name of my dog. No commonplace name like that for me. My hound had a more unusual name. Prince. Valiant Prince.

Muth was my mother. "Muth" was short for "Mother" in my early talking days, and it stuck.

Her name was Eleanor and somehow she looked just like an Eleanor. She was one of your genuine dark-haired, black-eyed Irish beauties. And when she turned those eyes on you, whatever she wanted she got. That must have been how she got my father, whose resistance to feminine charm was like butter to a warm knife.

Just as my dad was firm in every sense, my mother was soft in every sense . . . and never very well. She died in her fifties. Perhaps it really is possible to die of a broken heart. Possibly she never achieved what she hoped for, either from my father or from life.

She had vague theatrical aspirations induced by having been raised in a theatrical boarding house by her grandmother, who had been some sort of seer or outdoor-show, fortune-teller type. Apparently she possessed what is now known as ESP, and like all ESPredicters, she hit it right just often enough to establish some credibility. These triumphant prognostications were looked upon with great awe. Her misses were, naturally, forgotten.

At a very early age, Mother worked in the stocking mills, then had a few insignificant parts in some insignificant theatrical productions. Then one day a man about town, an older man named Edward Leo McMahon, came to the boarding house to visit a man my mother knew only as Sport. It wasn't long after that that McMahon was going places with Eleanor instead of Sport.

No question about it, Dad was something of what was once called "a roué." That's why Muth always felt she had to travel with him. And that's why there was never any real domestic continuity in our home life. But what home life there was, when we had it, was good.

While I feel a meal isn't complete unless it is preceded by a couple of martinis and includes a good beer or the appropriate wine and an after-dinner drink, neither my mother nor my father were, in any sense at all, drinkers. The only early recollection of liquor I have is when Muth, who was a very good bridge player, used to have "the girls" in on certain afternoons for a friendly little game. Or during my father's very serious poker games with some serious two-fisted drinkers. Two or three of Muth's "girl" friends did pretty well with the sauce, too, as I remember. So there was always plenty of booze available. When I'd come into the room there would be the usual "isn't he cutes" and then Muth, who always said she felt there should be nothing mysterious or forbidden about booze, would allow one of her guests to give me a sip of whiskey "so he won't crave it later."

When I told this to Johnny he said, quietly, "She should see you now."

This I must protest. He's given me a great reputation as a lush. I'm not. I'm a drinking man. I admit I like to drink . . . a lot. Certainly I drink a lot more than Johnny does or can. As he's said over and over again, three drinks and he goes bananas. But I'm a much larger man. I can absorb a great deal. And I like to.

I'm not addicted. As Mark Twain said when asked if he

thought he could ever give up cigar smoking, "I can give it up any time I want to. I know this to be true. Because I've done it hundreds of times."

Actually cutting off my liquor supply is my best way of losing weight quickly. I recommend it to everyone. For those who don't drink, I have only one thing to say, "You don't know what you're missing."

But if Muth and Dad didn't drink very much, they smoked up an inferno. To the day she died my mother puffed through over three packs of Camels a day. Dad was a more sophisticated smoker. He liked Lord Salisbury cigarettes. They were oval in shape, came in a box, and Dad went through about four boxes a day.

I often wonder if the fact that both my parents were such heavy smokers is why I don't smoke at all. This once kept me from being the smokesman for Liggett & Myers.

I'm sure there were a lot of disappointments in my mother's life, and it's possible I was one of them. Maybe she felt guilty about all the time she traveled with Dad, leaving me in boarding school or with Katie. She'd had a hard time at my birth and never let me forget it whenever I did anything to displease her. "And to think I almost died to give you birth," she would say.

It makes a small kid feel warm all over to hear his mother say something like that. But now I know, it was born of the sadness in her life. Most of the time she was very loving, kind, and considerate.

She was about seven or eight years younger than my dad who, in true Irish tradition, married late. So he was a little older than most men when he had his first son and only child. As a result of this, and because he was away on business a lot, Dad and I were never as close when I was a boy as we grew to be later in life when we became a little closer in age by virtue of experience.

Incidentally, "Dad" was what I called him. He might have liked being called "Guv," if I'd thought of it.

He was a large, aggressive, domineering man whose motto

was "Always walk into a place as if you belonged there. Look like you belong and everyone will think you do." That stood me in good stead after I graduated from high school, got into college, show business, and the Marines.

If you "look like you belong" you can walk right past a ticket taker with three or four friends following you, saying, "They're with me," and nine times out of ten the perplexed ticket man lets you all go through wondering who you are. If he actually stops you and asks who are you, just give him your name in a loud clear voice as if you're saying Abraham Lincoln or Howard Hughes, but never stop moving right along. Over and over again I've worked my way through situations I didn't know anything about by acting "as if I belonged."

Another one of Dad's personal mottoes was "Always measure up." Do what people expect you to do and if you have people working for you do as much as you expect them to do. You can't ask them to "measure up" if you don't. These are the things I've tried to instill in my children—"act as if you belong" and always "measure up." Another is, when you're looking for a job, answering questions, "Tell them what they want to hear."

KATIE AND THE BIG BLOW

For me, living with my grandmother, Katie, had success written all over it.

My father was her favorite son. That made me the son of the man who had gone out into the world and occasionally brought it back to her instead of staying in Lowell, with his other brothers, in the plumbing business.

She called my dad Eddie. Everybody did. And if Eddie got what he wanted when he came home to the big house in Lowell, his son got it in spades redoubled. Sometimes her Eddie would telephone all the way from St. Louis or New Orleans. And when her hero came to town everything at Katie's stopped and paid him heed.

He was a great storyteller. Maybe it would be a yarn about what had happened in Toledo the day before when the police were trying to evict him and his operation from a building for a mere matter of nonpayment of rent. It was sheer harassment; Dad would make it clear that he had no intention of not paying the rent. "But," he asked his audience, "how can you do that when you have no money?" When the police didn't understand this, rather than embarrass them with the logic of his position, he left town in the middle of the night. Katie got far more fun out of listening to my dad's stories than hearing his brother's talk about the scarcity of number 7 nuts.

Not only Katie and I lapped up my dad's stories of derring-do in his exciting world of carnivals, circuses, state fairs, fund-raising promotions involving all sorts of gambling and show biz gimmickry, my plumber uncles and their wives did too, and so did my Aunt Mary, who helped Katie with the house. Their Eddie was the family's window to the world. I kept my nose pressed against it from the very start of me.

Dad would blow into town from some faraway place, fill Katie's enormous kitchen with loud talk, pick her up with a hug, swing her around, and say, "Come on, Katie, we're going to Montreal." Katie wouldn't ask when, where, why, what for, or for how long. She'd just say, "I'll get my hat." Women wore them in those days, and they fastened them on with hatpins. I remember wondering as a child how Katie could stand poking that pin into her head as she seemed to do when she put her hat on.

And when Aunt Mary heard Katie say, "I'll get my hat," she automatically went into Katie's room and packed her bag for her.

Aunt Mary, who is still alive as I write this, was a rather shadowy figure beside the magnificent Katie, but I was very close to her, too, because even more than Katie, Aunt Mary understood what I was aiming to do. She was the youngest of Katie's children and closer to my age.

They had a "day" for me back in Lowell and I was happy that Aunt Mary was still around to enjoy it with me because we made a big thing of her. The event was called A Regatta, I was the guest of honor, and there were all the usual things, including parades.

In one of these I rode with Frank Sargeant, who was then Governor of Massachusetts. I'd never met him and didn't know what kind of man he was. But I soon found out the gimmick was that we were to ride on the Budweiser wagon drawn by the Clydesdales. Well, we were riding along and it seemed as if every man and woman along the line of march were hollering, "Hey, Ed! I went to school with you. I was in your class."

Man, that must have been some class! I don't recall it being that large. The population of Lowell is about ninety thousand. The police estimated that there were between three and five hundred thousand people at the Regatta. All hollering that they were in my class. That's when I found out that the Governor was my kind of guy. He turned to me and said, "You bastard, don't you ever come back here and run for Governor." Poor guy got beaten that year. But then he came up with something as we were riding along behind those beautiful animals that I'll never forget. An interesting crack for a man in his type of work. He said, "You know, Ed, I feel right at home here. I've been in politics all my life. And here I am riding behind eight horses' asses."

Another event of the Regatta was the restaging of a man-on-the-street-type broadcast that I did with a fella named Tom Clayton. Tom was my idol when I was an announcer in Lowell. I wanted to be just like him. He could ad lib and everybody loved him. I was just the announcer on the show.

Well, they re-created this show live. Tom came out of retirement and the manager of the station, Mr. Sullivan, came down from Springfield to participate. Like all Sullivans, he was a brave man . . . *the* brave man who took a chance and gave me my first announcing job.

But I've wandered away from Aunt Mary. Jerry Lewis joined me at the Regatta and he and I were riding in the big parade. Aunt Mary was riding in front of us in a convertible.

Well, Jerry and I had a big sign made and put it on the hood of the car. It said, "Who are those two guys riding behind Aunt Mary?"

It was a great gag, I thought, but Aunt Mary made us take it off the car.

I think I still get up early every morning, because when you lived in Katie's house, with Katie working her culinary magic, all your senses were attacked at five thirty every morning. There was the sound of washing being done in an antique machine that I suspect one of my uncles built out of spare parts. It shook the whole house like a passing locomotive. The smell of bacon sizzling, biscuits in the oven, coffee boiling, and the sound of houseful of plumbers noisily anxious to get an early start affected your whole being. Your olefactory sense told your stomach you were hungry and the noise of the machinery and the people whetted your curiosity. So you were out of bed and into action in a hurry.

To top the whole early-morning anthology of sound and smell was the irresistible aroma of blueberry pie. By quarter to six Katie would have four or five of them in the oven along with a few loaves of bread. And there was always a special little loaf in its own tiny pan for guess who.

My recommendation to any kid planning to have a nice permissive childhood is to have loving parents who come to see him often, treat him with generosity and affection, and leave him in the care of an infatuated grandmother.

In 1937 a real rouser of a hurricane hit Massachusetts and Lowell took it right on the chin. That hurricane stands beside my experience in the Tunnel of Love as one of the most exciting happenings of my youth.

When the storm started to come in I was at football practice. It began getting windier and windier until the ball was being blown so badly it was impossible to throw passes. We had to quit playing. The wind finally became so stiff you could almost lean against it. Walking was practically impossible. But it was a kick to go with the wind and let it blow you along.

None of us kids knew it was a hurricane. But we knew we were into something very serious when suddenly there was a big noise and right before our eyes the side of a building blew off. It was a fantastic sight. It was as if some little girl slid open the front of her doll house, which just happened to be a factory. We could see the people still at their machines. It happened so suddenly they didn't even know the wall was gone. As we watched them the roof of a three-story house not far away blew off. Finally, hurricane or no hurricane, I went home to supper.

Night came on and the high wind continued. All my pals were out in the hurricane and I felt I had to be with them. Naturally Katie tried to talk sense into me and keep me home. But she knew this was a position she had to take but could not hold. Finally, on my absolute guarantee that everything would be all right and that nothing would happen to me, she allowed me to leave the house.

Later I was to make her the same guarantee before joining the Marines.

Once outside, with a flashlight in my hand, I walked the streets where trees had fallen and were still toppling over, as if I believed my own guarantee. Finally I reached the park where my buddies and I hung out and there they all were, each with his own flashlight, just standing there doing nothing, getting news flashes and rumors from the men of the National Guard, which had taken over the city to prevent looting . . . possibly by kids like us. They wouldn't let us go anywhere and finally put us all in their truck and escorted us to our various homes with instructions to stay there.

It was a night of adventure and it taught me that Katie understood what so many wise, strong women know, that a boy has be allowed to seek adventure or he will lose his self-respect.

MY HIGH SCHOOL DIPLOMA

Dad couldn't have picked a worse time to give in to my pleading that he let me handle the mike on the sound truck he had circulating around Lowell and environs plugging the big Fourth of July celebration he was promoting for the Kiwanis Clubs. He called his lash-up an Aerial Circus. What this really meant was that it was out in the open air, no tent. High-wire people, guys on swaying poles, jugglers, and the fella who jumped from a ninety-foot platform into a damp blotter, all worked under the bright blue sky or the twinkling stars. If it rained, everybody took a bath.

Along the midway there were plenty of chances to drop a bob or two if Lady Luck turned her back. Gambling at that time was legal. I have never understood why gambling ceases to be sinful when its games are run for charity. There were Big Six wheels and Blackjack wheels and enough bingo games to supply long evenings of entertainment to all the churches in a small diocese. The event, under my father's adroit promotion, had mushroomed from a two-day stand into eight hilarious days of fun, excitement, thrills, and not a little drunkenness on the part of those citizens who felt you couldn't have a party without a drop of the sauce that makes all mankind kin—when it doesn't turn them into brawling, blithering idiots.

So this is what I'm plugging, live mike in hand, sitting in the back of a van as it tours the streets of Lowell and environs. It occupied a lot of my time during the day and early evening,

73

time stolen from regular studies but mostly from rehearsal for the high school graduation ceremonies.

I had tried to cover this absence by making a deal with another McMahon in the class, Lawrence McMahon. When I turned up absent, he was to hold the seat just ahead of him for me. That is, when they all marched in and took their chairs he'd save the seat between him and the person ahead of him. It was worked this way because E. McMahon came before L. McMahon. What neither of us had covered was the possibility that I wouldn't even make the actual ceremony.

Comes June 30, I was cruising the countryside around Lowell, extolling the magic that the yeomen of the territory would enjoy on the Lowell Common on July the Fourth. That day we stayed out a little longer than usual and the traffic in Lowell was a little heavier than usual. My ballyhoo was getting weaker and weaker as I wondered whether Larry would hold my seat for me. My mother, who knew a lot about vaudeville, had told me about a comedienne she admired whose name was Sylvia Clark, the Little Clown. Mother particularly liked one of Sylvia's songs, "It's Hard to Do the Shimmy When There's Murder in Your Heart." Until this moment, late for my graduation, stuck in the back of a truck trying cheerily to urge people to come to the fair, Miss Clark's little bit of philosophy had only been a joke to me. Now I realized its true and deep significance.

Finally we pulled the truck into the parking space near school and I rushed into the auditorium. The audience and the class had all assembled. The ceremonies had started.

I grabbed my mortarboard cap and robe and headed for my place on stage, trying to put the robe on as I went, which was hard to do because I was carrying that crazy square hat. I never thought to put it on. While doing this I was trying to find where L. McMahon was sitting and to see if he'd saved the seat for me. I saw him. He had. And I headed for that space, trying to get there unnoticed.

It's not easy for a guy as tall as I was to be inconspicuous. I must have looked like a juvenile Ichabod Crane as, robe flying, I crawled over my fellow graduates. People began to snicker. As my inconvenienced classmates were letting me go by, some of them dropped things they were holding. I was brought up to be polite, and stopped to help them pick these items up. The giggling grew louder.

Finally the headmaster, Mr. Ray Sullivan, who was speaking, turned to see what was going on behind him. He saw me just as I was reaching my seat and putting my mortarboard in place, carefully adjusting the tassel to the proper angle. The moment he saw me the audience saw that he saw me and there came one of those sudden silences that sometimes mysteriously overwhelm an audience. In this silent impasse I sought for a hole where I could hide. There was none. I felt obligated to rise to an occasion I really hadn't planned. I gave Mr. Sullivan a little salute. It was not a smart, military-type, respectful salute. It was more a sort of "hi fellas" type of wave that you just don't throw at a headmaster. It got a helluva laugh.

Now I began to think of the trouble I was in. What would happen when my name was called and I walked up to accept the sheepskin? Would Mr. Sullivan hand it to me, hit me with it, or tear it up? *M* is in the middle of the alphabet and there were about a hundred students in the class. I suffered while some hundred or so kids were called and honored.

Mr. Sullivan said something to each graduate as he handed him or her the scroll. I wondered what he'd say to me. I thought of George E. Stone as he took that final walk in the movie *The Last Mile.* Nobody ever walked as slowly as I did to receive the certification he had worked so hard to win. After what seemed like a week I was actually approaching Mr. Sullivan. He held out his hand. If I took it would he break my wrist? The next thing I knew we were shaking hands and he was saying in a loud, clear voice, "Glad you could make it, McMahon."

This got a big hand from an understanding audience. I wanted to grab the mike and tell everyone what had happened. Instead, I leaned toward the mike and blurted out, "I wouldn't have missed it for the world." Even Mr. Sullivan laughed. It was my first ad lib, the first time I felt the thrill that all performers feel when they get a big laugh saving a bad situation. What was even more important, I'd spoken on a mike and I wasn't hidden inside a truck. People could not only hear me, they could see me.

ANNNND THEEEERE THEY GO . . .

After being a mike man on the sound truck, followed by the bizarre events of my high school graduation, I began to climb on my father's back to let me really go to work for him . . . or somebody . . . at one of his bingo games . . . or somewhere. All I wanted was a live mike in my hand.

Even my dad, who flattered no one, not even his own kid, admitted that I'd handled the truck job well. How was he to know that what he really had was a "Paul Douglas"? Besides the truck trick was the second job he'd given me that I handled with alacrity and aplomb.

In response to my urging he let me sell bingo cards at a game he was running for the Royal Order of Moose. This didn't seem to me to be a very demanding job. People who wanted to play bingo came to the Moose Hall for that purpose. As I saw it they couldn't play bingo without cards. So I felt the cards sort of sold themselves.

But I figured a way to make a little more cash on the cards than the other sellers were making. First you have to picture this bingo setup at the Mooses' place. There were tables and chairs and long counters wherever they could fit them in. And for those who couldn't find places at tables, we had free lap boards. People with these sat on the floor or on the stairs, anywhere they could put it. You never saw so many people playing bingo, some of them with as many as eight cards in front of them.

To sell the cards Dad started me out with four dollars in change plus of course the cards that were supposed to go at ten cents each, two for fifteen. That's what all the other sellers were calling. Not Ed. I was hollering, "Only winning cards here, folks! Ten cents apiece. Buy two, three, or more and double, triple, quadruple your luck." Not a word came out of me about two for fifteen. Mine were the "lucky cards." They sold at ten cents straight.

There was nothing illegal about it. As advertising men would say I was "offering a benefit." Mine were the "lucky" cards. I was carrying on in the good old American tradition of putting in more thought and more effort to make a harder sale. At the end of the evening, to my father's astonishment, I was holding about a buck and a quarter of extra nickles for myself after accounting for the cards I'd taken out on the two-for-fifteen bookkeeping system.

Mother was terribly impressed with how clever I was. Dad, I think, started a small account in a local savings and loan association to cover bail money I might need in the future. I guess this first little bit of free enterprise selling moved him to allow me to try working on the truck that, in turn, after graduation, made him decide to help me get the kind of summer job I wanted.

I remember Mother saying, "I don't want Edward in the bingo business. It's bad enough that I've had to spend my entire married life in homes furnished entirely in bingo prizes. I don't want any wife of Ed's ever to have to do that."

The first game of bingo I participated in—I'm told—was in Atlantic City. Dad had a big bingo layout on the boardwalk. It was a real bingo palace, big and ornate. If they'd built a Las Vegas casino in the early twenties it would have looked like Dad's Atlantic City operation.

I was so young at the time that Muth used to wheel me to and from the place in a baby carriage. The trip was supposed to be so Edward could see his father.

Actually when the game closed there was nothing to do with the money but carry it back to the hotel under me in the carriage and put it in the hotel safe until morning. It was probably the Traymore Hotel. And the baby carriage served as sort of a

Brink's truck for transporting the loot. It was the safest way to carry considerable cash. They pushed me along the boardwalk, late at night, feeling perfectly secure because in those days no one was about to rip off a baby.

But Dad, while knowing my compulsion to have a mike in my hand, still resisted getting me work as a bingo caller. It's a very stylized kind of spiel, and the one thing it doesn't need is the kind of midway come-on that separates the bourgeoisie from their cabbage. In a bingo game the separation has already taken place but the effort on the part of the separator is to give a little of it back to the separatee.

Apropos of "giving a little back," my dad had a yarn about a carnival character he used to know. When the going got tough he'd find the name of a racehorse that was due to be destroyed for some reason or other and run a raffle for him. Who wouldn't wager fifty cents to win a thoroughbred? The deal might not have held much appeal for city folks with no closet room in their apartments for a horse, but it was big at county fairs and in barbershops around Middle America's farm country. "What," you ask, as everyone did, "happened when the winner found out he'd bought a ticket on a dead horse?"

"No problem," Dad said. The guy just gave the mark back his fifty cents.

"And speaking of horses," which is the comedian's and carny spieler's way of dovetailing from one subject to another, it was at Salisbury Beach outside of Boston that my dad got me a job calling the ponies.

Dad was acquainted with a concessionaire named Gene Dean, who was head of an outfit called Mulcahey & Dean Concessions. They owned and operated some shows and rides along the beachfront and also rented space to what you might call a series of floating bingo games. These traveled around playing carnivals and other available midway areas. And I can't wait to tell you about them.

The job Dean gave me was with a mechanical game called the Sport of Kings. You've seen the setup, a row of tables that look like a battalion of pinball machines. Actually, that's what they were. The job they gave me was counterman. That meant I made change so people could play the machines. They put in a coin and were given an allotment of balls which they tried to roll into certain holes at the end of the table to advance the horse that was "theirs."

The winner received a handsome prize which cost the operators, for tops, the money from two machines. The rest was overhead and profit. And, believe me, the overhead was light. I know because I was part of it. But the pay didn't matter. What mattered was getting my hands on the mike that was in the hands of a man who was calling each race as it was played.

While I was walking around making change I learned the patter and the horses' names. By being a little pushy I managed to make relief mike man in a couple of weeks. And right then and there the foundation was laid for the line I hope you hear every evening: "Annnd Nooooow Heeeeere's Johnny!"

The machines would all be active. The game would start. The balls would roll. The horses would start to move and the lucky players would hear me saying, "Annnnd theeeere they go. . . . Out of the gate it's Farfetched . . . Farfetched followed by Aerial Toy and Regal Lily." I kept that patter going, calling the action as the balls fell into the holes and the horses changed positions. "As they come into the clubhouse turn it's Regal Lily moving into contention. Baby's Boy is making his move now with Aerial Toy pushing Farfetched on the rail. It's a dingdong finish . . . and the winnah is . . . Aerial Toy by half a head."

Then, whoever had Aerial Toy got the baby doll or the lampshade or whatever other tacky item of merchandise was the coveted prize for that game.

I'd been doing this type of calling for about a week and, although I didn't know it, Mulcahey and Dean had people spotting me. Finally Gene told Dad, "This kid's got a voice. He'd make a helluva bingo announcer. Let me put him on the road."

Dad had misgivings about sending a teen-age kid skylarking

around New England with a bunch of carny grifters but he figured there was no time like the present to find out what kind of stuff I had. So he okayed the deal and off I went with a traveling bingo game. The Paul Douglas surrogate with the Clem McCarthy patter was on his way to becoming a bingo announcer.

It turned out that the Clem McCarthy style was about as much like bingo calling as boogie-woogie is like *Rigoletto*.

HEADING FOR MEXICO, MAINE

I'm sitting in the back of a truck headed for Mexico, Maine. I'm part of a bingo game. I'm started on a career. And again I'm filled with that feeling of anticipation and apprehension I felt in Bayonne when, with some other kids, I explored the musty black interior of an abandoned tunnel of love.

Only now two full years of steady residence in Lowell, where I made friends and became part of the high school scene, had given me a confidence I would have lacked had I not, for instance, been on the editorial staff of the Lowell High School *Review*. "Editorial staff." Sounds classy, doesn't it? What I did was run a column in collaboration with a boy named Bob Reilly. (He's my daughter Claudia's godfather.)

Bob and I ran a sort of advice to the lovelorn column. Our byline was Gardenia Reilly and Lollypop McMahon. By calling it an advice to the lovelorn column, I'm giving Bob and me all the best of it. We actually were the Rona Barretts of Lowell High. We'd reveal who was sneaking out at night with whom and, if possible, warn them if their family was suspicious of their shenanigans. It was a very popular column. We did a whole lot of investigative reporting.

The day the *Review* came out, the first thing everyone turned to was Gardenia Reilly and Lollypop McMahon to look for their names. I often wonder why we both didn't get black eyes or bloody noses every publication day. The only thing that saved us, I guess, was the majesty of the press or, possibly, my size.

Robert Benchley was my literary idol in those days and I'd try to write the same sort of things he wrote, imitating his style. I remember being very proud of one such piece. It was on the art of "O" filling. This was something you did on telephone books, in booths, while waiting for your number or during examinations while waiting for whatever personal god you thought was watching over you to come up with the answer to the first question. I started the piece way back in ancient times with the art of "O" chipping, which was practiced by vandals who would go around Rome in the dead of night and chip the centers out of every "O" in the names on the statues.

Just a little background on the scared passenger on the back of a bingo truck. It was my first experience with truck travel and I can tell you it will never take the place of flying United or even going by Greyhound. When you're traveling on a bingo truck you've hit the absolute low in transportation.

The rig is always so packed with gear that there's very little room for people. This is true no matter how big and successful the game is. The bigger the game, the more gear and the more people. And it never occurs to a bingo operator to get a bigger truck.

A bingo truck is a little world of its own the way, I imagine, a covered wagon must have been. It carries everything for living and doing business with the emphasis on the latter. There are tents and tent poles and the planking needed for counters; stools for the players to sit on and the sound equipment with which to call the games. There were horses and lumber you could build into a pyramid platform on which to display the prizes. There were yards and yards of black velours to cover everything and lighting equipment to glamorize the prizes displayed against the black velours. Then, of course, there were all the prizes, the blankets, the lamps, the dolls, the ashtrays, and gadgets of all kinds, plus the equipment for running the game, the cards, the barrel full of numbers, and all manner of essential trivia like tools, batteries, extra light bulbs . . . we even carried a little cash so that we could start doing business the moment we got set up. No need, if a player handed us a dollar bill, to run over the fairgrounds looking for change.

I finally wound up operating a bingo game so big we had our own semitrailer rig, which I drove. But that's another story. On this excursion to Mexico, Maine, the vehicle we had was a stake truck with what we called a wool rack. Maybe it's a standard name in the truck business for a storage area that extends over the top of the cab. Maybe bingo men gave it that name because that was a convenient place to carry the blankets that were among the premiums offered. However it got its name, a wool rack gives a truck more carrying space.

There also had to be some space in the truck for the personnel of the outfit and whatever luggage they carried, which was never very much. The number of people, of course, depended on the size of the show. First there was the boss, a man named Frank Sullivan, or maybe it was Gallagher. They sound alike. Last names of people with bingo shows are quickly forgotten because they're seldom used. Frank was a hard-drinking man, which was good for me because he was the show's mike man. He rode up in front, traditionally, with the driver, who doubled on the job as a counterman. There was one other counterman, a checker, and me, the *assistant* counterman and *apprentice* mike man. Already I was two different kinds of man.

There was really room for none of us in the truck except Frank, who sat in the cab with the driver. And as the night grew chillier and I pulled the blankets, which would become premiums in the morning, around me, I resolved to be either the driver or the boss who rode in the truck with him if I stayed in the business. I became both.

BLACKIE

Like most growing boys I instinctively sought the facts of life at its source, girls. At first they were hardly the facts. They were the probabilities, and they come to me from a man named Blackie, whom I met while trying to sleep in a bingo truck on the way to Mexico, Maine, who told me of the possibilities. His avuncular guidance stalled my first headlong and inexperienced efforts at investigating that mysterious force that holds the world together and sometimes blows it apart. I am speaking, of course, of sex. There's an innocuous little story that can be told in the most mixed and straitlaced gatherings, at church picnics, and at the family dinner table. For those who understand it, it's funny. For those who don't, the laugh that follows the punch line offers a suggestion of things to come.

Two little boys had hiked seven miles into the country to a secluded valley where, they understood, there was a nudist camp that was causing a lot of discussion and controversy around town. Why this was so, perplexed them. So, like all little boys, they went to investigate.

They had succeeded in pushing through the undergrowth left there to protect the campers from just such prying eyes as theirs. And when they came close enough to see the people in the camp policing the area, washing bedding (I almost wrote clothes), cooking meals, playing volleyball, they decided that one of them would crawl a little closer to watch at a more advantageous range and then crawl back to report to his buddy. Their one fear was that they'd be caught in the act of sexual espionage. They didn't know the penalty for voyeurism (they didn't even know the word) but they were not about to find out.

So, as one lad looked and the other stood guard, the sentry, unable to contain his curiosity, called softly to his observer, "Are they men or women?"

"I don't know," came back the answer. "I can't tell. They haven't any clothes on."

Today, the kids would have had a hard time telling which was which if they'd *had* their clothes on. But, roughly, that could have been me when I began to veer off down that dangerous road that leads from puberty to adolescence. I only realize now that I didn't become conscious that there must be a very basic difference between boys and girls—other than wardrobe—until I became aware that the girls were beginning to develop bulges I hadn't noticed before. These I found very attractive and interesting.

I learned exactly what they were in the back row of one of Lowell's better movie theaters. I did this, along with several other young men of my own age and a nubile young lady whose curiosity about the difference between the sexes plus an inner urge to participate in exploring that difference made her available for what turned out to be a gang feel. The girl seemed to enjoy her part in the exercise and let it go as far as she chose, which was far short of what, we had yet to learn, was our objective. We did discover that the most amazing things were concealed under the frilly feminine fashions of the day.

It was the discovery that there were certain girls who would let you cop a feel and certain girls you wouldn't dare try it with, plus the myth that "there are two kinds of women, good and bad" that kept me fairly straight. By that I mean relatively inexperienced, for what, by today's standards, was a long, long time. It wasn't till I went with the bingo game to Mexico, Maine, that I even learned certain earthy and gamey words that are now the backbone of the merest high school freshman's vocabulary.

That I didn't allow sex to become the dominant motivation in my life was due to Blackie. He became my mentor and adviser as long as we both toured the bingo circuit together.

Mexico, Maine, was, and probably still is, just outside of Rumford. Rumford, in spite of the fact that it had "rum" for the first syllable, was dry. Under the Maine prohibition law, local option or something, drinking was not permitted . . . except in the back of the barbershop and in almost every room in every house in town. You just couldn't buy the stuff legally either by the bottle or by the gulp.

If you were thirsty, you went to the barbershop, walked past the two chairs, through the door in the back, and there was the bar. There, too, frequently was the sheriff. It was to this blind tiger, as it was called ("speakeasy" was a city word), that Blackie took me on my first lesson of his learn-while-you-earn course in what, for lack of a better word, must be called manhood.

There was something pitiful about this man, part Indian, who had been an aerialist, one of the elite of the circus world. He had fallen, injured his back, and the country doctor who fixed him up in whatever community the accident happened was no Marcus Welby.

His back had been repaired so badly that he walked with a stoop, a broken man who went into bingo because it was part of the carnival-circus life he could not bear to give up. I don't know what might have happened to me if it hadn't been for Blackie.

On our arrival in Mexico it turned out we had joined one of the toughest carnivals on the road. The night before a guy had been killed by another guy. He got angry and hit his friend over the head with a sledgehammer. That smarts!

The carnival had closed for the night and the wake was going on when we pulled into the grounds and started setting up to be ready to start calling bingo bright and early the next morning. This was hard work and all five men in the troupe including Frank, the boss, worked at it. It meant raising the tent, setting up the counters in the interior and the display table in the back, hooking up the PA system and the lights that would make the prizes look prettier than they really were.

We did what they told me was good business and I was enjoying the whole new experience tremendously. I was beginning to feel at home among the people, the sights, and the smells of the carnival and I wanted to be 100 percent one of them.

One evening during my break, Blackie found me standing in a line of men and pulled me out of it so fast he almost broke my arm. Most of the men on the line were sailors, railroad workers, fishermen, and the like, and Blackie said, "What are you doing in this line? What do you want with a tattoo?"

I told him it seemed to me to be the manly thing to do. "That's not what makes a man," he said, "and you'll never be able to get rid of that damn thing. What do you want with it? A person like you isn't going to be traveling with bingo games all his life."

At first I was mad but when I finally realized the favor Blackie had done me, I didn't make a move around that carnival without first getting Blackie's advice and okay.

Every boy stepping into a new life should be able to step into it with a "Blackie" to guide him.

UNNNNder the BEEEE . . . NUMMMbah SEVV-un

By daybreak in Mexico, Maine (sounds like a song cue), we were all set up and ready for business. It was "opening night" for me in many ways. I was really on my own, far away from home. (Another song cue.) I felt I had finally pointed my life in the direction I wanted to travel.

Besides starting a career in the carnival business, I had joined the show with special instructions to my boss, Frank Sullivan, from *his* boss, Gene Dean, to "break in McMahon as a bingo announcer."

I was wearing the uniform, the outfit worn by all bingo countermen—black pants, white shirt, and a little apron. In the wide pocket of this we put the change we made from selling the bingo cards. I was cool. I was ready. I knew what my job was and I was prepared to be the best there was in the world at it.

What I didn't know was that Frank was one of those boozers who could drink and drink and you never knew it until all of a sudden, he wasn't there.

To get the crowd and get the game rolling it was common practice to offer a few free games with extra prizes. You gave people free cards and sacrificed a few impressive prizes. This attracted crowds and got the marks really interested. All of a sudden we'd start charging for the cards. We'd lose a lot of our crowd, but enough bought cards and stayed to see what would happen, mainly those who had won. They were enough to keep things going. Bingo, like any other game of chance, is one you can get hooked on. And that's how we made our money.

After Frank had called three freebies and one game for cash and things looked pretty good, he suddenly had an acute attack of parchedness. He called to me, "Hey, McMahon! Take the mike!"

"Already?" I thought to myself, but I walked over with all the confidence of a guy doing the last mile. Frank handed the mike to me saying, "You take care of it, kid." The mike was so heavy I could hardly hold it. It was never designed to be hand-held. It was one of those old-fashioned things made to be on a stand. But there was no stand, so we held it.

I took this heavy scepter of sound and in a moment I became that combination of Paul Douglas and Clem McCarthy who had wowed 'em with the Sport of Kings concession at Salisbury Beach. "Here we go, folks," I began as I drew the first number from the barrel. "And it's number twenty-three, folks . . . number twenty-three under the *I* . . . keep your eye on that, ladies and gentlemen, as we go on to the next big number for someone and it's under the *N*, folks . . . it may be the beginning of the *N* for someone and the number under the *N* is number fifty-two. And now we're rolling with number twenty-three under the *I* and number sixty-two under the *N* . . . and now, friends, we come up with a great big fifteen under the *B* . . ." And so I babbled on.

Anyone who would rate this as successful bingo calling would classify the maiden voyage of the *Titanic* as a pleasure cruise. It proved to be about as popular with the players as the flood was with the people of Johnstown. Our players began melting like snow drifts under a warm spring sun. They were actually walking away from cards they'd paid for without finishing the game.

I was, of course, covered with what I now know to be flop sweat—that awful feeling of damp distress for which there is no cure. Every experienced comic has his own way of dealing with it, for even the most experienced comedian meets an audience, now and then, that does not agree with any of his ideas on what is funny.

Jerry Lewis falls back on sure-fire physical stuff that he used years ago . . . and that's some falling for a man whose bones may be a little more brittle than they were when he first met Dean Martin.

On the rare occasion when the jokes Shecky Greene is working on strike an audience as less than hilarious, creating what is generally known as a lull, Shecky resorts to ripping off his clothing. He throws his things on the floor like a bad child, he stamps on them, violates them in every possible way, until he awakens the audience to the subtlety of his humor. He'll gladly sacrifice a $350 suit to keep a $20,000 gig from bombing.

The worst example of flop-sweat hysteria that ever happened on *The Tonight Show* was the night when Dick Shawn felt he wasn't getting the reaction that time had taught him he should be getting from the material he was using.

So he started attacking the furniture. He overturned chairs, the sofa, and finally Johnny's desk. This could have been a lot worse than it was—but better for Shawn—if Johnny had been caught sitting there without pants. Sound silly? It's possible.

Sometimes when he has to make a quick change for a Mighty Carson Art Players sketch or something else that calls for costuming, he'll just wear his shirt and jacket because it takes too long to drag off a pair of trousers.

The only thing I can think of to top Shawn's mighty effort to demolish *The Tonight Show* set was a little job Dom DeLuise worked up in an attempt to show Johnny a trick with a raw egg. It didn't go exactly as planned—or maybe it *did!* It went all over Johnny's raw silk jacket.

Picking up another egg from a bowl standing by in case of an emergency, Johnny broke it on Dom's dome. Then began the great *Tonight Show* Egg Throwing Carnival. Burt Reynolds and Art Carney got into the act, and it made an omelet of the whole stage, assuring itself a place in any *Tonight Show* retrospective right alongside the tomahawk-throwing bit as executed by Ed Ames. The target was a life-size cutout of a man, and Ed managed to sink the tomahawk right in the center of the cutout's manhood. I have never heard people laugh so long and so loudly.

Meanwhile, back at the bingo game, the people who stuck till the game was over picked up the kernels of corn we gave them to use as markers and threw them at me with encouraging remarks like "Where's the other guy?" And "You stink!"

"The other guy" had disappeared into the bottle. We found him in the back tent surrounded by enough empty fifths to supply a small distillery.

My first effort to step into a man's shoes that were much too big for me had ended in disaster. I don't know how I would have handled myself if it hadn't been for my mentor, my guardian angel, Blackie, on the carny trail.

"Take it easy kid," he said. "Call a few free games and lose that radio racehorse-type spiel. That's not what those players want to hear. All they want are the numbers slow, loud, and clear, the way Frank calls them. Try to imitate Frank, he's one of the best in the business."

So I called a few free games, imitating Frank. It wasn't all that great but it was better than what I'd been doing. And I slowly improved as I got the hang of it and Frank's rhythm and intonation became easier for me. By the end of the evening I was going good. The following night Frank was still off somewhere, a fugitive from AA in a souse's stupor, and Blackie was running the operation.

When we opened in the morning he said, "You call it, kid. By the time we closed last night you were doin' okay." The day after that, a wire came to Frank telling him to close up the game and return to Salisbury Beach. It also said that McMahon should report to Whitey McTaag in Chatham, New York. I didn't know whether it was good news or bad. I didn't know Whitey McTaag, never heard of him, and I had no idea where Chatham, New York, was.

It turned out that they'd had scouts listening to me in Mexico and when they pulled the show back because Frank was non compus bender, they sent me on to another one of their bingo spots.

This set me up just great. I now had Frank's patter down cold and I thought of myself as the Babe-Ruth of bingo callers. I knew that only time was between me and a bust in the bingo callers' hall of fame whenever they established one.

Meanwhile, back in Mexico before I left for Chatham Blackie and I had made contact with a couple of the girls in the show. After closing we'd go over to the blind tiger barbershop, walk through the door into the back, and settle down to several rounds of Pickwick Ale. That was really the beginning of my life as it applied to drinking and dames. I loved it. I loved the carnival, I loved bingo, and while I was in this loving mood, it was lucky that along came some congenial girls.

Sunday morning I caught the bus for Troy, New York, where I changed to another bus for Chatham. Once in Chatham I had no trouble finding the carnival; it was part of the county fair, and when I reported to Whitey McTaag at the Mulcahey & Dean Concessions, I found he had a much bigger setup than the one I'd just left. Next to that dinky game McTaag's was the Taj Mahal. Unlike the game I left it wasn't even the only one on the midway. Things were very competitive. Good bingo calling would pay off against bad.

McTaag had ten countermen, twenty people working the show. The prizes were bigger and looked more lavish. The experience I'd gotten with that little show was comparable to what a vaudeville act got playing a split week in Union Hill, New Jersey, before going off on the big time. I was convinced I'd learned my trade. I was ready to be relief mike man on this great show.

What I didn't know was that Whitey McTaag really was the greatest bingo caller around. Where Frank had just been very good, Whitey was a superstar. Something else I found out was that Whitey never needed relief. His throat never tired. It was leather. You could use it to sharpen razor blades. He'd take a cold drink and a bite of a sandwich between games while the checkers and the countermen were setting up, and go right on calling. Nothing ever stuck in his throat. This, I knew, was from experience and practice. What puzzled me was that he never had to go to the bathroom.

While I was waiting for some miracle to come along and cause Whitey to fracture his larynx, I wandered around the midway, checking up on the techniques of other bingo callers and memorizing such high-class spiels as those for the hermaphrodite, the geek, the girlie shows, the magicians, and the fire-eaters.

Finally the day came. Luckily I was around. Whitey called, "Hey, McMahon!" and handed me the mike.

The tables were full. He'd really gotten things rolling. His rhythm had the customers hypnotized. He had them all hooked on promises he'd made between games, "Three games from now comes the big bonus special!" Nobody knew what that was, but Whitey made it sound as if it were worth waiting for or why would he make such a big deal of it?

If you really analyze it, the whole trick of calling bingo is to get the rhythm going and finally heat up to something sort of like the old Southern prayer meetings where everyone gets caught up in the swing of the thing. When it's really working it's great to hear. And that's where Whitey was when he called me.

As he handed me the mike he just said, "Pick it up from here." What a thrill. The big time at last. I was following the great Whitey McTaag. I carried on and I thought I was doing fine. But before I'd finished the first game I saw him hurrying back from the toilet tent. He stood and listened to me call one more game. Then he took the mike from me and said scornfully, "You call yourself a bingo announcer!"

I was crushed, but I knew what had happened. I hadn't kept my eye on the ball. I'd wandered all over the midway listening to barkers for all kinds of shows that had nothing to do with bingo calling and I'd listened to a few bingo callers who weren't in the same league with Whitey. I got mad at myself, once I'd isolated the trouble, and resolved to show Whitey I would be as good as he was.

I did absolutely nothing all day but watch and listen to Whitey. I practiced his rhythms, his inflections, his pronunciations. I mimicked the way he'd pick each little numbered ball out of the cage, hold it up dramatically for a moment and then, even more dramatically, call the number on it.

I watched him and, kidlike, I prayed that his vocal cords would get knotted or something. Nothing serious enough to kill him, just maim him in the throat. Then, as if in answer to my uncharitable prayers, he actually did get laryngitis. It renewed my faith in prayer and from then I worked as his relief man.

I should have been very grateful to Whitey but I don't think I ever was. I never liked him. I respected his professionalism, his skill, but there was never any warmth between us although we toured for several weeks together. It was during that tour that I learned how a bingo concession operated, which came in handy when I got another wire from the home office of Mc cahey & Dean to join another bingo game as mike man; not relief mike man, THE mike man.

The mike man, of course, was usually the manager of the show. But on this new connection I was just to be mike man. The manager wasn't good at it, but he was great at picking the best location, setting up merchandise displays and the other tricks of operating a bingo game.

I could hardly wait to find a postcard, bum a penny stamp, and send word to my dad that I'd made mike man. It didn't occur to me until this very moment, as I'm writing this, that Dad might have engineered my whole meteoric career.

STELLA WAS WITH IT

During a political campaign, Senator John Tunney of California, to prove a cost-of-living point, spent only $1.25 a day for food for a period of seven days. Of course the dollar today buys considerably less than it did when I was sixteen, back in 1939, when I earned and lived on $10 a week.

Senator Tunney found it tough to get by on that.

How, then, did I make $10 buy not only my victuals but all the other little luxuries so dear to the heart of a growing lad? Surprise! It was easy. I only remember yearning for one thing when I was on the road with the bingo people. It was a shower.

A bingo game's complete lack of ablutionary facilities caused me great anguish. I felt this so strongly that I created my own facility which earned me the sobriquet, "the Shower Kid." My urge to be Mr. Clean led me to carry a little rig which I invented and set up outside the tent everywhere we played.

I'd hook this up to any water outlet I could find or, if worse came to worst, set up a tank above it and be able to take a quick shower whenever I felt grimy. I sometimes wonder why my keen sense of how to convert a good idea into a buck never moved me to make my portable shower available, at a nominal fee, to other members of the carnival community. Possibly I did and don't remember. Maybe they weren't interested. Many of my co-workers used to go for days, each day growing more gamey, until we came to some town that had public baths.

Had I not attained the status of mike man, I wouldn't have been able to get away with my portable shower. It might have been considered too ritzy. But a mike man has status. I also had a very deep voice and I looked about four or five years older than I was.

Now about the living expenses. They really were negligible. I slept in the bingo tent. We all did. We slept on the bingo counters and display tables, using for our mattresses, sheets, blankets, and pillows the Beacon blankets which we offered as prizes. I have since slept more comfortably.

This use of blankets as sleeping equipment was, I'm sure, why every bingo game used them for prizes. In the morning you'd fold up your bed and put it back in the display with the rest of the tacky goodies your patrons gambled to win.

Arranging this stuff—kewpie dolls, hassocks, ashtrays, baby swings, lamps, pocket knives, lighters, key chains, and dishes, you had to make it look like treasure. Doing this bordered on an art. It had to look like gifts under a Christmas tree. We even carried a couple of baby spots which, properly placed, made what was about one hundred dollars' worth of merchandise look like a million.

Dad told me how he and his partner used to build their prize displays. He and a man named John McClay had a bumper game in a place called Rendezvous Park in Atlantic City where Convention Hall now stands. The spot where year after year they fail to elect Bert Parks as Miss America.

When I got out of the Marine Corps after WW II it was John McClay's son who gave me my first job, and John McClay himself was best man at my wedding.

"There was always a lot of wear and tear on the prizes," Dad pointed out, "and the problem was to give away the ones that had been damaged without having the mark come back and complain about it."

McMahon and McClay solved this problem by putting damaged articles in the most prominent spots of the display. They'd make a scratched ashtray, by the way they placed and lit it, look like something in Tiffany's window. Then, when you had a winner and you gave him his choice of any article he wanted, nine times out of ten he picked the dented thing you were featuring.

McClay would then say to my father, "See, I told you everyone would want that. We should have taken that down." Then they'd go into an argument that would convince the winner that he'd shrewdly picked the most valuable prize on the lot, óne that was just up there as a come-on, not supposed to be won.

Finally, McClay would give in and say, "Well, okay, if he really wants it let him have it."

"He won it fair and square," Dad would say and then he'd make a big thing of climbing up to get the item. By this time the guy was so embarrassed about causing so much trouble that even if the prize fell to pieces in his hand he wouldn't beef.

That's an example of the way my father always tried to make something out of nothing. That's a pitchman's great skill and it was part of Dad's personal credo, "Always make a stumbling block into a stepping-stone."

The cost of food when you're with a carny can be almost nothing. You can go into town and buy a cheap meal or you can live on hamburgers, hot dogs, peanuts, popcorn, and tonic—that's what New Englanders call soda and Midwesterners call pop—which you can get for nothing just by saying to the concessionaire, "I'm with it."

How about that expression "with it"? Sounds more like the mid-seventies than late thirties, doesn't it? Today everybody wants to be "with it." With what is never very definitely defined. On the midway it means "with the carnival."

It was through my friend Blackie that I first found out that I could get things free on the midway by saying I was "with it." This came to pass because of a provocative performer in one of the girlie shows, a lady named Stella. She worked for a concession that employed the services of a Patch.

Every carny of any size, if it hoped to do uninterrupted

business, had on its payroll at least one character they called the Patch. This citizen was generally a lawyer, more generally a disbarred lawyer, who acted as the fixer for the show and generally doubled as the advance man.

He'd get into town ahead of the outfit, see that they got a reader . . . a license . . . look over the moral attitude and climate of the community, see what had to be done to meet the financial needs of the local lawmen who might overlook certain legal formalities and, in short, take care of every detail to ensure a smooth, bust-free run. Incidentally, as far back as the thirties you were in for a "bust" if the "heat" was on, which meant you might get an unscheduled visit from the "fuzz." So you see, in the seventies even our slang is nostalgic.

If he did his homework properly, the Patch had hardly anything to do when his outfit came to town but protect it from members of the citizenry who felt they had a grievance.

Sometimes if a carny joint was working strong—a "joint" is a stand and "strong" means outside the law—if a wheel was rigged or a girlie show was showing too much of the girlie—it would carry its own Patch.

Then when a mark felt he'd been taken or a bluenose saw a kootch show that made his cheeks so red they clashed with his proboscis, the Patch went to work.

Incidentally, a "mark" is a customer or anybody who can be taken. I think the word comes out of criminal slang meaning "target for tonight." A "shill" is a guy who works for a joint and pretends to be a mark to attract business.

Getting back to the Patch, if a mark starts beefing, making a scene, it's his job to wander up and move him out. Sometimes he'd do this by identifying himself as a concerned citizen who saw the whole thing and is anxious to help the mark keep everything on the up and up. He puts his arm around the mark's shoulder, saying, "Come on. Let's go see the manager. I'll back you up. I'll do better than that. I know some newspapermen in this town. We'll talk to them. They'll get your story and your picture in every paper from coast to coast. Everybody in the country will know how this show took you. That'll kill their business everyplace they go.''

Before they get to the manager's office, the mark sees himself as just that, identified nationwide but more particularly in his own hometown as a rube who can be taken by any city slicker. He reneges on seeing the manager, saying, ''I think I'll wait to see my lawyer before I talk to the manager.'' Then he splits and that's the last anyone hears from him.

Of course when a carny was carrying a show like Stella's the word got around that the Patch wasn't traveling with them just for the ride. People coming out the back of the tent when her show ended (you went in the front and came out the back, so possible dissatisfied customers couldn't communicate with those waiting to get in) the exiting marks let it be known that Stella really separated the men from the boys. This was something I devoutly wanted to have happen to me.

When Blackie saw me standing on line, waiting to get in to see Stella work, just as when he'd seen me on line waiting to get tattooed, he pulled me out and said, ''Lemme explain something to you, kid. When you're with it, you don't go to the girlie shows.'' Then Blackie explained why the people who were with it never went to the girlie shows. The audience that paid to see Stella work was an impersonal bunch of strangers. She never really saw them and, from the info I gathered about what she did, they spent little time looking at her face. But if you were with the carnival, as I was, she'd see you all the time and you'd see her and the proper respect that one co-worker must have for another co-worker would be flawed.

When you think about it, a carny company is like a little invading army. It is mandatory upon everyone to respect his fellow workers and be able to respond when the cry ''Hey, Rube!'' means one of his people is in trouble. This usually meant trouble with the townies, and that would mean the show would be run out of town. Sometimes there'd be a ''Hey, Rube!'' because Stella promised more than she delivered. What she actually delivered I can't tell you.

I never caught her act. I never knew exactly what it was she did for that extra "four bits, the half part of a dollar" that got you in to see her work. I just adored her from afar everytime I saw her walking around the midway fully clothed. I guess it was for the best. To this day she has my deepest respect.

While Stella was enjoying my respect, there was another girl from her show who got my deepest appreciation, if I may call it that.

Every stand like Stella's had what they called balley (to rhyme with "alley") girls. This didn't mean that they danced on their toes. Their toes were not the focal point of their terpsichorean activities. They were the outside show, the girls who wiggled up a storm and gathered the crowd while Stella was stripping on the inside.

The talker—barker—would be spieling, "Here they are, ladies and gentlemen, the most beautiful girls this side of Paris, France, and I don't have to tell you smart people what the girls do in Paris, France!" The music would start and the girls would start to squirm. "Just a minute, girls!" The music would stop. "Don't give them too much for nothing!" The girls would stop. "You want more? All right, ladies, give the good people one more little sample." The girls would go-go-go again. After a moment of frenzy, "Now, then, folks, the little ladies are going inside to prepare for a show the likes of which has never been seen outside the privacy of a sheikh's harem."

As the girls wiggled their little behinds going into the tent, the barker went on, "Go right in, folks! No waiting. Show starts in just one minute. You can't afford to miss it. A show like this (he looked furtively in both directions) may never pass this way again."

Generally speaking, the balley girls were much younger, prettier, more attractive in every way than the older women who did the show on the inside. These, like Stella, had been in the business for generations. Sometimes they really delivered and stripped to show a lot of what they had. Often, when they did, you wished they'd kept it a secret.

As luck would have it, one of those balley girls took a fancy to me. She'd hear me calling the bingo games and when she had a break she'd wander over and sit and listen and I'd show off for her and between games we'd talk. We got better and better acquainted and, of course, neither Stella's show nor my bingo game went on all night.

This chick was a very experienced doll. She'd been around a lot longer than I had. And as some girls (and lots of older women) so often do, she seized an opportunity to initiate me into a realm of activities I couldn't even have guessed at if I'd watched Stella every performance.

As I look back on that earthy, lusty, pretty, and now name-less young lady, I think my experience may be similar to that of many a young man who thinks of himself as the aggressor in matters of love. Not so. No way. The female is always in command. She knows where the man is going and decides what to do about it—when, where, and how. There's an old saying, "He chased her till she caught him." That's what that balley girl did to me and I'm forever grateful to her.

I TAKE MY PICK—AND SHOVEL

After graduation from Lowell High School and my first summer with bingo games, I wanted to continue my education at Boston College. Those were the days when everybody didn't have to go to college. It had not yet become necessary to have a BA in order to get a job that any high school graduate could handle. But I wanted to go to college in the worst way and, as the old joke goes, it looked as if that would be the only way I'd get there.

My father was sick. We'd fallen on hard times and what little money I'd sluiced away from my summer on the midways was needed at home. So was any other money I could earn. I had to go to work. The job I looked for was the one that would bring in the most loot.

World War Two had started and the buildup was on for our eventual entrance into it and to increase our ability to supply those fighting Hitler. I became a member of a construction gang that was working on a defense establishment at Fort Devens, Massachusetts. My qualifications for the job were my height and weight, which added up to muscle. They handed me a pick and a shovel and I used both. The day was long; the pay was good. Very good! And that was my main objective.

Later I found I could earn even more by becoming a carpenter's helper and I switched jobs. That was great. I not only got more dough, I augmented my rudimentary knowledge of simple carpentry, and got to be pretty good with hammer and nails. But even as a common laborer, I was able to make

103

enough to bolster the family bank account and take a course that I hoped would start me on a show biz career.

The fountainhead I went to for the know-how that would make me a second Paul Douglas was the Emerson Speech School in Boston, a school once famous among thespians for its courses in the evolution and execution of elocution. During the day I labored with my hands. At night I studied how to make my voice work for me. The course of thirteen weeks cost $35. It wasn't much, but it might have been the best $35 I ever spent.

The first thing they had you do when you started was make a recording. Then you attended classes in speech and how to control your voice, given by antiquated actors. Like all courses in how to do something that must stem from a basic talent and a lot of enthusiasm, Emerson's was not all bad. On the other hand, it was only as good as each individual student made it. If you came in with nothing, that's what you finished with. If you came in good, you finished better.

At the conclusion of the course you made a second recording and compared this with the record you made when you entered. It was always better. It figures. Thirteen weeks of constant practice had to count for something.

The big trouble was that the instructor of my class was an ancient Shakespearian ham who, instead of training us to talk to a few people in a living room, which was what radio called for, gave us the kind of speech training you need to project to the last row in the balcony. And by this time I was hip that there was no use in throwing my voice up there because I knew what went on there. The last thing they needed was a guy shouting at them.

Nevertheless, I remember how much work they put in on our class to get us letter perfect in the first commercial we were supposed to do. I don't know whether there actually was a product called Praise Linoleum. I doubt it. But we sure sold it. "You'll like the way Praise displays linoleum." That was it. Like all good commercials it suggested something but said nothing. What good was it to know how Praise displayed its linoleum? What people wanted to know was how the stuff stood up under your feet.

While I was taking this course I continued to be the only non-immigrant in a gang of construction laborers who had never found time to learn much more English than the few words they needed to find and keep a job. Oddly enough, most of these were of the four-letter Anglo-Saxon variety. They used today's great American four-letter word as a noun, an adjective, an adverb, a verb, a pronoun, and a participle— which was hard to do because they didn't know what any of those things were.

Soon, like every other adolescent, I was doing the same thing, trying to be a man by peppering my talk heavily with the same gamey words my colleagues used, words that have since become part of every grade school kid's vocabulary. Not mine.

People who know me best will attest to the fact that I rarely ever use what, for lack of a better euphemism, I'll call the language of the streets. I rarely swear and never use obscenity unless it's absolutely necessary for the punch line of an absolutely fantastic joke. My conversation, I've been told, sounds as if I grew up in a nunnery. Okay. You talk your way and I'll talk mine.

This antiseptic vocabulary has helped a lot in radio and TV. Unlike many men in the business, I don't have to be constantly on the alert that I might let a word slip that would get me bleeped, embarrass a sponsor or, perhaps, type me as a bawdy rogue. I may be. But why advertise it?

Shortly after I began working with the hard-core work gang, I became straw boss because I spoke and understood English better than they did. When the boss gave an instruction I understood what he wanted done and had the patience to make it clear to my colleagues. And they loved to listen to me. My Emerson Speech School language was a source of unending pleasure to them. Everytime one of their compatriots would pass our operation driving a dump truck or a cement mixer they'd holler at him, "Hey! Wanna hear somebody talk? Listen." The truck would stop and they'd say to me, "Hey, Ed, go ahead and talk something."

Embarrassed and self-conscious, reverting to my best Emerson School delivery, I'd say, "What do you wish me to say?" This broke them up. But they liked it and they liked me because I represented what they wanted their sons to be someday. They'd try to talk about it at lunch and they'd share their wine with me. They called it Cellar Red. By the time lunch was over, with the garlic and the wine, they were sleepy and I was bombed and very little work got done. And I was not only talking like them, I was doing what they did. I asked myself why. Why should a guy who's trying to become a speaker, a talker, a communicator, imitate the language of the gutter? I thought about it for a while, then, just as one gives up smoking (which I never had to do because I never smoked) or drinking, which I've done several times, I gave up swearing.

CARNY ISN'T ART

The second summer I spent in the bingo game business was tremendous. To begin with, I became an experienced hand. I'd learned the trade. I knew how to arrange displays and light them so they'd look like a million bucks. I knew how to pack a truck so it wouldn't topple over taking a turn for the worse on the highway. You have to trim a truck just as carefully as you do a boat, so this was important. I knew enough about the business end of the game to be a manager. And I'd become a first-rate mike man.

So they fitted me out with a truck, gave me five guys, all the equipment I needed, and about three grand in prize merchandise and I was ready to roll. This time we were not playing just any little county fair or lodge promotion we could get into. We were traveling as part of the Coleman Brothers Circus. It wasn't really a full-fledged circus although we did have animal and aerial acts, but it was a very large, circus-y type of carny.

It was this circus atmosphere that got me. All my life I'd loved circuses. As a little kid I was the one who pestered my grandmother to let me get up at four in the morning to watch the circus roll into town in two or three special trains, unload in the railroad yard, truck their gear across town, and set up on the fairgrounds in time to do a matinee.

Even as a grown man I thought watching the circus train pull in and unload—elephants first so they could help with the rest of the equipment—was a joy reserved entirely for country kids. Then in New York, while doing *The Tonight Show*, I talked to some men who were born on Manhattan Island and grew up in New York. They told me how they used to do the same thing I did, going up to the marshaling yards in the Bronx, watching the circus unload, and then following the parade down Fifth Avenue early in the morning to the old, original Madison Square Garden.

One of these city fellas told me a story about a friend of his who was a cub reporter on the old New York *Tribune*. It may be just as well that I don't remember the young reporter's name. Being the youngest guy on the staff, he was selected by his editor as being the most likely person to cover the color story on the arrival in town of Barnum & Bailey.

The show was scheduled to pull in around four in the morning and this presented the young man with a problem. Like all men his age during prohibition, his life was dedicated to drinking the Volstead Act into oblivion. And everybody, particularly every young reporter—those were the days when it was stylish for all newspaper people to follow the pattern set by Ben Hecht and Charles MacArthur—had his own special speakeasy.

In view of the circus' early arrival and his dedication to the elimination of the 18th Amendment, he saw no sense to going home to Brooklyn for two or three hours and then journeying all the way back to Manhattan and up to the Bronx. So he checked into his favorite speak, told them he had to be up in the Bronx at four A.M., told them to see that he made it, and ordered a double.

There are certain results attendant on sitting for several hours in a saloon. As the time passed it got very drunk out. By the time the barman reminded him of his early-morning date, the cub was fairly gassed. "Thank you," he said to the barman. "Good-night," he said politely to the head of the establishment, walked out, hailed a cab, and said to the man at the wheel, "Drive up Fifth Avenue till you come to an elephant."

I'm told that in prohibition days in New York, this kind of instruction didn't phase a hackie. Our hero, bombed but not enough to make him forget his job, sat back in the cab and began folding a piece of copy paper and fumbling for the stub of a pencil with which to jot down notes on whatever seemed to him to be newsworthy.

Suddenly, at 112th Street and Fifth Avenue, the cab pulled to the curb. The driver jumped out and began sprinting east on 112th as if he'd sat on a cactus.

His surprised fare hollered after him, "Hey!"

Then, about a block away, coming down Fifth Avenue, he saw an elephant leading blocks and blocks of Barnum & Bailey circus. The reporter wrote his story not on the circus, but on what it must feel like to a cabdriver to suddenly find out that he is in on his drunken fare's hallucinations. The reporter got a raise on the basis of the unusual story. Which proves it's always good to take a little drink before you go to work.

When the circus came to town in Lowell, you didn't have to take a cab to find an elephant. It was just a short walk and what you did when you got there was carry water and do all sorts of menial jobs in exchange for a ducat to see the show. But to me the unpacking and the setting up was the real show. It's an art.

When a circus leaves town, as each act finishes for the night, it packs up and boards the train. The acts that are needed first for the next matinee in the next town are the last to board. These are generally the midway shows. They have to be set up and working to balley people onto the lot and keep them interested until the job of raising the big top and setting up the main show is finished.

At the outbreak of World War Two, when the Army suddenly found it needed a lot of extra transportation people with heavy logistical experience, I'll give you eight to five the first place they looked for them was in circuses and traveling outdoor shows.

What fascinated me was to see the boss of the outfit walk into a big empty field, look around for a few moments, get the feel of the prevailing winds and the slope of the land, and then drop a handkerchief. That's where they drive the first stake.

Everything was measured and set up from there—main tent, sideshows, cookhouse, dormitory tents—if they happened to be staying more than one day. These were for those who don't sleep on the train or hadn't brought along their own trailer sleeper-dressing rooms. Only the biggest stars had such luxuries.

Suddenly I was actually traveling with a circus, seeing my childhood fantasies coming true. And on top of that, I was the boss of my own concession. Well, not exactly my *own*—but *boss* of it. How big can you get at seventeen going on eighteen?

I was even free to leave the Coleman Show anytime my dad had a promotion going somewhere and wanted me to help him. When Dad's job was over, I'd hook up again with Coleman.

One of the problems of running a bingo game or any sort of game of chance in Massachusetts, at that time, was an organization called the Watch and Ward Society. This was a bluenose outfit that arrogated unto itself the job of evaluating and censoring whatever it deemed immoral. Immorality was anything they defined it as being. A friend of my father's, who seemed to have only one name, Jake, explained how the organization got its name. They watch, he said, for any activities that might give the public pleasure and then they ward them off.

The Watch and Ward Society would not allow bingo on Sunday. Problem. What do you do on Sunday with nothing but an inactive bingo game? I went into vending soft drinks, using the bingo stand as headquarters. My people would circulate among the throngs watching the outdoor aerial acts, particularly when Captain Divo plunged from a 125-foot tower into a bowl of oatmeal. The good captain's tank did look terribly shallow, but it was an illusion. It was about six feet deep and the bottom was a thick layer of sawdust. Nevertheless, if he didn't do it right, he'd cream himself. "Ah, the world of illusion," as W. C. Fields might say.

As the people got the roofs of their mouths sunburned looking up at the acrobats, my operatives would circulate among them offering, "delicious salty roasted peanuts and hot buttered and deliciously salted popcorn." We'd huck this stuff for half an hour or so as the crowd developed quite a thirst at the thought of all the salty stuff or because they were nibbling it.

But there was nothing to drink because I controlled it. Finally, when everyone's tongue was hanging out and their mouths felt full of cotton, I called in my peanut and popcorn people. They refilled their trays with bottled goods, changed their hats to ones that said, "Iced Cold Coca-Cola," and went out to a tidal wave of thirst-quenching business.

There was nothing basically new, or wrong, about stimulating the soft drink trade by offering people salty stuff. For years bars have been giving away free salted peanuts and potato chips to tempt the appetites of and stimulate the thirst of the tipplers. It's one of McMahon's rules of salesmanship: If there's no normal demand, create one.

Nellie Coleman was the wife of one of the Coleman Brothers. She saw to it that the moral standards of circus life were not breeched. She wouldn't allow any woman with the show to wear slacks, shorts, or very short dresses when not working. No matter how undressed they appeared in the show, no matter what kind of smutty talk or suggestive actions were part of their act, when they were off duty they dressed like ladies.

I am giving away no secrets when I say that these gals weren't doing *Mrs. Wiggs of the Cabbage Patch*. They were offering what was pretty raunchy stuff for those days. But of course, nothing compared to now. And, I may add, there was nothing too awfully straight about most of the games, although I wouldn't say they were exactly crooked. What I would say is that it was awfully difficult for the customer to win. He rarely even got everything he thought he had paid for.

In spite of some rather hardnosed moral attitudes, circus and carnival people are, at heart, nonconformists, outside the mainstream of society and completely wrapped up in the life they lead, with a language and a communications system all their own.

If you ever approach two guys talking and you hear one of them say something about "CB," it's a safe bet they're carnival men and it's a probable eight to five that they were talking about you.

CB is the code for change the subject. I've told a lot of my buddies about this and we use it among ourselves all the time. It comes in very handy.

It works like this. If someone's talking to me about someone and I see that person coming our way, I'll cut in with, "Say, I just remembered, the initials of the guy you asked me about are CB." That's pretty obvious to anyone in the know. But it means nothing to an outsider. If your pal is really with it, you can try being really subtle and simply say, "DeMille."

A code word the carnival pitchmen use a lot is "motley." When one of them is being relieved, as his relief approaches the block he'll say, "Dr. Motley was looking for you." They get relieved every hour and the word "motley," no matter how it's used, tells the new man that for the past hour it's been a rotten group. An hour's as long as any man's throat can stand pitching, that's why they measure their time on the block by hours. The block is the platform on which you stand, dominating the crowd.

And if the new pitchman wants to know what kind of business the stand's been doing, he may be told, "It looks like a liner." That means they grossed about fifty bucks in the hour.

A line is fifty . . . fifty cents . . . fifty dollars. A double line is a hundred bucks. A big liner is five hundred. Forget about a thousand. In an hour the subject never comes up.

When I was working on the midways the drifters of the outdoor show biz kept in touch with each other through a magazine called *The Billboard*. In those days it was largely a circus- and open-air show sheet. Today it concentrates mainly on the music business.

Out of curiosity I went to the public library and looked at

some microfilm copies of old issues of *The Billboard* and the two columns that I remember as getting the heaviest reading among the people I knew. They were *Midway Confab* and *Pipes for Pitchmen.* The former was a way of telling friends and co-workers whose whereabouts you didn't know, where *you* were. The *Pipes* column dealt heavily with the pitchman's business problems—where things were good, where bad, where the law was tough, where it could be bought. I loved to read those old columns of *Pipes* because when I came out of World War Two that's how I started earning a civilian living—as a pitchman.

In the *Pipes* column of April 6, 1940, I found the following item that even I don't understand:

DOC PHILLIPS has been working gummy and flukem in Huntington, W. Va. for the last two weeks to good takes. "This town is wide open," he writes, "and the reader is only an ace note. There are three other pitchmen here working med and sharpeners. Leo (Pete) Ashworth is laying the blocks right and left. Would like to hear from Doc Anderson and Jess Mitchell. Also Doc Gullett."

Another item says:

PIPING IN from Texarkana, Tex. after his hardest winter in 40 years, Eddie King says, "I am mushing signs and pitching cards and am doing all right. Pipe in, Harry Tucker and Omar Thompson. Was sorry to hear that Doc Burdick was ill."

Maybe you'd like this one:

DEWITT SHANKS scribes from Paris, Tex., "I have been down in southern Louisiana and Texas trying to dodge the snow and cold but with little success, as it really hit Dixie this winter. Two prominent boys among the med fraternity took a shake recently in Texas and one in Arkansas for adulteration. I have permanently retired from the med game and am presently operating a crew with fair success."

Apparently those two "boys among the med fraternity" who took "a shake" in Texas threw a scare into Ole DeWitt.

As I sat there reading all those old pipes from pitchmen from all over the country, I was interested in reading that there was a Thomas P. McMahon working the northwest at the same time, apparently, that I was working bingo in New England. He wrote to Bill Baker, who ran the *Pipes for Pitchmen* column to say he was

. . . still working Seattle and pickings are quiet. There are several peddlers working in and out of Seattle and the reader is $5 per month. But the stinger is, you cannot work where the money is as they roust you around the side streets.

In the *Midway Confabs* column there are things like this:

"After a successful season with Liendar's Great Shows, I tried some winter trouping with my Strange But True Show," pens Sailor Harris from Ashdown, Ark. "However the weather helped me decide that it's time to put the canvas away until the grass is green. We're in quarters but will begin active work soon."

Then there's the carny language which is kind of a Pig Latin involving the insertion of the syllable "eeaz" after the consonants in a word. Thus "talk" becomes "teeazalk" and "carny" becomes "keeazarneeazy."

"Leeazet meeazee geeasive yeeazoo aneeaze exeeazameeazull of heeazow eeazit geeazows." That, obviously, is "Let me give you an example of how it goes." Try it on the kids.

Among the sideshows with the Coleman outfit was a hermaphrodite named Diana Franko, Half Man-Half Woman.

I don't know how on the level Diana Franko was as a half man-half woman, but I can tell you this: One day I was strolling over to a water hydrant to get a pail of water to activate my shower and my way was along the backs of the tents occupied by the "human oddities," sometimes vulgarly called freaks. There was a person in the pretty pink plumage of a lady—pink dressing gown with feathers, frills, and a little bit of fur at the throat and wrists, standing before a mirror and a basin full of water—shaving.

I was the manager of the bingo show but I was also a boy of seventeen and the sight shook me up a lot. What kind of a world had I gotten into where there were people I couldn't tell whether to shake hands with or kiss?

A SEMI-SUCCESS

I went down to the beautiful Balboa Bay Club one weekend to try out an act I was preparing to open at the Tropicana Hotel in Las Vegas, co-starring with Vicki Carr.

So that our acts wouldn't conflict, Vicki promised not to drink if I promised not to sing. Then she heard me sing and decided to drink. She then insisted that I sing before she did, so as to give the audience a comparative picture of how the art can be handled.

After I rehearsed with the band in the morning, the late Joe Flynn, his wife and two boys, and some friends of mine were invited by Bob Miller and his wife, Sharon, to join them for a ride on Bob's several hundred-thousand-dollar prizewinning single-mast racing sloop. It was a pleasant day and the harbor was full of all manner of small craft darting around like flies on a stagnant pond. Suddenly Bob said to me, "Know how to handle a boat like this?" Now, I'd handled lesser craft but never anything like the one we were on. But I knew he wouldn't have asked me the question if he didn't want to give me the honor of taking the helm. So I did what my father taught me always to do, "Tell 'em what they want to hear." I said sure.

He moved over and left the wheel free for me to take. Now I'm zigzagging through the bay to avoid all the speedboats, starboats, excursion boats, fishing boats, and ferries as we're heading for home when I get my second surprise. As we approach the mooring, I'm about to turn over the conn to Bob when he says, "Take her in."

I was told later by those who know Bob very well that this was a great honor, that he never lets anyone but himself or his skipper moor the craft. So I was happy we went in fine. If I do say so myself, I did a nice job. Of course, Bob was standing right at my elbow telling me what to do. Even so, the slip gives only about two feet of clearance on either side. It's fairly close. I was proud and the rest of the guests gave me a standing ovation. They were all standing . . . ready to jump.

I mention this incident only because as I was nursing this eighty-two feet of sleek racing craft into its narrow slip, I saw myself trying for the first time to back a semitrailer into the loading bay at the New England Toy and Novelty Company in Boston, as a small group of old-time, professional truck drivers watched me critically. It came about this way.

As headman, manager and mike man of a bingo game I had several people under me. One of them drove the truck while the rest of us slept as we traveled between dates. One day Gene Dean, my boss, showed up to check on how we were doing and said to me, "Ed, can you drive a truck?" I knew he wanted to hear that I could because I also knew that our truck driver had been taken very seriously smashed. So I said, "Sure."

Then Dean said, "I mean a semitrailer."

I said, "So do I." I said this with the assurance that only a bluffer who didn't really know the problem, who had never in his life driven a semi, could get into his voice. What a piece of acting.

"Well, you're the trailer driver on this outfit from now on," said Dean. "It pays fifteen dollars a week extra."

"Fine," I said. And at that very moment on the Narragansett Racetrack where the bingo game happened to be playing, a brand-new semitrailer driver was born.

As John Wayne and Gary Cooper always say in every picture they're in, "A man has to do what he has to do." I knew the thing I had to do, and quick. It was to learn how to drive a semi. I sauntered over to where several of them were parked and said to the drivers, "How do you run one of these rigs?"

I've learned that skilled people are always proud to explain what they do well to people too naïve to understand that what ignorance makes look hard is really easy. For the next couple of hours I learned all about the four speeds forward and two in reverse, about double-clutching and all the other ways, means, and nuances of piloting ten tons along a highway at sixty miles an hour. Then they gave me some dry runs in place. It was a little like working in a flight trainer, which I was to do a lot of when I was training to be a fighter pilot. Finally they actually let me drive around a little, let me practice backing up and parking, and by the end of the week when it was time to move on, I was ready.

I'd learned all the tricks of packing one of the smaller trucks, so the bigger job presented no problem. I got everything balanced fine but I learned a couple of stops later that just getting it balanced wasn't enough. You had to get it all in.

This came up when we received a shipment of new merchandise and had to move out with more than we moved in with. It's tough but you work it out. Finally, you earn a big sigh of relief when you get the doors closed and locked and you take off.

To make everything dandy for me, that first time I drove a semi from Narragansett it was over the mountains to northern New York. It was quite an ordeal handling that rig for the first time with an actual load, at night over strange and winding roads, with an ETA I knew it would be hard to meet. Luckily the men asleep in the back didn't know it was my first time at the wheel of such a vehicle or I might have had the same problem Captain Bligh had to deal with.

Driving the semi proved to be great training on how to do without sleep. You start setting up as soon as you arrive at a new location. As soon as you get the game set up, you start to play. So, being a truck driver, manager, and mike man, there were long stretches of time when I didn't get any chance at all to sleep. My ability to keep rolling the way I do today may stem from those sleepless weekends. Looking back on it, it seems to me to have been the most grueling work I ever did.

But it was lucrative. On one day during the Labor Day weekend we took in $1,500 in nickels.

Then, and this gets me back to mooring Bob Miller's boat, there came that time I had to drive the semi into Boston to the New England Toy and Novelty Company to pick up some prizes. This company had its landing dock located in such a way that you had to back down a narrow alley. I'd never tried such critical backing. It just hadn't come up. Naturally I made a couple of bad starts, and having a few regular drivers standing around giving me the critical eye didn't make it any easier for me. But when I finally got the rig in after a few bounces off the curb and the wall, one of them said, "Well, you made it, kid."

"I'm just learning," I confessed.

"We know," he said. "It'll get easier."

There's a fine camaraderie among truck drivers. They're a very maligned bunch of men. There's hardly anyone who's done much cross-country driving who hasn't, at some time or other, been given a helping hand by a friendly truck driver. I'm proud to be one of them.

PRESIDENT OF ALL THE FRESHMEN

One of the things I'm most proud about is being a colonel in the United States Marine Corps. Almost as far back as I can remember I wanted to wear the Globe and Anchor. At first it had something to do with "the halls of Montezuma and the shores of Tripoli." I was interested in finding out where they were.

It all started because I went for the ads. The Marines were the crème de la crème of the military. And to be a Marine fighter pilot was to be with the crème de la crème of the corps—the Fi-est of the Semper Fi, which is short for the corps' motto, Semper Fidelis.

As the cloud of World War Two hung over us, Dad pointed out that if I wanted to be in Marine Corps aviation, I'd better get myself enough college to make me eligible. I don't know whether he said that to delay my entrance into the war, but it was good advice. So to get into college, instead of being drafted, I enlisted in the V-5 program. This was a crash college course that led to a commission in the Navy. Since the Marines were a branch of the Navy, I could get the two years necessary for aviation training and switch to the Marines. It was a great plan for me and I kept hoping the Navy would cut down on the years of college needed so I could get into active training. They didn't do that, but during my freshman year at Boston College they came up with an accelerated program that enabled you to do two years in a year and a half. I jumped right into that action. I remember I was majoring in physics and I immediately switched to electrical engineering because I thought I'd need that more and I was right.

Freshman year at Boston was a spectacular success for me. It even had a spectacular beginning. That summer on the road with the bingo game had ended in a blaze of glory. Besides making extra money for doing three jobs, I got a $550 bonus. And I just made it to college in time to register, came right off the road in the big old bingo truck. Believe me, that wild-looking carny rig didn't go unnoticed in the parking lot.

It was probably the first vehicle of its kind to roll through the sacred streets of fashionable Chestnut Hill, much less to stand parked in the Gothic shadows of dear old Boston College. But there it was, right alongside all the classy convertibles of the young gentlemen who made up the student body.

In passing it's interesting to note that all it cost to register at that time—and the fee included lab charges and everything—was a mere $550. How many dads today wish they could buy a year of college for their kids at that price? A semester at a private school for my son Michael cost almost five times that.

I've parked my rig and I'm on way to register. I'm aware that there's a guy following right behind me. As we came to a doorway through which you could see out onto the parking lot, he said, "Get a load of that crazy truck! Who'd come to college in that?"

"Me," I said. "I'm Ed McMahon."

He was a little embarrassed, but he put out his hand. "Glad to know you, Ed. I'm Frank Dwyer."

And that's how the future president of the freshman class and the future vice-president of the freshman class got to know each other. We're still friends.

Jimmy the Greek would have just laughed if anyone had asked him what the odds were that a bingo mike man, Ed McMahon, a day hop from Lowell, would get elected president of the freshman class at Boston. These are the things he'd have to weigh.

(1) In the class was a guy named Charlie Rogers, a big-man-

on-the-campus type when he graduated from Boston College High, where he had been president of every one of his classes, freshman, sophomore, junior, and senior. On that alone he looked like a shoo-in to be elected president of his freshman class at college—just on the basis of experience.

(2) I was a day hop, a low-class type of person looked down on by those Olympians who live on campus. There were a number of us Lowellies and we drove into Boston every morning.

What I had on my side was the hustle and experience with people that I'd gained working the bingo games and with the construction crew. From the circus and carny folks I'd learned that you can sell almost anything if you go about it in the right way . . . and work hard enough. Maybe it was this that prompted my gang of day hops from Lowell to talk me into running against Charlie Rogers. Charlie made the same mistake Thomas Dewey made when he ran against Harry Truman. Dewey saw the election as a milk run. He overlooked the hustle, the earthiness, and the fighting spirit of Give-'Em-Hell Harry.

I guess there were a lot of types such as myself, new to Boston College, brought in by the V-5 program. Guys who realized that if they wanted to fight for their country on a higher level than GI Joe, they had to get an education. It was these people plus my buddies from Lowell who banded together to work for me. We came up with a great slogan: "Everybody's Sayin'—We Want McMahon." Not one single soul had been heard to say this. But did anybody really ever say "Tippecanoe and Tyler Too"?

The election was run off just after the midterm exams. Those were the days before ball-point pens, the days when, if you didn't blot the ink that poured out of your Waterman pen before you turned the page of your examination blue book, you smeared the whole thing. It was important to include a blotter in your writing material. But most guys were so busy scribbling items on their cuff they forgot about the blotter.

So right before each exam one of my campaign workers

would be at the door of the examination room passing out small blotters. It was a nice gesture and it completely wiped out the opposition, which had never thought of such aggressive campaigning to become president of a freshman class. Each blotter had printed on it, "For President of the Freshman Class . . . Everybody's Sayin' We Want McMahon."

Now you may be wondering what became of the shy McMahon, the loner nobody knew, who talked to nobody? Well, that character got lost somewhere along the carny trail. As president of all the freshmen I continued the kind of thinking I'd learned as manager and mike man of a bingo game. I'd become a talker. I'd learned how the barkers operated. They knew how to attract and interest people and, although there are upperclassmen in every college who will deny this, freshmen are people.

One of the big things I did during my term as president was to change the character of the freshman dance. The college had just been given the Liggett Estate. I saw this as a beautiful acknowledgment of the college's role in causing students to acquire thousands of headaches, which led them to Liggett Stores to buy aspirin. But it was a magnificent estate and the college had not yet found a use for it.

I saw this spacious mansion with the driveway sweeping up to it, huge double doors that opened into a center hall with a winding staircase as an ideal place to hold our dance. It sure beat having it in the usual rented ballroom of a downtown hotel.

For openers, the place would cost us little or nothing. We could use what we saved on rent to throw a more lavish affair. I took the matter up with the dean of freshmen. He thought the idea was good, but couldn't be worked out. But he said he'd think about it. He did and decided that he was right. It was impossible.

Then I approached the dean of men. He took it up with the dean of freshmen and together they came to the conclusion that it was not the right year for such innovative procedure. In addition to this, I was told, the college had not yet decided exactly what they wanted to do with the Liggett Estate. I suggested that while they were deciding we might run a dance there. They told me this would be utterly out of the question.

I moved on up to the dean of the college and presented my case. As their president I was determined to get the freshman class something they'd never had before. It was not until the dean of the college sent me to the president of the college that I began to see that famous light at the end of the tunnel. I pointed out that the mansion belonged to the school and the freshmen were part of the school. Q.E.D. the mansion belonged to the students as much as it did to the faculty. That did it. I promised that if we did anything to hurt the house we'd have it fixed and the deal was set.

Man, that was the best freshman dance Boston College had ever seen! A guy would drive up the beautiful approach to the place, his date, very impressed, sitting beside him in whatever kind of conveyance he could afford. And as she stepped out, he turned his wheels over to a fella who parked the car for him. I'd arranged for a valet parking service and the kids who ran it made themselves a nice piece of change. The bigshot approach to the place made overtippers even out of freshmen.

When they entered the house and got a load of that center hall and that majestic staircase with dancing in the room on one side of the hall and refreshments on the other side they thought they'd walked into Tara and began looking around for Scarlett O'Hara. I can close my eyes right now and see all those guys and gals sitting on that staircase singing and laughing and making a little polite love. It was sensational. I guess it was my first big social success.

CAREFREE COLLEGE DAZE

My college days were about as much like the ones I saw in the movies back when Jack Oakie, Skeets Gallagher, and Richard Arlen were packing the pigskin for dear old Paramount, as Patsy Kelly is like Greta Garbo.

For openers, I studied. You had to, to stay in the V-5 program. I carried a very heavy load—calculus, physics, chemistry, biology, an English course in (would you believe?) poetry, and German. That was the killer. Three years of German were required in the course I started in my freshman year.

On top of all those classes I was functioning as a very gung-ho freshman class president, trying to pick up a little extra scratch for walking-around money and working to put some bread on the table in Lowell. Then came the weekend when I was supposed to have a little time for the pursuit of those pleasures so dear to the hearts of all freshmen—girls. There was one in particular, Madelaine, whose last name I'm omitting in order to spare her any embarrassment.

To help finance the Madelaine project and meet the cost of living problems in Lowell, I had several things going. One was the car pool from Lowell to college. I picked them up at home, took them to school, and returned them in the evening for three bucks a week. Five passengers, fifteen dollars.

Five were all I could carry in my Hudson Terraplane. What a name for a car. And, it seems to me, almost the entire fifteen bucks went right into keeping that Terraplane running. I figured that, at least, the car was self-supporting and I needed it in my other activities such as Madelaine and my job with the Canteen Company.

This was an outfit that serviced the vending machines in the mills in all the little towns like Lexington and Concord. Every night, like Paul Revere, I'd ride into Lexington and Concord spreading candy and peanuts, making the rounds of the machines. This was my main source of revenue. And it had an ancillary benefit. With all those candy bars and other goodies in the back of my car I was very popular among my fellow students. Of course it cost me money to hand out the stuff, but I was president of the class and how else can a politician act?

My third activity was football. But I had to give that up for reasons, I like to tell myself, of health. This did not mean that I was against getting my arms and legs broken. It was that I needed money more than a big block *B* on my sweater.

I actually made the second team. But this presented problems. One of these was the first team, which broke down into eleven small problems, each of which was bigger than me.

That was the time when Boston College had seven men on the All-American Team. Two years before they'd beaten Tennessee in the Sugar Bowl. That team was so great there was talk of an exhibition game with the Chicago Bears. It would have been the first college-versus-pro-football encounter. But it never came off in spite of serious talks. The amateur-pro problem must have blocked it.

Anyway, Boston had a red-hot team and I was on the second, or lukewarm, team. I was second-string end up against a couple of descendants from that tea party that was such a great social event one year in Boston. They were Charlie Furbush and Rocco Canelli. They had just instituted a maneuver where the right guard, in this case Canelli, would pull out of the slot, get the ball from the quarter behind center, and cut around Charlie Furbush's end. Furbush was supposed to glance off me, sort of finesse me out, and then go for the secondary while Canelli bulldogged his way through me.

Rocco Canelli weighed 260 pounds. I, at that time, weighed a mere 195.

When Rocco started running at me he'd holler, "Geronimo!" (He thought he was an Italian poet-general.) Naturally I had to make some attempt to stop him even though I knew this would lead directly to the infirmary. Nevertheless, I tried. Once in a while I succeeded. It was very painful. Most of the time I'd just get a hand on him or grab a hunk of his jersey. On the few occasions when I did make a clean tackle, Denny Meyer, the coach, would walk over to Rocco and say, pointing to me, "See this man?" (He never called anyone by name.) "See the size of him? Now let's see that play again."

Let it be no secret that I didn't stop Rocco the next time. And it loomed evident to me that if I were going to indulge in that kind of football, get my homework done, carry out my commitment to my car pool, spend part of the night filling canteens in the nearby factories, and see Madelaine over the weekend, only one thing would happen. I'd die.

So I gave up football for my own good. Some who saw me play say that it was for the good of the game.

It would be wrong to underestimate the time I spent on my car pool. True, I had to make the trip anyway. But I didn't have to make five stops each trip. There were no thruways in those days. The trip was through the city streets of all the little towns that surround Boston and defend it from contact with the outside world. Each way was a slow and tiresome twenty-three miles or so.

At night, after my homework, I'd start on my rounds of filling the vending machines. I had it down to a fine point of efficiency. I'd have been the joy of any time and motion man. I filled the machine, polished the mirrors and the bright work, and moved on to the next machine in just eleven minutes. Some of the factories had three or four machines and, with the time it took to go from one to the next, I never got to bed before three or four in the morning. I never could have done it if my experience as the Poo-Bah of the bingo game hadn't trained me how to go for long hours with little or no shut-eye.

I'm not changing the subject when I say that a couple of years ago, before I became a member of their Board of Governors, the Bedside Network gave me their Man of the Year Award. The Bedside Network is a large group of stage, film, TV, and radio people who regularly visit Veterans' hospitals to bring the men entertainment in which they themselves participate.

The people of the Bedside Network supply scripts, props, and material so that the vets can amuse themselves by pretending they're Tony Orlando, Bob Hope, Flip Wilson, and all the other personalities and characters they see on TV and hear on radio. And they give their performances for the rest of the patients in the hospital.

It doesn't sound like a lot and, in point of the amount of effort it costs the people who are doing it, it really isn't much. But the pleasure, relaxation, and change of pace it offers the vets is immeasurable. I only mention this because when I accepted their Man of the Year Award, I did so "In the name of thirty nameless men for whom, at one time, I was the sole source of entertainment and I thank God, thanks to the Bedside Network, that things have improved since then."

Those thirty nameless men were patients at a Veterans' hospital that was my only daytime vending machine stop. On my way home every Wednesday I'd make my car pool wait while I did those machines. This was usually between four and five in the afternoon. I gave those machines my best eleven-minute treatment. But as I was hustling through the job, anxious to get on with all my other myriad commitments, I noticed that I had an audience of twenty-five or thirty men. At first I thought they were waiting to use the machines. But, unlike those in a steel plant I serviced, the hospital machines were never entirely empty. After about three trips it dawned on me that my audience was just that. They weren't waiting to use the machines. They were just watching me for entertainment. I was their big weekly change of routine, a show to watch on Wednesdays.

It is in memory of those men that I am still and will always be active in the Bedside Network. But there's more to it than just helping the men put on their own plays. Sometimes, in showing up at a hospital, you get into a situation which makes you feel, here but for the grace of God, I'd be.

I was visiting St. Alban's, a mental hospital on Long Island. Every so often they have a happening involving what they call "the hot seat." It's a form of therapy. More or less the same thing is done in the drug rehabilitation scene. Someone is put on this "hot seat" and has to answer probing questions fired at him by his peers.

I was standing in the back of the room watching one of these sessions and thinking how awful it must be, yet how mentally purging, when the psychiatrist in charge standing next to me said, "Okay, Ed. How'd you like to have a go up there in the hot seat?" The next thing I knew I was being questioned by about a hundred and fifty men—all more or less mentally disturbed.

Some of the questions were nothing. But one round hit me very hard. "You were a naval aviator in World War Two and in Korea, weren't you?" came the question.

"That's right."

"You were a Marine fighter pilot?"

"Yes," I said. I'd been warned not to volunteer any information, just to answer what was asked. Lawyers tell you the same thing.

"Don't you think all Marine fighter pilots have a desire to die, have a wish to be killed?"

"I think it's possible that they may have some symptom of a death wish, otherwise why have they volunteered to tangle with death? The odds of living through a war are not very good in the fighter pilot business."

"Then you admit that you have a death wish."

"I think there's a difference between a willingness to die for a cause and a wish to die. There are certain things, for instance, that I'm willing to do but I don't wish to do them." Then a thought struck me and I asked, "Were you a naval aviator?"

"Yes, I was."

Suddenly everything was cleared up for me. He had a

conflict within himself over a death wish he thought he had but had not fulfilled.

It's not easy to walk through a big building full of men in various stages of physical and mental incapacity, men from possibly ninety years old down to mere boys of eighteen or nineteen. Most of them have been, or can expect to be, there all their lives, the wrecks of war, the rubble of humanity after the bombardment is over. Buildings can be rebuilt. Economies can be rebuilt. But things happen to men when they play at war that can never be put right again. And that applies not only to those visibly wounded in body and spirit.

There are thousands of "healthy" veterans, a contradiction in terms. No one can be in a war and come out totally healthy. He may be a hero for a while and then all he has are some memories that could be so unpleasant he doesn't want to think about them or talk about them. They haunt him and he lives alone with them.

But let's get back to the kid working his way through college servicing vending machines at night. Things were different on the weekends. On Saturday and Sundays I serviced the machines at the Bethlehem Steel Yard. The guy who serviced the machines five days a week was so knocked out by the weekend he couldn't handle it anymore, had to rest. So the job went to a college boy who wasn't doing anything all week, anyway.

Bethlehem was working on war materiél—parts of tanks and that sort of thing. They were at it night and day and they had twenty-four machines for the enormous work force. At my speed of eleven minutes per machine it came to four hours and twenty-four minutes to service the bank of twenty-four. This meant that by the time I'd finished the last machine I could start all over again at the front of the line where there'd be people waiting to buy something. Between every couple of servicings I'd have to zap out to the car and get more merchandise. That was Saturday. I just kept filling machines until I collapsed or ran out of merchandise, whichever came first.

There was only one reason this Saturday routine exhausted me—Madelaine. Friday was our big night. I'd known her in Lowell. Then, when I started going to college, I met her again in Boston. She was beautiful. A model who was always turning out to be Miss Press Photographer or Miss Drink Your Milk or Miss Have Your Eyes Examined. She seemed too rich for my blood in Lowell, too stylish. But when I ran into her on the street in Boston—don't get the wrong idea from that phrase—we hooked up together and it became a thing, a rather modified thing. But we saw a lot of each other.

Every Friday night we'd go to the Totem Pole. That was the rendezvous for people our age in Boston. All the top-name bands played there—Glenn Miller, Casa Loma, Guy Lombardo, the Dorseys. There was no better spot to romance a girl on a tight budget.

The place had been a carousel and they'd put in a band shell, decorated it with mirrors, and there was a gallery of sofas where you could sit and watch and listen to the music and maybe get in a little discreet necking. The whole evening, including a couple of hot chocolates and two hot dogs at Howard Johnson's later, came to a heavy buck thirty-five. But it was our big night. Reinforced by those hot chocolates and the franks, we'd neck until maybe four o'clock. But that's as far as it would go. Just heavy necking. Then I'd take her to where she was living in Boston, zap back to Lowell for a little shut-eye, and then go into my Saturday routine at Bethlehem. Saturday night I slept. Sunday I did the Bethlehem bit all over again. But Sunday evening Madelaine and I went to the movies.

I've gone through this whole bit of how I hustled my way through Boston College—or as far as the war would let me go—because it seems to me to be the answer to a question Johnny is always raising when he can't think of anything else to say. "Ed, why are you into so many different things?"

The answer is, I just can't help it.

The McMahon nature and the McMahon finances were always such that extreme action was always indicated. Finally, today, when things aren't so bad, I can't break the habit. I don't know if I'd want to if I could. I like a lot of variety.

One thing I can't figure out. Why, when I was hustling around filling all those vending machines and dating Madelaine, why in the world wasn't I smart enough to do what today's kids would do? Why didn't I have Madelaine helping with the machines? And today's kids would have gone much further with Madelaine, too, than I did. Today the thing to do is marry the bird and let *her* put you through dental school.

THE VICTORY BALL

I've been asked many times by my family and friends why I do some of the dangerous things, unnecessary things I do, like flying with the Blue Angels or possibly taking off in a hot-air balloon. By the time this book reaches your hands, I'll take the odds I will have done some gliding. Hang gliding is the new big thing and maybe I'll take a crack at that, too. And before I go to that great big broadcasting studio in the sky, I may even try sky diving. But I don't know.

Why? Well, it may be because I have a funny feeling that I, a nut about being on time for appointments, forgot to show up for a date with destiny.

The event that could have been my closing night on Mother Earth went blazing off without me. Ever since then I've felt I was running on borrowed time, that maybe something had gotten so snafued that it might never get straightened out and that eventually I'll be able to do a gentile version of Mel Brooks' 2013-year-old man.

The year I was president of the freshman class happened to be the year it was the freshmen's turn to host the annual victory ball for the football team. At that time Boston was so sure of having a championship team that there was never any doubt about the need for such a ball. Boston had not even been scored on. It was the hottest team in the country and there was every indication that the victory ball at the Statler Hotel was going to be the big, número-uno, don't-miss event of the collegiate social season.

By tradition it was to follow the Holy Cross game, an annual feature of the Thanksgiving Day weekend to wind up the whole, clean-slate season. I was addedly interested in this team because it was the one I would have been on if I hadn't dropped out for financial reasons.

In order to get an idea of how hot the competition was each year between Boston College and Holy Cross, take the USC-UCLA game, the Notre Dame-Army game, the Harvard-Yale games of yore, and mix them all together in Yankee Stadium with the old Yankee-Brooklyn Dodgers games and you'll get some idea of how strong the feeling ran.

Everybody was anticipating a massacre. There were some who were willing to bet that Holy Cross wouldn't even show up.

Naturally at the box office it was a bust. Who wanted to pay money to watch a snowplow push through a pile of slush? Holy Cross people didn't want to see an encounter that would make the charge of the Light Brigade look like a victory. BC people were embarrassed about their powerhouse going against Holy Cross's team, which had lost every game it played.

Only a handful showed up to see the game which ended 55 to 12 . . . in favor of Holy Cross. It was the world's outstanding example of what overconfidence can do to a good ball club. It should be printed in red in the record books.

There was no joy at the victory ball at the Statler Hotel that night. The crestfallen team showed up for a few minutes as a courtesy to the freshman class and then split. The players were then supposed to go to a big shindig being thrown for them by one of the alumni at a nightclub across the street from the hotel. But they didn't show up there at all.

People were leaving the victory ball so fast you'd think the next thing on the program was a cholera plague. The gloom was so thick it stuck in your teeth and gummed up your eyeballs. The only reason I stayed was because, as the host, I had to wait for the last, slightly smashed, disappointed rooter and his date to realize they weren't having any fun.

The affair had about reached that point when a guy came

rushing into the room as the orchestra was just winding up a set and all he could say was, "Ed, you won't believe it! You just won't believe it!"

"What?" I asked.

"You won't believe it! You just won't believe it!" he kept repeating hysterically, and rushed off, motioning me to follow him. He led me to the suite I had at the hotel, headquarters for the dance and, as we dashed through the door, he pointed toward the window and said, "Look!"

I did. Across the street was the nightclub where I thought the BC team had gone and where I had a reservation. I really didn't believe it. Lined up on both sides of the street as far as the eye could see and, I found out later, in all the cross streets, were trucks, every conceivable kind of truck that had a back door. There were bakery trucks, laundry trucks, ice trucks, furniture trucks, pie wagons. They were all being pressed into duty as ambulances.

The nightclub across the street was the Cocoanut Grove, famous now for a flash fire, one of the worst in history, that took the lives of over four hundred people. I might have been one of that ill-fated four hundred if Holy Cross had not defeated BC.

ONWARD WITH MIKE AND TRANSIT

My first official communication as a member of the United States Navy was to go home and wait for orders. I'd finished my V-5 work. The next move was up to the Navy. They had to find a place for me.

So, while waiting to hear, I managed to parlay my experience miking college shows and dances into a job with WLLH in Lowell and Lawrence, the Synchronized Voice of the Merrimack Valley. Isn't that gorgeous?

The station held auditions in the assembly hall of Lowell High School. Hundreds tried out. Everyone who could talk thought that was all you had to know how to do to be on the radio. When the audition was over I came in second. The winner was Ray Goulding of Bob and Ray.

Many people still comment on the similarity in our appearance as well as in our voices—same timbre, same tonality, same cadences. Luckily Ray was so good that it wasn't long before he left Lowell for Boston and that's where he met Bob Elliot.

When Ray left, I replaced him. I was on the air continuously from six in the evening until one in the morning. Great training. I did everything—news, weather, sports, special interviews. I even used to do my own live remote in Lawrence while I was still on the air in Lowell. Nobody told me that you can't kill two birds with one tone.

They didn't have tape in those days but they did have big sixteen-inch glass records that would take a full half-hour program. I'd put one of these on in Lowell, hop in my trusty Ter-

raplane, drive the few miles to the Hofbrau House in Lawrence, do a fifteen-minute live show from there, and get back
in Lowell in time to sign off the show. I even remember one of
my magic lines from the live show at the Hofbrau House. Get
this. "While Dick Stabile is off in the service of his nation, the
lovely Gracie Barrie takes baton in hand to lead the band in
that ever-popular ballad of loneliness. 'I'm Gonna Sit Right
Down and Write Myself a Letter.' "

As I look back on myself, bicycling between two radio
shows, one in Lowell, one in Lawrence, one recorded, one
live, the most interesting thing to me is that I also did my own
engineering. It wasn't really hard because that's what I'd
studied at BC. But I wonder what would have happened if the
record player had broken down in Lowell while I was singing
the praises of Dick Stabile in Lawrence. Or what if my trusty
Terraplane had fallen apart between the two towns?

Sometimes an engineer helped me on the Lowell shows.
Some help! Once he'd set a mike level there was only me, no
orchestra to bring in or anything, so he'd keep himself awake
trying to break me up. He went to great lengths to do this. His
most eleborate scenario was when he hung the station manager in effigy.

I was doing a sports broadcast. One of those things like Ted
Husing and Mel Allen used to do. Older readers will remember. It was a fifteen-minute thing called *Sports Headlines and
Heart Beats*. The copy came from a syndicated service and I
just read it.

I was up there doing this pathetic thing about how some ath-
lete overcame insurmountable hardship to become a cham-
pion, and in the window of the control room I saw a little doll
that looked just like the station manager marching across the
windowsill to a tiny gallows. All kinds of nonsense went on
like that in radio, where the listener couldn't see what was
happening. And it still does in television. I've been reading a
commercial on *The Tonight Show* when someone, who shall
be nameless, has crawled up under the camera, which was
only shooting the upper half of me, and given me a hotfoot.

The fact that I can generally handle this sort of thing is due in part to my early training with that engineer in Lowell. Now, if I break up during a commercial, it's not called incompetence. It's called personality.

A lot of unexplained personality hit the TV tubes one evening when Buddy Hackett decided to apply one of his Las Vegas gimmicks to the staid and austere halls of television. It's Buddy's practice, when playing Vegas, to come out during the first half of the show when James Darrin or Eddie Fisher are working, clad only in a bathrobe. Hackett's feet are bare and his whole deportment leads the audience to believe that any minute he might tear off the robe and go streaking out through the back of the room.

Well, I'm once again proving what kind of dogfood dogs like best when I look up and see Buddy standing beside the camera starting to do a striptease. Now, this is in the commercial area. The audience can't see it. But I can't avoid seeing it. So little by little there comes an extra chuckle in my always jovial voice because I don't mind telling you watching Buddy take off his shirt, zip down his fly, take off his pants and then his shorts is not something you can easily ignore. I mean, Buddy Hackett fully dressed looks pretty funny. Shut your eyes and try to visualize what I was seeing. It could make this an X-rated book.

But working at WLLH was only my night job. The days were hanging heavy on my hands because I wasn't making any money, and there's nothing more of a drag than waiting for something to happen if you're not busy. So I applied for a job with the War Department as a civil engineer's helper. Little did the department know that any civil engineer who got me for a helper needed more help than he realized.

I got the job because, again, I adhered to Dad's advice to "tell 'em what they want to hear." It was in Bedford, Massachusetts, where they were lengthening the runways and generally enlarging an Army Air Corps field. The guy who was interviewing me for the civil engineer's job asked if I'd ever been a rod boy. I didn't know a rod boy from a breeches buoy, but I said, "Sure!"

"Have you done any chaining?" he asked. Again, "Sure!" All I knew was that he was talking about surveying because I'd picked up a little info about that in college. Then, just as I'm giving this guy answers that would lead him to believe I'd worked with a surveying crew, in comes an assistant crew chief foaming at the mouth. "We can't do any work!" he screamed. "I'm short a rod boy. He claims he's sick. Holding up the whole project!"

"You got a lot of luck," said the man I was talking to. "I'm just hiring a rod boy." I didn't bother to look around to see who he meant. I knew.

"Well, come on," the crew chief said to me. "If you're the one he's talking about, let's get going." Over his shoulder he told my interviewer, "Make out the applications later. We've got work to do."

We're on a truck heading for the job and the word TROUBLE is flashing on and off like an electric sign right on my eyeballs. My new boss is still fuming mad and I know that's not going to help me when he asks me to do something and I don't know what he's talking about.

Finally, as we're approaching the work site I muster up enough courage to say, "Look, sir, I don't know how to do this job." He pulls the truck to a screeching halt. There's a transit setup and people standing around waiting. He takes several long, deep breaths, turns and looks at me, and says very slowly, "What do you mean you don't know how to do the job?"

"I've never been a rod boy. I don't know what 'chaining' means." I could see the blood rushing to his cheeks. I went right on. "Listen. I'll learn quicker than anybody you ever saw if you'll just give me a chance because I need the job and I'm smart."

He thought for a minute, came to the conclusion that a guy who was willing to learn was better than no boy at all, and reluctantly said, "All right. We'll see how it goes." I was delighted. Always, in the back of my mind, the alternative to being a radio announcer was being a civil engineer.

For the curious, in the simplest terms, "chaining" is a term of measurement in surveying. It is placing markers at fifty-foot intervals, the length of the chain. Simple!

It wasn't long before I learned how to function in a surveying crew and, with McMahon's luck, after six weeks the assistant crew chief who hired me got sick and they gave me his job. It was the beginning of what happened to me all through my career in the service. I think I got the crew chief's job not because I knew that much about surveying but because I was tall.

So I was a radio announcer at night and a surveyor by day and it's coming up to Christmas. Any minute I expected to hear from the Navy. And even with the two jobs money was in very short supply around our house. Dad was sick and Mother was very blue. I'd hear her talking to friends on the telephone—"We're not going to have a tree this year. Edward's a naval cadet and he's liable to be called any minute. There just won't be anything to celebrate. So why have a tree?"

About a week before Christmas Day something happened the way it does in the movies. We were extending a runway and were going to have to cut right through a little clump of trees. And there in my transit I saw a beautiful blue spruce. I pointed to it and told the crew, "That one's mine." Then I grabbed an ax and chopped it down. The whole grove had to go anyway. You can imagine the excitement when I brought it home that night. I'd stopped and bought some lights and some trimming and when I came in with this stuff it was almost like something out of Dickens.

"I've changed your plans," I said to Muth. "We're having a tree." It was the best we ever had—a great Christmas.

Six weeks later I got a call from the Navy.

FIRST COMMAND

There's a war on!

Suddenly the words of the Constitution have become operative.

In their obligation to their country all men have become equal.

But no man wants to be less equal than the next man.

Little did I know, when I chose to become a naval cadet, that I would be the equal of no man—no enlisted man, no CPO, no rating, no commissioned officer. Even a civilian had more status. Right off I learned that a naval cadet's standing in the naval hierarchy was zilch.

But just as you try to get yourself the best place on any line, just so you want to enjoy the best you can get in the service of your country. They don't tell you, when you become a naval cadet, that the best is yet to come—after a lot of hard work.

You've made your choice, however. You know as well as anybody that it's a waste of national resources for a man with demonstrated leadership—bingo caller, president of his class in college, radio announcer, and DJ—to become a follower. You were about to learn that less than a follower, as a naval cadet you had become a doormat.

Nevertheless, your reasoning was sound. It seemed unpatriotic to let yourself be drafted. That's the way I looked at it. An earlier and more juvenile reason was my great desire to be a Marine fighter pilot.

But this took certain qualifications and the Navy had given me the time and the opportunity . . . to meet these. I felt

141

ready. I wanted to get in there. There were three men, Hitler, Hirohito, and Mussolini, who gave my country something to fight against, something I understood and hated.

So I waited at home, worked night and day at two jobs for two reasons: (1) To keep busy, (2) To make money. Then the call came. The Navy told me where to go and what time to be there. Suddenly, like when you're sitting in a dentist's office, the hurt vanished. Only at the dentist's you can jump up and split, saying, "Damn! I forgot all about an important meeting. Tell the doc I'll be back anytime he can catch me."

You can't do that with the Navy. When they tell you to be at the Fargo Building in Boston at seven A.M. on such and such a day, that's where you'd better be. And so, with my heart in my mouth and more qualms than a man needs when he marches off to war, I went to the Fargo Building.

It wasn't the way I'd seen it in all those glamorous pictures of the War Between the States. No band, not even a drum and bugle corps, led my regiment up the circular driveway that led to the old family mansion and waited there as I solemnly shook hands with my father, kissed my mother, all my aunts, and then all the coquettes in the neighborhood, who spent a certain part of every day rallying round to kiss Johnny good-bye as he went marching off promising to come back either carrying his shield or on it. It was nothing like that with me.

There was no family mansion. And this was a different kind of war, a war of machines rather than men, which was why I had to go to college for two years to get into it.

What I actually did was say good-bye as cheerfully as I could, grab a toothbrush and shaving gear, and head for the bus to Boston and the Fargo Building. There began the waiting, which is the first essential of any war—everyone knows "hurry up and wait."

There were 150 of us at the Fargo Building when we dressed up in a ragged line for roll call. One hundred and fifty out of thousands screened from that area. Each had taken a rough exam, which I breezed through because I'd majored in physics and electrical engineering. So there was nothing they could throw at me in the way of math that I wasn't able to field. English, too, was a piece of cake. I knew more words than I knew the meaning of, but I knew how and when to use them.

The physical tests I'd rather forget about. Finally we were all lined up and I almost sank through my shoes when the sergeant, after calling the roll, looked back through the list and barked out, "McMahon!"

"Yes?"

"Yes, *sir* is what you say, Mac. And you step forward, smartly, when I call your name."

I stepped forward, smartly. "Yes, sir!"

"You're in charge of this group. You'll take them to Texarkana, Texas."

I didn't have time to wonder why he picked me. But hindsight told me it must have been my voice. Obviously I was accustomed to using it. And it came out sounding like the voice of authority. This is something you learn calling bingo. "I have *num*-bah sev-ven in the *bee* line"—when you said that, people knew what they had to do and did it. And I don't think it hurt a bit that I was six feet three.

My first job with the Navy was one I didn't like. It put my peers, so to speak, under me; hence, as things go in the service, against me. And my superiors treated me as a naval cadet, which is one who has no place at all in the world of men. So the cat who always wanted to be "just one of the guys" just wasn't.

I was the leader of 150 gallant naval cadets from the Boston area entrained for Texarkana, which seemed like a ludicrous place for the Navy to train people. I had their train tickets, their food chits, and every one of their problems. All my training traveling with a carnival concession was called into action. Most of the men had never been more than fifty miles from home. Their mothers had taken care of them. I became their mother. I knew complicated things like how to release a guy who locked himself in the john on the train.

I was constantly calling the roll, keeping track. Keeping

peace. Keeping up morale. One guy loses a food chit. I get him another. Another guy loses a food chit. I have no more. I give him mine. But he doesn't know it. A million things can happen taking 150 kids by train from Boston to Texarkana. One of the things that happened was that we passed a train going the other way taking 150 naval cadets from Texarkana to Boston. That's the way they run wars.

The trip took between three and four days but I got them there without losing a man. We were met by the commanding officer of the preflight training camp. I lined up my Coxey's Army, called the roll, turned, saluted, and said, "Cadet McMahon reporting, sir. All present and accounted for."

A PILOT DECISION

The first time I saw Texarkana in the first year of WW II, it did not strike me as the ideal place for a honeymoon. This was as it should be, because my relationship with the United States Navy was no honeymoon.

You see, for my stay in Texarkana, and for sometime afterward at various other places where I learned various things about various aircraft, I was being tutored by the Navy but was not actually a member of it. I was going through a weeding-out process. My commitment to the Navy was only half the bargain. The Navy wanted to find out if I was worth bothering with, if I could possibly become a pilot. Not until they made up their mind about this would they actually enlist me.

The Navy started out by teaching us to fly Cubs as a way of wiping out anybody with a fear of high places, a susceptibility to motion sickness, claustrophobia, or inability to remember which was his right and which was his left hand while flying in an upside-down position.

Texarkana was the first stop along a trail of Navy installations, each designed in its own way to eliminate a person from pilot training and syphon him off into a pair of thirteen-button (now extinct) bell-bottom pants . . . or the infantry.

Just to give you an idea of how successful this distillation process was, out of my group of 150 who left the Fargo Building in Boston, only two, of whom I was one, got their wings. It all happened gradually. Guys would drop out along the way for different reasons. Occasionally because of death.

At each new installation you had to decide whether to continue training and ultimately join the Navy or whether you'd prefer to drop out.

Those who dropped out could then continue to try to be pilots by joining the Army Air Corps. Those who stayed in the Navy program, and ultimately failed to make pilot, went back to "go." They had to start all over again as seamen second class at the Great Lakes Naval Training Station.

I had to make my decision while I was at the third and last of a series of preflight schools, which happened to be the University of Georgia in Athens.

I arrived there as just another cadet with no command responsibilities. I hoped I could keep it that way. I realized that I needed all the resources I had to concentrate on the job of winning my wings.

But my freedom didn't last long. In the first regimental parade held, I was standing at attention when I heard, "Cadet McMahon, front and center!"

I executed the maneuver as ordered as I heard the officer in command say, "Cadet McMahon, you have been selected to be cadet regimental commander. Take charge!"

It had happened again. As far as I could see or learn, solely because of my size and the sound of my voice, I'd been given a command.

This was anything but great, because my stay in Athens was one tough assignment. The training at Athens was more Spartan than Athenian. It was the place where the final decision had to be made whether or not to stick with the Navy or switch to the Army.

So Athens was where the Army bombed the Navy. Every day they zoomed low over the campus and dropped thousands of pamphlets suggesting that we quit the Navy program and join the Army Air Corps. This, they pointed out, would assure us that we'd never wind up as seamen second class at the Great Lakes Naval Training Station.

The Army's pitch was to make it sound as if it were a lead-pipe cinch to get your wings with them while, as we had discovered, it was no roll in the air to win them from the Navy. As one cadet said to me as we panted from one class to another on the double, "I wouldn't trade this training for a million dollars. But I wouldn't go through it again for ten million."

We were jogging along the cinder track that ran from the north campus to the south campus. We called it the Burma Road. Just as Boston men went to Texarkana for training and vice versa, all the cadets who lived on the south campus had all their classes on the north one and, again, vice versa. We used to pass one another running back and forth. The road was our first activity of the day and the last at night—always on the double.

They had other little goodies for getting us into great physical shape—if we lived through them. They had a little deal called a "pack test." Very simple. They strapped a bag of sand weighing one third of your weight to your back. When I hit Athens I weighed about 180 pounds. This meant I carried a sixty-pound bag of sand.

Carrying one third of your weight, you had to step up onto a bench twenty-two inches high. That's about like stepping onto a bed. You had to do this, right foot, left foot, both feet up, for five minutes. If you think it doesn't sound like much, try it. The Navy figured it as complete exhaustion. It was their little way of finding out how you'd stand up under stress—and they are welcome to it.

When you finished the test they'd see how long it took you to recover, checking your pulse, blood pressure, and all other vital signs. You took this test the first day and you had to pass it the last day if you expected to get your wings. You never forgot this detail as you took the test to the rhythm of a drumbeat. Even if they'd gotten Buddy Rich and Louis Belson alternating on drums they couldn't have made anybody enjoy it.

When I finally passed and left Athens, I'd dropped five pounds, was down to 175. I wish I could make it now. But not by doing the pack test.

Naturally, living conditions were delightful. I wouldn't say ours were cramped, but if where a man lives is called his quarters, ours wouldn't have qualified as dimes. The rooms, originally built for two, were furnished with two double-deck bunks.

Reveille sounded at five. You got up and had to be standing beside your bunk all shaved, dressed, polished and ready, holding all your bedclothes in your arms as if you were about to take them to the laundry. Then you waited for the inspection officer to come along. This was done so you wouldn't just crawl out of bed and put things back smooth and nice. You had to make your bed all over again each morning from scratch. Then the inspecting officer dropped a quarter on the bed to see if it would bounce. If it didn't, look out!

Following this, to get everything shipshape you mopped up the room, doing it so that when you were finished you could reach the mop into the closet and close the door without leaving any footprints. It took quite a bit of doing. But working together, my buddy Buckwheat O'Neill (don't ask me why I called him that) and I (he called me Alfalfa McMahon) got the job done. This sort of thing went on for three months—the pack tests, the running back and forth along the Burma Road, and policing your room. But no airplane flying. The day was filled with plenty of athletics, however. There was football, soccer, swimming, and baseball and you had to get your "S" for superior in all of them. It was a grueling three months. And for the whole three months the Army continued to bombard us with their propaganda for the Air Corps.

But they didn't get me with their guileful blandishments. I'd been brought up on the technique of sales pitches. So I wasn't one of those guys who wandered around the campus in his spare time—about ten minutes a day—staring at the Army's offer and wondering what to do, wondering whether the Army really was easier, which it was difficult to believe. While no one really had his heart set on becoming seaman second class after all the preflight work he'd put in, no one wanted to wind up as a pilot in the cavalry.

The real reason I didn't make the switch was because I'd grown used to outdoor work and the possibility of ending up as a pilot in the cavalry, as explained in the joke, was for 100 percent indoor work in barns with a top sergeant commanding you to pile it here or pile it there.

It wasn't that I disliked horses. It was that the Army's arguments that you'd be better off with them than in the Navy seemed to me to be exactly what a pilot in the cavalry had to shovel.

THE HEAD MASTER

Denton, Texas, took its place among the world's great seats of learning as the site of a normal school called Texas State Teachers College. It was while she was attending this school that the lovely film star Linda Darnell was discovered and transported to tinsel town. This robbed a whole bunch of Texas tykes of a really neat teacher. All this would have made little difference to me if it had not been for events that took place just before the arrival in Denton (from Texarkana) of 150 naval cadets still under my command.

We came to Denton while there was trouble, to paraphrase the song in Meredith Willson's *The Music Man.* I say trouble right there in Denton, Texas. And the trouble was—to continue as Willson might have—a nasty mess, and that ends with *s*, and that stands for sex.

To bring it right down to the bottom line, the group of naval cadets that had moved out just ahead of us must have been a horny lot and, I might add, for good cause. A great many of the girls in Denton were just as attractive as Linda and, like her, were built to maximum feminine specifications. What went even further was that many of them must have been more than eager to explore the ways of a man with a maid. As a result, Denton was suffering an epidemic of unplanned parenthood among their unmarried daughters.

To stop this epidemic the city fathers insisted that the Navy confine its cadets to quarters. That meant us. It was like busting the next two people to enter a bank after it had been ripped off by Bonnie and Clyde.

Naturally, as the appointed cadet commander of this quarantined group of eager young men, I was held personally responsible for the situation and my popularity sank to an all-time low. The only man who took more flack than I did was my immediate superior, a lieutenant whom I shall call Ginguzzler. He was more than a bit of a lush and, like me, he was lonesome. We were drawn together the way a fifth of Tanqueray will inevitably gravitate toward a bottle of dry vermouth.

So every evening the lonely lieutenant would seek me out and, as his guest, we wandered around the town looking for trouble and occasionally finding it. At regular intervals the college would run dances for the girls. Always a good place to find trouble.

Originally the dances were held so that the girls could meet some boys, which is always part of the learning process, therefore acceptable practice at a teachers college. But, with the town boys all off at some distant cantonment and the local trainees confined to quarters, the dances were less than successful—at least emotionally.

It was frightening to walk into a dance, with Lieutenant Ginguzzler, an officer and a gentleman, hence privileged, and find maybe a hundred women and only six men who were never likely to be drafted. They were at Teachers' College to learn to play the violin and that is what they were doing at the dance, supplying the music. Have you ever danced to a violin sextette?

I leave it to your imagination to figure out what happened when a young, tall, moderately attractive cadet commander and his slightly squiffed but impressively sea-dog-like lieutenant walked into this harem. It was fun while it lasted. But that sort of thing could not be kept a secret and before long the young fliers in training, with whom I had to associate daily, were treating me as if I were Hitler's nephew. I was between Scylla and Charybdis, wherever that is. I didn't want to offend my commanding officer and I didn't want to be on the hook with my peers.

Finally I said, "Lieutenant, you know I have a helluva time when I'm out with you. What could be better than being one of two men in a college full of babes? But I've also gotta live with the guys. Right now they all have little McMahon dolls that they're sticking pins in. So either I've got to quit going out with you or, better still, you fix it so the guys can get out and spread themselves around a little; arrange it so that I can take them all to the dance this evening."

What came out of this was a compromise. My group was to be let out on its own for three hours on Saturday afternoon and three hours on Sunday afternoon. No sooner was this announced than the Saturday-evening dances became matinee dansants. As everybody knows, a healthy young American man, if he's clever, can get into a whale of a lot of trouble in three hours on Saturday afternoon and three hours on Sunday afternoon.

I have always thought it was peculiar that a guy could be out the entire day with a girl and neither one of them is in any way compromised. But let him be out all night with her and her old man starts to polish the family blunderbuss that he uses annually in the Thanksgiving Day Pageant.

Now it came to pass that there was a young lady student who was majoring in the art of the dance. She had a pretty face, lovely long legs, and a mind that, had she been born thirty years later, would have drawn her into the Women's Lib movement. She was a free soul and she liked me very much.

One Sunday afternoon when we came back from a long ride in the country in her Packard two-seater with the rumble seat, we sat outside for about five minutes longer than my leave. I hoped my friend the lieutenant would take the cue and he did.

When he saw me, the head honcho of the outfit walking in five minutes late, he said in a loud voice for all to hear, "McMahon! You're late. Five minutes late!"

"Yes, sir. I apologize."

"Apologies don't go in this man's Navy. You're busted. You're no longer commander of the cadets."

"Very well, sir. Will that be all, sir?"

"No, that's not all. From now on you're captain of the head."

He had not only relieved me of my command, he had sent me to the bathroom. As head of the head I had gone from the top to the bottom of my class. But by doing what he did, the lieutenant had fixed everything up for me with my pals, and I appreciated it.

I appreciated it so much that to this day when I'm at a night-club where there is a captain in charge of the head handing out soap, towels, and possibly a small squirt of Binaca, I am a very heavy tipper. I understand what it means for a man to humble himself and I try to help him compensate for his lack of status by trying to make him independently wealthy.

Even outside of the head I'm an overtipper. I have found that a little money properly placed gets you remembered. And a man who is remembered in places that are tough to get into always gets in. McMahon's law says, "A little overtipping now and then makes bigshots out of little men."

PENSACOLA—IT'S THE REE-AL THING

I suppose it was typical of the Marine Corps that there seemed to be no way of entering its aviation arm but by fighting your way in. First you had to join the Navy. Then you had to qualify for flight training, mentally and physically. This was followed by three preflight schools before you could get on line to get your wings. When you finally got them you had to transfer from Naval Aviation to Marine Corps Aviation. If you didn't join up when you were very young, you reached retirement age before you got into the air.

My three preflight schools were at Texarkana, Texas, Denton, Texas, and Athens, Georgia. From there I went to Pensacola, Florida, where actual flight training began in earnest. But there was a little trap between Athens and Pensacola. It was an installation near Dallas that was lovingly called by those who were to become its victims, "E Base." "E" stood for elimination.

At E Base they made the final determination whether you went on to Pensacola or up to the Great Lakes Training Station as a seaman second class. Traditionally one-third of those who made it through all the other training steps were washed out at E Base.

There we were taught to fly a Steerman biplane, known affectionately as the Yellow Peril. You flew these for five or six hours every day. You were taught stunts and aerial acrobatics of all kinds so that these basic maneuvers weren't new to you if you should make it to Pensacola. During all this flying you were required to pass four tests known enigmatically as the A Test, the B Test, the C Test, and the D Test. Once successfully through the D Test you'd bought a ticket to Pensacola. If you didn't wash out there, you got your wings.

I've recapped all the effort, mental and physical, you had to exert before the Marine Corps would commission you to fly one of their expensive fighter planes in action to prove that the Corps didn't want you to die dumb. And of all the things you weren't dumb about, the main thing was death. I saw a few of my buddies killed in training. It was not a good feeling.

At Pensacola, before I got my wings, one of my mates flipped over and lost an eye. Another friend lost a hand in an accident. To say the least, it made you apprehensive. Yet you went on and on and if you were lucky you survived and got your wings. I almost didn't.

This was not for any sensible reason, not because of any lack of knowledge or skill, but because of what, for want of a better word, I now have to call chivalry. When knighthood was in flower and all that sort of romantic stuff, over a girl I scarcely knew. This all happened when I was what they called an "end of the road" trainee.

I was just six weeks away from winning the wings I'd promised to bring home to my grandmother. Clearly it was no time to do anything that would get me washed out and, believe me, I didn't plan it that way. But there was a "tarmak" at the base who kind of looked up to me.

A tarmak was a sort of cadet in waiting. He was not yet allowed to fly. But they kept him around, working on planes and so forth, to familiarize himself with the machinery and the procedures. This was over a year after I'd started my training and they now had more cadets than they knew what to do with.

This lad's dad happened to have quite a bundle and his kid meant a lot to him so he decided to come down to Pensacola and spend New Year's Eve with his son. There was just one hitch. The boy didn't get leave on New Year's Eve. He wasn't due for any and they weren't making any special deals for rich young tarmaks.

The old man took it philosophically and decided to have his son select some of his buddies to be surrogates for him at the New Year's Eve bash that was being held at the Edgewater Beach Hotel. It was once a very fashionable spot, the kind I have since learned to like very much.

There were, of course, lots of uniforms and champagne was the posted drink of the evening. Everything was fine. The finest thing about it was that my young friend—fully a year younger than I was—had selected me to take his place.

Another very fine thing was that he had a very pretty sister, whom I shall call Natalie, that he hadn't told me about.

I was all dressed up in blues and having about the best time I'd had in months for two reasons: (1) Natalie seemed to like me, (2) I'd happily forgotten that among all military uniforms cadets were shunned by enlisted men and scorned by officers. Next to any cadet, Rodney Dangerfield would have been the most respected man in the room. Busboys were doing better than we were. And to top it all, I found out that Natalie was engaged to be married.

But I rose above all this. I was there, she was there, and we were dancing; she in the state of Florida, me in a state of euphoria. I think I took up residence in this state when Natalie said, "See this lieutenant walking toward us? Don't let him cut in, please. *Please,* don't let me dance with him." The loot was a lieutenant JG, but at that point I became a giant, senior grade, and damn being a cadet! A fair lady had put her trust in me. I patted her shoulder reassuringly with my right, white-gloved hand and prayed that the lieutenant—I'll never forget his name, Koontz—had his eye on another girl—or dropped dead.

I felt a tap on my shoulder and I changed my prayer. I prayed that I'd drop dead or that it was General MacArthur. I felt sure Natalie wouldn't mind dancing with him. Unfortunately, the general was busy elsewhere and it was, as I suspected, Lieutenant Koontz. What he said was, and in a boorish tone, "I'm cutting in, Cadet." And he sort of pulled me away from Natalie.

Now that's not the sort of thing you do to a very physically fit young Irishman who has had several glasses of champagne. I shrugged free and said, "No, you're not, lieutenant!" Then Natalie and I continued dancing.

She gave me a little special hug of appreciation and if my head had swelled any more my scalp wouldn't have fitted me.

In a moment the lieutenant came back and gave me a shove. Then everything hit the fan. Here was an officer and a gentleman and a soon-to-become officer and gentleman about to engage in a brawl.

What actually took place was the same as what happens in a baseball game when the batter runs out to take a poke at the pitcher. Both teams swarm onto the field to protect their buddy from possible expulsion from the game. On one side the cadets were holding me. On the other side Lieutenant Koontz was being restrained by more levelheaded junior officers. My host was saying, "I'm sure this can be straightened out." He didn't know Koontz and he didn't know anything about the Navy.

Koontz just pointed his finger at me and said, "I'm going to find out who you are!"

"You don't have to, Lieutenant," I snapped at him. "I'm Cadet McMahon"—which was about as smart a thing to do as trying to hold an alligator's mouth open with a toothpick.

Then, with the sudden realization that my whole career was about to go down the drain because of a girl who was engaged to someone else I excused myself and left the room.

There was nothing to do but wait for the ax to fall. One week went by. Nothing. Two weeks. Nothing. Early in the third week I walked into a lecture on the radio operation of a new plane we were going to fly and who is giving the lecture? My old friend Lieutenant Koontz. Only he had been promoted to full lieutenant.

My first tactic was to find out if he remembered me. We'd both been drinking that night. I raised my hand and asked a question. He answered it without showing any sign of recognition. I figured I was over the hill and home free. The luck of the Irish had held. I was floating on air. But I came down to earth fast when I got back to the barracks, where I found my name posted to report to the commanding officer.

It was an invitation I couldn't refuse, and after the usual cordial exchange of salutes, I saw lying on his desk, spread out before him, my whole career as a cadet. Fourteen months, every record, every picture, every report, every exam score. The complete dossier.

"McMahon," he began, "you have been recommended for washout on six counts!" Then he started to name them—drunkenness, disorderly conduct, disrespect to an officer, insubordination, and two I've forgotten. It could have been stupidity.

"As I look at your record," the CO went on, "each place you've been stationed you've served as company commander. Each place but here. Why?"

I explained what had happened at Athens, which was hard for an officer to understand unless he'd kept in very close touch with his men.

The CO looked at me long and hard for what seemed like a week and a half. Then he rubbed his chin the way Harry Carey used to do in the movies, kind of cocking his head to one side and said, sympathetically, I thought, "Son, you're in a lot of trouble." This was not news to me.

"Will I be washed out, sir?"

"I hope not," he said, giving me a little low-cost insurance. "The only thing I think you can do to prevent it is to go and have a talk with Lieutenant Koontz."

"Yes, sir," I said, feeling this was the worst possible thing I could do.

"He's running the tower today. See him up there. That'll be all for now, McMahon."

Salute. About-face. Out.

I'd be compounding my felonies if I didn't do what the CO told me to do. So I dragged my tail over to the tower, grumbling to myself about a fink like Koontz, who would do the kind of thing he did. But I kept walking and I kept climbing to the top of the tower and soon I heard myself saying, as if it were a movie I was watching, "Lieutenant Koontz, I'd like to talk to you, sir."

His face was completely without expression as he said, "Yes?" Meaning, what's left to talk about?

"I'd like to ask you a question, sir."

Another, flat, questioning, "Yes?"

"What would you do, sir, if the following thing happened?"

As I started to tell him about Natalie's panicky request not to let "this officer coming toward us dance with me." Then I realized I was talking to the very man the girl was violently rejecting. But I was trapped, so I went on with the story and finished. "In a situation like that, sir, what would you have done?"

To my surprise he said, "I don't know."

"That was my dilemma, sir, and the way you cut in irritated me." I explained why. What could he do to me that was worse than everything he'd done?

"I don't know what to do, McMahon. You certainly displayed . . ." and he catalogued all his charges against me. "I just don't know what to do."

"I'd certainly hate to have this ruin my career in the Navy, sir. I was counting on it to help me get through college if I make it through the war."

"What college do you plan to attend?"

At that moment the McMahon luck snapped back into gear. I said, "Yale, sir."

Koontz's face lit up. Without knowing it I'd told him what he wanted to hear. "Well, McMahon," he pontificated, "you have to watch your deportment at Yale. It's a very special school. I went to Yale and I intend to return there."

I'd told the truth, of course. I'd always wanted to go to Yale. I'd been accepted there. But I couldn't go because I couldn't find a job in New Haven. This ran through my mind as Koontz kept me standing there while he mulled over what he should do about me now that I was a potential Yalie.

Finally he said, "All right. I think I understand your predicament now. If you've learned your lesson, if you'll behave yourself, I'll have you put on probation.''

"Thank you, sir,'' I said, saluted sharply, did an about-face, and split.

It meant that for the last six weeks before I got my wings—with girls falling all over one another to date the upcoming ensigns and second lieutenant Marines—I was confined to base. This might have been all for the best. It was during that last six weeks that I made application for the Marine Corps, which brought on a whole new rash of tests.

The first thing the Corps wanted to know was why you wanted to get into it, what you thought you had to offer. Then they wanted to know why you wanted to be a fighter pilot and what you thought qualified you for such work. To find this out one of the things they did was to present you with yet another questionnaire that was part psychology test to determine if, instead of a fighter pilot, you might not make a better bomber pilot or a skipper for a seaplane.

As I answered some of the questions honestly, I knew it would hurt my chances of being picked as a fighter pilot. All I had to do was lie a little. But I didn't. I'm proud of that. There were questions such as, "Would you strafe women and children in the street?" I answered "No!" There was, "Would you shoot a man in a parachute?" I answered, "No!"

I wound up in land-based bombers.

So I went to the psychological board in Pensacola and explained, using each of five carefully selected questions as examples. "If I'd answered this dishonestly, I'd be a fighter pilot," I said. "But I really don't think you have to shoot a guy in a parachute. I'm not out to kill *him*. My job is to cripple his plane. I'm not out to shoot down innocent women and children who have nothing to do with the war, who are actually victims of it.''

This, you must remember, was long before Vietnam when nobody knew who was and who was not a combatant.

The upshot of it was that the board asked me to write them a letter explaining my feelings and why I answered the questionnaire the way I did. The letter got me transferred to the fighter command.

I was given a short leave and ordered to report to Lee Field in Jacksonville, Florida. I had two weeks and I figured to cut a handsome figure around Lowell in my new Marine blues and my old Terraplane, which I'd put up on blocks the night before I headed for the Fargo Building in Boston. I'd taken out the batteries, taken off the tires, and done everything so that when the war was over I'd have a car.

When I walked into the garage, no car. I stormed into the house and the first person I saw was Mother. "Where's my car?"

"Oh, that," she said. "I sold it. I got fifty dollars for it!"

I was stunned. I couldn't believe it. The wife of a carnival pitchman, the mother of a bingo caller, had been hustled out of a car worth several hundred dollars in the war economy for a mere fifty bucks, a car that wasn't even hers.

"Did I do wrong?" Mother asked, as if she knew she had.

All I could think to say was, "You might have held out for sixty." What good would it do to get mad?

THE OTHER SHOE

When I arrived at Lee Field there were about four hundred newly commissioned ensigns and some Marine second lieutenants who, like myself, were learning to fly what was at that time the Navy's hottest fighter plane, the Corsair. It was referred to lovingly as "the killer." And it was. The day I arrived at Lee three men lost their lives in training accidents. What a welcome!

The name of the Navy lieutenant in charge of the group I was assigned to was Radford. It occurred to me that he had done exactly what I did when I went on the road with a bingo game. He too had followed in his father's footsteps. Lieutenant Radford's old man was Admiral Radford.

I just mentioned that to emphasize that my commander was all Navy, very gung ho. Along with everyone else on the base he did everything possible to instill in us newly commissioned fighter pilots a spirit as close as possible to the fanatacism of the Japanese kamikazes, yet consistent with our principles of democracy.

In fact, the big joke around the base, the one that everyone heard the day he arrived, was about the kamikaze recruit being briefed by his commanding officer. "You will," said the commander, "be trained to be the best pilot in the whole world. You will be given a Zero, the best airplane in the world. When you have mastered every one of the hundreds of maneuvers this fine plane can perform, you will be given your great assignment. This will be to take off from one of our honorable carriers, proceed to a designated United States war-

162

ship, and fly your plane directly into the bridge or down the forward funnel.''

The briefing officer paused to allow the Japanese pilot to digest his orders. He then concluded, ''You are, of course, prepared to do this for our honorable emperor.''

The flier waited a second, then leaned forward, putting both hands on his commander's desk, looked him right in the eye, and said, ''Are you out of your f——mind?''

The gag was no joke at all to the Navy men who had stood on deck, on the bridge, or been in the engine room or gun turret when one of those suicide pilots went to meet his ancestors. There were many of those who came to tell us about the experience, to inspire us and to psych us up to making whatever sacrifice might prove necessary.

Among these was the Marine Corps' first fighter pilot hero, winner of the Congressional Medal of Honor, Lieutenant Joe Foss. Joe, who returned from the war and became governor of South Dakota, among other things, gave us a big pep talk and had us all on our feet cheering when he said, ''I'll see you all out there!''

We had been taking very heavy punishment in the Pacific. We'd lost a lot of men, planes, and ships in the battle of the Coral Sea. A new replacement squadron was needed at once. So I figured my time at Lee was limited, that I'd be shipping out pronto.

In a war, particularly one you're losing, you have to do a lot of improvising. The way they improvised a new fighter squadron was to create one out of all the flying instructors at Lee Field. These were the men who were teaching the latest tactics. They were up on everything. Who could be better? What choice was there? It was logical. A first for the Navy.

What happened to me after that defies logic but follows form. Again I answered roll call and heard, ''Lieutenant McMahon, step forward.''

''Yes, sir.''

''Lieutenant, from this moment on, you are the flight instructor for your group.''

I saluted and said, "Yes, sir." But what was running through my mind was the question, "What kind of a Navy have I gotten myself into?" Since there was no way of getting out of it, however, I made the best of it, followed my father's advice, and did my best to "walk in as if I belonged."

I studied. I read. I practiced. I stayed one lesson ahead of the men who came in with me. I was getting, as well as dishing out, the most important part of what would add up to, when finished, about one hundred thousand dollars' worth of pilot training.

And there was one compensation for all the extra work and danger I encountered as an instructor. I had under me officers from other branches of the Navy taking flight training for one reason or another. But don't get the idea I gloried in a feeling of power to be, in a sense, in command of men who were years and ranks my seniors. I didn't. It scared me. Except in one instance.

Who do you think showed up at Lee and wound up in my training group? Yep! Lieutenant Koontz.

It is impossible to describe the indecent satisfaction it gave me, having Lieutenant Koontz face me every day and never giving him an indication of what my intentions were. In his heart he must have felt that any minute I would wash him out as he had threatened to do to me. The temptation was there. All I had to do was sign a paper. Any pretext would do . . . or none. I could just state that I considered him incapable of becoming a fighter pilot. He would have no recourse.

To this day I am proud that I never said a word to him—confining my revenge to letting him suffer in uncertainty. I never dropped the other shoe. And I never saw him again after he left Lee Field. I hope he had the same good fortune in the war that I did.

Me.

Ringmaster Jack Sterling (top), myself, and Chris Keegan preparing our clown faces for another *Big Top Circus* TV show from Philadelphia.

One of the early television shows in Philadelphia. From left to right: Sandy Stewart, Jack Valentine, Don Prindle, me, and the Tommy Ferguson Trio.

Playbill for *The Impossible Years* when I filled in for Alan King.

Carmel Quinn and I starred in the musical *Wildcat* with the
Kenley Players, Warren, Ohio.

Agog over Marilyn Monroe.

Here I am with Father Gilbert V. Hartke, head of the Catholic University Speech and Drama Department.

Sharing the spotlight as Santa Claus with Mitzi Gaynor on her Christmas special.

During a break in the filming of *The Incident,* I receive instructions from director Larry Peerce.

On the *Tonight Show* the Duke, John Wayne, ignores the boss to make a big man out of the second banana.

Jack Grant, prop man for
the *Tonight Show*,
outclassing the boss
(except for the sneakers).
That's Shirley Wood on
the right, one of the
show's talent coordinators.

Jerry Lewis being Jerry
Lewis as guest host for the
Tonight Show.

Don Rickles, holding
George Segal's banjo,
takes a moment to dissect
me one more time.

Muhammad Ali weighing in
on the *Tonight Show.*

A night of superstars, Sammy Davis, Jr., and Mickey Rooney.

Joey Bishop convulses the great Jack Benny on the tenth anniversary show.
(Photo by Richard Nairin.)

Listening intently to British actress Diana Rigg.

The night the *Tonight Show* greeted the Divine Miss "M," Bette Midler, was indeed one to remember.

Doc Severinsen and I get ready for the Fourth!

Claudia (left) and Linda (right) on one of the early trips to Los Angeles.

As a jealous McLean Stevenson looks on, I'm being kissed by one of the loveliest of the lovelies, Doris Day.

One of my youngest fans.

Catching up on the news on the daily commute back from Las Vegas at the height of the Watergate scandal—the headline reads NIXON QUITS.

Yours truly on the special "Ed McMahon and His Friends Discover Wet at Cyprus Gardens."

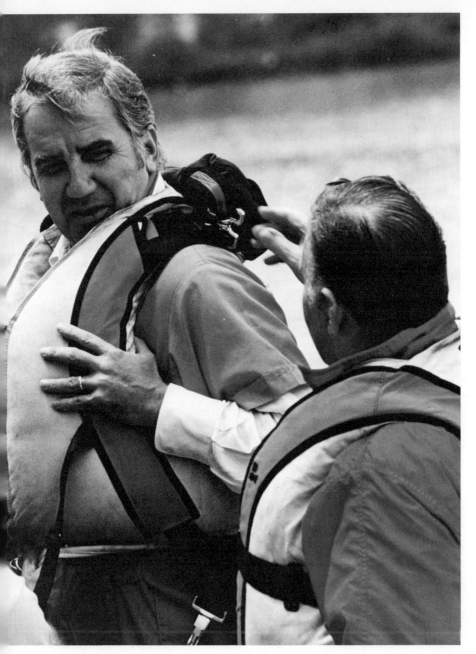

Donning a parachute before one of my frequent trips aloft.

A very big moment in my life—opening night in Las Vegas.

SAVED BY THE BOMB

I had put in twenty-two months at Lee Field as an instructor and test pilot when we reached that point in the war where we were beginning to turn it in our favor. Instructors and test pilots were under heavy pressure to accelerate the training of new fighter pilots, "chicklets" we called them, who had just won their wings.

So there was an ongoing need to use every available plane every moment of the day. One day a Corsair that had lost a wing and been rebuilt came in but it couldn't be used until it was thoroughly tested and certified safe. My group needed that plane, so lucky Ed had to test it.

The moment I got it off the ground I knew there was something wrong with it. It was unstable. I couldn't get the newly repaired plane into a level position. Even with the stick all the way over I remained at about a 45 degree left bank. This is a very bad and very tiring way to fly an airplane if for no other reason than that it means you can't land without shearing off a wing.

The book solution to that problem was, jump! A man is more valuable than a machine. I started to climb and set the craft on what figured to be a safe course over the Everglades, where it could crash without doing any damage to anything but a couple of alligators, which had not, at that time, been designated as an endangered species.

With everything set, I pushed back the canopy and was about to jump when I felt the wind coming at me and saw the nothingness beneath me and said to myself, "To hell with this."

I closed the canopy and told the tower I'd changed my mind and was going to try to bring her in for a landing. The ground's position was, "You're the boss. You're the pilot. Do what you think best." For the next few minutes what I thought was best began to look worse and worse.

Below me, as I made my first tentative pass over the field, I saw the emergency vehicles assembling—the "meat wagons," our name for the ambulances, the fire trucks, the crash wagons—lining up along the runway with their red lights flashing. They were all waiting to take care of me in whatever condition they picked me up.

It crossed my mind, busy as I was, that they might marshal all that rescue equipment a little more discreetly so as not to add to the rescuee's nervous burden by making him any more aware than he already *must* be of what his fate *might* be.

I became more and more tired as I made pass after pass at the runway and then chickened out. After about the tenth or eleventh time I figured the best plan was to pop my wheels at the last minute. This, I hoped, would lift the wing long enough to let me land before the wing came down again. I knew this maneuver figured to cause a ground loop and what happened to me (and the plane) after that depended largely on luck and was the problem of all those wagons with the flashing red lights. It took several more passes before I got my guts up as the emergency worsened because I was not only running out of strength, I was also running out of fuel. So, on the next pass, I mentally shut my eyes and did it!

Sometimes—generally—a landing gear will give on a landing like that. Sometimes, if it cartwheels, the plane will catch fire. But I had put the whole matter in charge of whatever Account Executive up There was in charge of the McMahon business. I'm happy to say, he turned out to be a good man to have on my side.

The plane hit the runway, wandered all over the field like a drunken sidewinder, and finally came to a halt, tilted on one side, minus the malfunctioning wing but with the pilot whole and okay.

My buddies in the squadron, knowing that Navy coffee has the same medicinal quality often ascribed to chicken soup, handed me some hot java in one of those handleless Navy mugs. My hands shook so from nervousness and fatigue that the coffee sloshed all over and burned one hand. I think to this day that I'm the Navy's only crash victim hospitalized for damage from scalding coffee.

It was right after this that I figured combat couldn't hold any more perils than being a test pilot and instructor.

It was suggested that a carrier be commissioned with only Marine fighter pilots. Usually there were about three Marine pilots integrated into each Navy fighter squadron. So this new 100 percent Marine lash-up figured to be a very hot potato. I wanted to be in it.

This made no sense because I was married while at Lee Field and my wife, as such things sometimes happen, had become pregnant. Naturally, after I'd put in for this combat duty—but only after—we talked over how it might turn out. Considering some of the narrow squeaks I'd had, I argued that it was clear a change of some kind was indicated.

In the end we said all the usual emotional and highly charged things that pass between men who are about to go to war and women who can only console themselves with that classic cliché, "At least I'll have your baby." The movies didn't make that up. People actually said it.

That I'd be checked out for the all-Marine carrier was never in doubt. I was fully qualified to join the outfit which was shaping up on the West Coast. All I had to do was to hang around Lee Field testing planes as they came in until the new carrier was ready. Every day seemed like a month.

Finally the day came. I was asleep in the test pilot's shack awaiting my next assignment to arrive when a phone call told me that my orders had come to ship out for the West. By a strange coincidence that happened to be the very same day we dropped that deadly egg on Hiroshima.

I had twenty-five days' leave coming before I was due in California. I started this leave knowing full well that the war must be nearly over and I'd missed it.

On the third day of my leave we dropped the second bomb on Nagasaki. The following day Japan surrendered. A few days after that my orders to go west were rescinded. So there never was an all-Marine carrier in World War II and, as Bob Hope has said, I never left home.

As I write this I find myself experiencing a strange mixture of emotions, realizing that if we had not created and dropped that awful, unforgivable weapon, I might have died, along with thousands of other Americans and thousands of Japanese who were defending their homeland against us. On that basis it was the A-bomb that made this book possible, something new for which it can be blamed.

CHRISTMAS CAME IN APRIL

The place is Cherry Point, a permanent Marine Corps base in North Carolina.

Facing the colonel in command is a young second lieutenant, transferred from Lee Field because an atomic bomb canceled his ticket to Japan.

"You asked to see me, Lieutenant?"

"Yes, sir."

"What can I do for you?"

"I demand decent housing for myself and my wife, who is pregnant."

"You *demand* it, Lieutenant?"

"If I don't get it, sir, I'm leaving Cherry Point."

There must have been something about the boldness, the desperation of this, that grabbed the colonel's curiosity or compassion. "Suppose you postpone going over the hill with your pregnant wife, Lieutenant, until you tell me exactly what the problem is."

"When I arrived here, sir, there were no accommodations on the base for my wife and me. So we had to take a room at the Queen Anne Hotel."

Just the suspicion of a frown passed across the colonel's face. He obviously had some knowledge of the Queen Anne Hotel as a permanent home. Many of its guests only stayed a few hours.

"The place was noisy," the lieutenant continued. "My wife couldn't sleep, the room was tiny, oppressive, and uncomfortable. And the five dollars a day they were charging for it

185

was more than I could afford. After about ten days I was able to find a place in a little rooming house that offered only one advantage over the hotel. It was cheaper.

"As you may be aware, sir, this town is loaded to the gunwales with Marines. Every facility is severely strained. and the spots with the biggest problems are the eating places. No matter how much they charge it's hard to get in. No matter who you are, you have to stand in line for thirty or forty minutes, sometimes longer. There is nothing wrong with taking your turn, sir, but Alyce, my wife, just can't stand that long. Time and again she's been overcome with fatigue and violent spells of nausea just as our turn was coming up. The doctor has told me that this is normal to any pregnancy. He also tells me that going without food is not—not for her and certainly not for me.

"For the last three days we've been living on some cookies and a thermos of lemonade that we have in our room. This is very bad for a pregnant lady and worse, if possible, for a healthy second lieutenant who doesn't want to leave his wife alone if he can help it."

The colonel smiled and said, "Don't leave the base until you hear from me, Lieutenant."

"Thank you, sir," I said.

Would you believe that within a matter of a few hours I heard from the colonel and we moved into a quonset hut on the base. Now, anybody who's ever even seen a quonset hut knows that it doesn't compare favorably with the Plaza. But it looked like the bridal suite to us.

I immediately laid in a large supply of groceries, set up housekeeping, and started to plan for our first Christmas in "our own" home.

Then a career sergeant who had a great house on the base signed on for another four years for which he got a three-month sabbatical. When he took it we took his house. That's where we had our first Christmas and the coming of Claudia, who arrived four months later, in April.

April was very big for me that year. My first child was born and I accumulated enough points to get me separated from the service and transformed back into a civilian. If it had not been for a sympathetic colonel who winked at a second lieutenant's threat to go AWOL I might have been sent to the brig.

GETTING TO THE POINT

The first thing you do when you are separated from the service, if you have a wife and kid, is look for a job. To do this I headed for Atlantic City. To explain, let me remind you of the guy who lost his keys on West 45th Street around Ninth Avenue but looked for them in Times Square because "The light is better."

For me the light was better in Atlantic City because of my father's connections on the boardwalk. And sure enough, I landed a job almost immediately, giving away fountain pens. I was very successful at it.

Now, you say, what's hard about giving something away? Well, try to follow this pitch, which was successful in the days just before the ball-point pen changed the whole writing structure in America. Until they came along I was doing all right giving away the type of pen usually associated with the name Waterman. The pitch ran like this:

"You are all familiar, ladies and gentlemen, with the famous Waterman Fountain Pen . . . a familiar object in the vest pocket of every successful businessman. You are familiar, too, with the way this pen operates. Let me show you. You just pull this lever down, insert the point of the pen in a bottle of ink, let the lever go, and you are ready for many uninterrupted hours of writing pleasure.

"Now you have seen how this pen operates, and I am now about to shock you by announcing that I am not selling this expensive article for two dollars. Not for one dollar. Not for fifty cents. No. I am giving this pen away, ladies and gentlemen, absolutely free to every man, woman, and child who buys one of these absolutely necessary gold-finish pen points without which it is impossible to use any fountain pen.

"Now, friends, I can hear you saying to yourself, 'He's giving us the fountain pen but he's making us buy the point in order to get it.' This is not true, my friends. But show me a man who does not buy one of these fine, durable, gold-finished writing pen points at the minuscule price I am offering them today and I'll show you a man who doesn't recognize a good deal when he sees one, a man with no business sense whatsoever, and I know there are no such men in this gathering.

"You can see, friends, that this pen I am about to give you already has a point in it. So why should you buy this point I'm offering? What if you're about to sign an important contract and you drop this pen and bend the point? What if you get hold of some bad ink that clogs the fine point of this pen beyond repair? What if you're forced to write on rough paper that wads up and wrecks the point? What will you do?

"You will not be able to sign the contract. You will not be able to use your pen unless you have with you an extra point such as the one I am offering you now for only fifty cents. Now, friends, who will be first one to buy one of these extraordinary gold-finished pen points for only fifty cents and get this guaranteed fountain pen absolutely free?"

Could you, dear reader, resist getting that fountain pen absolutely free? Well, maybe you could. Times have changed. But I gave away an awful lot of pens until I switched to selling empty boxes.

"That's right, friends! You there with the pretty young lady in red, you heard me right. I'm about to sell ten of these empty boxes . . . just exactly ten . . . the specially selected ten I have piled right here on the counter . . . I'm about to sell these ten boxes only to ten lucky buyers at only one dollar each.

"Now I hear you saying, "Who's going to pay a buck for an empty box?' That's a good question. Not everybody would do that. Not your staid, conservative, solid, unimaginative man with no romance in his soul. But those of you who know that there's often more to a thing than meets the eye . . . those of you who can become fascinated, intrigued by an idea . . . those of you who wonder why a man would stand up before you and offer an empty box for a dollar . . . you will say to yourself, 'There must be more to this than meets the eye.'

"But there is a limit to the number of these empty boxes that I can sell at the price of just one dollar. Here they are. I will count them for you . . . one, two, three, four, five, six, seven, eight, nine, and ten! That's the limit."

At this point I'd pick up one of the boxes, look knowingly inside it, and smile provocatively at the crowd as if I wished they could see what I saw. This, was acting.

"Now, ladies and gentlemen, I say . . . I *say* . . . these boxes are empty. That's what I say. But I wonder if there are ten ladies and gentlemen among you out there who believe that I would actually presume to sell you an empty box, that I would be allowed to sell an empty box. So this is what I'm going to do. As each of you steps forward to buy one of these little jewelry boxes, I'm going to put one—the one you buy—on top of your dollar. When I have ten dollars covered by ten boxes, I'm going to ask each of you to step up here, open the box you bought, and find out if I told you the truth when I said the box was empty. Remember, I *say* these boxes are empty. Do you or don't you believe me?"

Believe it or not, in almost no time at all, I'd have ten boxes on top of ten one-dollar bills lined up on the counter in front of me.

"Now then, folks, I want each of you to step up here, open your box, and show everyone here exactly what you bought. You bought an empty box, exactly as I told you you would. Very well, ladies and gentlemen, what does that prove? It proves that I am an absolutely honest man. So you must believe me when I tell you that the very greatest item I have ever been authorized to offer here on the boardwalk of Atlantic City is this handy Morris Metric Slicer which I have here in my hand.

"Forget the two dollars these great little gadgets were made to sell for. I'm cutting the price in half. Just look at the way it slices these cucumbers, ladies and gentlemen. Is that great or is that sensational? With a machine like this you can slice anything so thin you could get a job with a tobacco company slicing calling cards into cigarette papers. And I'm about to give this little machine more use and abuse in the next two minutes than you would give it in an entire lifetime.

"It's guaranteed not to rip, rust, bust, split in the back, or smell bad in warm weather. Just a minute, what was that I heard? Did someone say cabbage? Thank you. Perfect stranger. Get a load of how this remarkable little machine handles your cabbage problems. For coleslaw, hot slaw, sauerkraut, or anything that may constitute your cabbage pleasure. Could I hear it for this coleslaw, ladies and gentlemen. But wait a minute, that's not all!

"Did you ever see a lady slice a tomato? She takes a poor defenseless tomato and plunges at it with a butcher knife. And the poor little tomato dies of a hemorrhage before it ever reaches the table. Now watch as I show you how this wonderful little invention handles your tomato problems. Look at those slices, ladies and gentlemen. Each one is so thin it's no wonder stingy people adore this little machine. Why I sold one of these to a lady in Bayonne, New Jersey, and it made one tomato last her all summer long. Look at those slices! And . . . wait a minute, ladies and gentlemen, that's not all!

"Today and for today only I'm including with each and every sale of this remarkable slicing machine a rotisserie cutter invented by the famous dean of the Parisian School of Potato Surgery. It was he himself who taught me how to use it. Any child can learn. Look at this!"

At this point I'd spin a potato on a spit in such a way as to produce a springlike spiral of potato that I'd pull out and let snap back.

"When company comes to dinner, spread it out. When they go home, let it snap back together again. One potato could last you a lifetime.

"And in addition to the slicer and the machine for performing miracles with a potato, I'm adding the juice-o-matic . . . here it is folks . . . all for one dollar.

"Plunge this handy little juice-o-matic spout into an orange, a grapefruit, or a watermelon like this. Take it with you on your way to work and drink the juice right out of the fruit on your way downtown. We don't supply the vodka. Stick this into a lemon and you have juice for a salad, a little lemon for your fish, a little lemon for your Tom Collins, and some for Mary and Jane Collins, too. There's enough for the whole damn Collins family. And wait till you try it on a grapefruit. Take this number two grapefruit. With this juice-o-matic you get enough juice to float the USS *North Dakota*.

"Who'll be the first to raise her hand and say, 'I'll be the first to give a dollar for those three marvelous kitchen innovations'? Lady over there? Thank you very much, my dear. And there's a man wants two. He's obviously leading a double life, the sly old fox. Good luck to you, sir. And thank you all for your enthusiasm. You have made this sale a success for both of us. And to those of you who didn't buy, I hope you won't regret the mistake too much in the future when you might want to become a little cutup."

As soon as the crowd had wandered away, I'd start the same pitch over again, beginning with the empty boxes to prove how truthful I was. No one would ever complain because a sucker never wants to be caught in the act of sounding like one. I made about 400 percent profit on every Metric Morris Slicer I sold, together with the other two items. And, of course, the dollar on the empty box was clear. Nobody ever took the box he bought.

It was a wonderful living for the summer, but my wife and my mother were sure it would lead to spending the winter in jail. Instead of that it gave me enough bankroll, plus what I got on my GI Bill, to register at Catholic University in Washington, D.C., where I planned to major in drama because I'd made up my mind that my future must be in the theater or the motion pictures, whichever came first.

BACK TO SCHOOL

The years have proved that in spite of the death, agony, and devastation that war brings on lands and peoples, there has never been a war that didn't advance the sum total of human knowledge.

The Trojan Wars, for instance, taught mothers that when dipping a kid in the waters of the River Styx to render the little nippers invulnerable to the engines of war, it is better to hold the boy by the hair of his head instead of by the heel.

One of the benefits of WW II was that it made it possible for me, and for thousands of other young men, to get or to continue their education through the GI Bill. To say that the Bill did this without any help from me would be to give it much too much credit. Like the story about a rubble-strewn vacant lot next to a parish house. One of the parishioners asked the Fathers if he could clean up the lot and plant a vegetable garden hedged around by a row of flowers. He was given the go-ahead and went to work.

By August the lot was blooming with lovely things to see, to smell, and to eat. And one of the Fathers said to the man who'd done so much to make it that way, "Isn't it wonderful to see what God can do?"

"Yes, Father, it is," was the reply. "But do you remember how it looked when God was on his own?"

Similarly, I'd never have graduated from Catholic University if the GI Bill had been on its own. It only supplied me with $90 a month. I had a wife and a little daughter. My rent per month was $93. It doesn't take a CPA to figure out that the

193

Bill alone couldn't hack it, that we couldn't get by unless Alyce got a paper route and baby Claudia took in washing. So I did quite a bit of hustling.

The money to pay my tuition and sundries came from selling articles of little value on the boardwalk at Atlantic City. But we needed eating money, dressing money, rent money, and walking-around money. I tried selling pots and pans from door to door. But that's hard, and you develop no steady customers. It's a one-sale situation. So while keeping the pots and pans on the fire, I looked around for something more self-supporting.

My natural inclination toward neatness and cleanliness led me to discover that the cleaning service that handled the college trade took five days. This was too slow for a man like myself with a limited wardrobe. They called themselves the Swan Cleaners and, as Groucho would say, "How they made a living, I'll never know. There wasn't a swan on the campus."

Acting on the belief that it was the inalienable right of every student and World War Two veteran to get a suit cleaned in less than five days, I made a few inquiries, scouted around, and found an organization called Jernigan Cleaners. It was off the beaten track, near the little flat in which we lived, and needed business.

I made a deal to bring them plenty of new business if they could do the work in only three days. Naturally I got a commission on every penny I brought in. All I needed was a good name for my newborn business.

At that time the boss sink-cleaner was Old Dutch Cleanser and everybody knew the slogan "Old Dutch chases dirt." So I climbed aboard and called my three-day cleaning service The Dutch Cleaners. I had some cards printed emphasizing the speed of the service and success was almost instantaneous in spite of the fact that some of the college authorities—probably because they were taking it under the table from the Swan Cleaners—tried to stop me from operating on campus.

The Dutch Cleaners was such a success that by the time I

graduated I had a partner helping to handle the workload. He was another guy at Catholic U. copying my action on another campus.

So we linked up. We had three trucks on the streets and were doing so much business that instead of Jernigan paying us commission we were paying him, at a very low rate, to handle our work for us.

Besides the cleaning business I did my pen-point pitch three days a week at Murphy's in downtown Washington. The trouble was that between the pens and the pants, coats, and occasionally vests, I was so busy I missed a lot of classes. This didn't keep me from graduating but it kept me from getting my masters, which I might have done with the help of some points I picked up at Boston College. Can you dig me as a philosopher?

Fulton Sheen was teaching philosophy at Catholic U. at the time I was there. Two other guys and I used to sneak into his class (which was hard to do) just to study his platform technique, which was as great as the sense of humor which endeared him to Milton Berle. Berle once said, while MC-ing a benefit, that he knew Bishop Sheen had arrived because there was a limousine outside with stained-glass windows.

I, who had become very ecumenical at an early age in Bayonne, New Jersey, sneaked in to catch the good bishop's act with the two non-Catholic pals I knocked around with, George Beebe and Arch Lustberg, one a Protestant, the other a Jew.

I think the mischief I got into with those two guys landed me in almost as much hot water as my cleaning business. The Good Fathers didn't look with a benevolent eye on students who blew as many classes as I did. There was, for instance, Father Hart. I was a member of his metaphysics class, which met regularly every morning at ten minutes after ten. Father Hart was a scholastic theologian who could no more understand my life-style than I could live his. So he would continually drop me from his class for absenteeism.

I couldn't afford to be dropped because I needed the credit, but more important, I wanted to learn metaphysics from Father Hart. So each time I was posted I took the action my father always recommended to anybody in trouble: "Go to the head man."

Father Ignatius Smith was the head of the philosophy department so I went to him. I told him the whole story of the cleaning business and the fountain-pen pitch and made the plea that no religious person could penalize anyone for showing industry and the will to succeed. The next thing Father Hart knew I was back in my seat at his ten-ten class.

That class was a polyglot group from all over the world. Sitting right in front of me was an enormous nun who'd been in China for forty years. There was a priest just home from the jungles of Honduras. Clerics of every caliber from every corner of the world were all around me. If anything had happened I could have gotten last rites in any of ten languages besides Latin.

When Father Hart took the roll the day I came back, all he said, with a sigh, was "You're back . . . again." A few days after that, to my surprise he said, "McMahon, please see me after class." This was astonishing to everyone because Father Hart talked to no one. He was just for listening to.

After class I went up to his desk and he said to me, "McMahon, what are you trying to do to me?"

"I don't know what you mean, Father."

"Why are you back in the class when you're overcut several times?"

There was nothing to do but introduce Father Hart to the world of commerce and competition. I told him about my extracurricular activities and that the cuts were frequently caused by my eagerness to squeeze in just one more cleaning pickup before his class. Frequently, I explained, when I did that, it turned out to be the day the lady decided to send the draperies. These meant a cool six bucks which was hard to turn down. So I'd wait while she took them down from the rods—often I helped her. And thus I was trapped by my own diligence and ambition. Then, rather than be a disturbing influence by coming to class late, I'd go on to pick up some more cleaning.

Father Hart listened with a naïve, unworldly bewilderment to the problems of the cleaning business and then to the problems and techniques of selling pots and pans and fountain-pen points. I told him about my wife and my little daughter and all my other responsibilities. Finally he interrupted me, mostly I think because he didn't want to hear anymore about my bustling world of trade, and said, "All right, McMahon. You may stay in my class as long as you keep up with your work. But may I give you a little piece of advice?"

"I would welcome it, Father."

He sighed, looked at me a long time, and then said, "Philosophy, McMahon, is for the idle man."

Think about that. I have. Many times.

From that day on Father Hart never called my name and I never missed a lecture. He just looked to see if I was there. One day he looked several times, which caused the huge sister from China to shift her position frequently. It wasn't that Father Hart's gaze bothered her. It was because that was the day my wife was sick and I couldn't find a baby-sitter. There was nothing to do but skip the class or take Claudia with me. The problem was how to get her in without re-perplexing the good Father.

He followed the same routine every day. He'd walk in, pull the hanging chain that lit the naked bulb over his desk, bow his head, cross himself, and bless us. Then he'd lead the class in a short prayer.

While the whole class was standing and Father Hart's eyes were closed in devotion, I sneaked in with Claudia. She was going on three. I had threatened her with punishments too terrible to describe if she made even one sound. Little girls can keep very quiet if they try (and if they're threatened) but they can't help squirming around a lot. It was this squirming that found its way into Father Hart's peripheral vision and made him glance in my direction. The shrewd sister from China, aware of what was happening, managed to move her big body just enough so that Father Hart couldn't see who was auditing his course. But I guess he did. His opening line was "Babes in arms and suckling babes, none are too young to learn metaphysics."

When explaining that I went to Catholic U. because they had a good drama department I forgot to add that they had a tiny theater. Apparently it's easier to build a drama faculty than a decent auditorium with a proper, well-equipped stage.

The dream of Father Harkey, who was the head of the drama department—actually the Father who fathered it—was to have a complete, perfectly equipped theater. I am proud that I was able to give his dream a great big push toward reality. I ran a sensational benefit that was ballyhooed with some of the greatest space you ever saw in the New York papers. It was the winter of '69/'70, the last show ever to be done at the famous old Capitol Theater, the home of the Major Bowes Amateur Hour and first of the great movie palaces to be built on Broadway.

As President of Catholic University's Alumni Association, I saw the swan song of that famous theater as an ideal setting for our big benefit. The trouble was, they had already started to wreck the enormous stage, which was one of the features of the house.

So much of the stage was gone that we actually had to build a false proscenium. But that was the only thing fake about the show. We had everyone you can name who was playing for miles around New York on our stage. And to let the town know that something big was going on we carpeted Broadway and wound up the whole thing with a champagne supper that got the biggies who were invited to get busy with their checkbooks.

Besides every Catholic actor who was ambulatory, we had Billy Eckstine and Johnny Carson helping out with the MC-ing and just to get things started right, I asked Alan King to open the show.

You know you've got some program when King's the opening act. Naturally I had to talk him into it. "I've got a million

Catholics out there," I said. "The only way I can win is to send out a Jew to get things started." Alan got things started in a great big way and because of that start Catholic University now has one of the most perfectly equipped theaters on any campus in the country.

PHILADELPHIA STORY I

I was soon to be graduated from Catholic U. The source of the loot that put me through didn't point in the direction I wanted my career to go.

I wasn't majoring in "theater" because it was considered a snap course.

Since my radio idol was Paul Douglas, who was at WCAU in Philadelphia, it crossed my mind that Philly might be the place to start. True, it wasn't exactly the theater capital of the world, but the bingo business taught me the danger of having your learning process too exposed. In Philly, I could learn in comparative privacy, then let my triumph in a small pond carry me into the mainstream. Good play, huh? And it had to work because I'd made no alternate plan.

John McClay, who'd been my father's partner and my daughter's godfather, had a son, John McClay, Jr., who happened to have an executive job at WCAU, which was just beginning to jump into TV along with all the other big radio stations of the country.

John had been a radio performer and had tipped me into a few jobs in radio. So I figured at the very least he could give me some advice.

After asking me what I wanted to do and hearing what he already knew, that I wanted to be an actor, John suggested that I ought to break into television by learning a little bit about production. That made sense to me.

"Don't worry," John said, "we'll find something here for

you. I don't know where, but when you're ready let me know."

While I'd been waiting to see John I was glancing through a copy of the *Bulletin* and an ad in the real estate section caught my eye.

NEW COUNTRY LIVING
DREXELBROOK
Tennis courts, swimming pool
Horseback Riding

The copy was so great that as soon as I'd gotten the assurance of a job from John, I followed the directions in the ad and headed for Drexelbrook. I took the subway, a trolley, and a short walk. And then I took a look at the apartments and fell in love with Drexelbrook.

Twelve hundred two-story apartments were under construction on what had been the High Top Country Club golf course. I looked at the plans, saw what I wanted, and put down a twenty-five-dollar deposit on a two-bedroom apartment to be ready in September.

When I got back to Washington and told Alyse about the apartment, showed her the handsome four-color brochure, and told her how I could take the trolley (and subway) to work, she pointed out that the twenty-five dollars I'd left at Drexelbrook were the last dollars we had.

While I was scratching for an angle to put us back in the black, Alyce was killing time putting together a scrapbook on Claudia. Cards and notes my wife had gotten since Claudia was born had been thrown into a big box to be sorted at some more convenient time. That time had come and for Alyce it was a sort of therapy.

Up to now I haven't mentioned a lady named Anna Cress. She was my mother's mother, my other grandmother. And even though she ran second to Grandmother Katie, because I saw less of her, she was quite a lady.

Well, among the things in the box was a card from Grandmother Anna saying how happy it made her to hear of Claudia's birth. It also made Alyce very happy to read the card because when she took it out of the envelope, out came an overlooked ten dollars. Sometimes you have to believe that "the Lord will provide."

There was nothing to do but celebrate our good fortune. And this sort of underlines my whole life-style.

We took the solitary sawbuck and blew it. We went to a place in Washington called Neptune's Grill. Drinks ran from twenty-nine to forty-nine cents. Martinis were thirty-nine. It was a cut-rate restaurant. I knew we could get in and out with the ten bucks and still have enough left over to pay the baby-sitter. It was a Quixotic way to live, but the next day things began to pick up. Some of my cleaning customers paid their bills. Maybe you could say that my motto has always been, "Rainy days are the ones when you can get into the best places."

To give you an example of the luck of the McMahons, the last Christmas I was in school at Catholic U. was one of our times of severest financial distress. I was trying out for a part in a play, trying to move in the direction I wanted to go. But this movement hurt my cleaning business.

It began to look as if Christmas would have to be played back at à later date. Then, one afternoon, walking through Hecht's department store, I stopped to watch a man who was pitching gyro tops. Remember them? They would balance on the corner of a box or spin on a string without falling off. Actually they were simple versions of the stabilizers now used on ships, planes, and space vehicles.

I was so fascinated with these things that I got to talking to the pitchman and we wound up making a deal. I bought a thousand of the gyros on consignment and closed the deal with a check postdated February. The Hecht Company knew me because I'd worked for them before so they okayed the deal. In four days I'd sold one thousand gyros, made one thousand kids happy, covered my postdated check with $250 of the money, given Hecht their $250, and the rest of the dough was ours.

So we drove to Atlantic City with a carful of gifts to spend Christmas with my mother and father. Of course they had loads of gifts for us and their granddaughter, so the holiday was kept in balance by the gyro tops.

The following year, on September 12, 1949, we moved to Drexelbrook and I went to work for WCAU at $75 a week. It was quite a cut from the money I'd been making through my conglomeration of projects. But as I saw it, that kind of money-making work was only a means to an end. The work at WCAU was the end. Actually, it was only the beginning.

Our move into our fancy, two-bedroom Drexelbrook apartment was extremely un-chic.

My mother gave us the furniture that had been mine when I was a boy. It was heavy, solid, and masculine, but not antique, just old-fashioned. There was a wardrobe, a dresser, and a bed. To help us out when we moved to Philly, they threw in a lamp, a bridge table, and a convertible sofa.

To get an apartment at Drexelbrook at that time, you had to prove that you were making at least $5,000 a year. That would be about $15,000 as of this writing. But by having assurances from WCAU that I was about to become a television star, I was able to bypass that requirement. I simply throw in those facts to emphasize that the place was considered a young executive's paradise.

The day we moved in, high-class moving vans were parked all over the area disgorging fancy new furniture and a few valuable antiques. We arrived with a dump truck, driven by me, and full of our mismatched goods. But we were welcome because the word had leaked out that I was a television star. Since very few people had yet seen TV, that sounded glamorous. As for our furniture and the way we moved it, everyone knew that all actors were eccentric.

PHILADELPHIA STORY II

Once in, we started to fix up the place by painting all the old furniture white with a green trim. It wasn't great but it was different. Of course we had Claudia's few things. She was still a baby. I think she slept in a crib longer than any child in the world because we could never get up the cash to buy a child-size bed.

The bridge table became our dining room table, and to take care of all the books we'd accumulated, I swiped some bricks from the construction, still going on, laid some boards across them (also from the construction), painted them white and, *voilà!* The bookshelves were the best and most modern-looking things in our apartment.

Then came the first day I appeared on television. John figured I was ready. It was an easy judgment. "Ready" meant available. He had nobody else around, no budget to hire anybody else. That was how many people became television stars. It was a time when, to star on TV, all you had to do was show up.

I was co-host on the first program I ever worked on. I was also co-producer. The "co" in front of your name, then, as now, meant you did all the work. It was a three-hour daily variety show starring a nightclub and vaude comic named Bob Russell. Next to this thoroughly showwise professional I could have come off with about as much class as an extra in a Tobey show. However, by combining the honest, down-to-earth approach I admired so much in Paul Douglas with the casual, forthright images projected by my two new idols,

Dave Garroway and Arthur Godfrey, I presented an acceptable contrast to the punchy Bob Russell.

But, get this, when I did this first show on TV, we didn't even own a set. I've told this to a lot of early TV stars and they all tell the same story. If you were working in television at that time, it meant you weren't earning enough money to buy one. But all the saloons had them. They drew business with shows like *Roller Derby* and *Wrestling*. During the day there was local baseball.

In order to catch my debut on the tube Alyce and baby Claudia had to go to a bar. Then Alyce had to talk the barman into switching whatever was on at noon to my show, *Take Ten*.

It was named after Channel Ten. It must have taken a lot of persuasion to get the guy to accommodate what looked like the most casual of customers. The baby couldn't be counted on for much more than a milk shake with maybe a drop of sherry. Alyce ordered a Dubonnet on the rocks with a splash of soda. But it worked out, because as soon as the lunchtime patrons of the bar learned that it was her husband Alyce was watching, they became involved. What else did they have to do? And they figured it was great sitting right there next to the wife of a real television star. Some thrill!

The gimmick I started out with on *The Take Ten Show*—you had to have a gimmick in those days and things really haven't changed much—was that as MC I never identified myself by name. Maybe I did this out of fear. But after a little while mail started to come in asking, "Who is that guy on *Take Ten*?" Whether or not to answer this was actually a matter of security. Why did they want to know? Should I tell? Finally, when it became obvious that they liked me, I began using my name.

That I went anywhere at all from *Take Ten* was due to the help I got from an actor, producer, director, and musician named Dave Kaigler.

And even with all the help Dave gave me, it's a wonder anybody at all saw me because *Take Ten* happened to go on against a guy named Bob Smith with a show called *Howdy Doody.*

Take Ten, then, was really the opening gun in my career toward becoming Philadelphia's "Mr. Television." They tagged me that because at one time I had thirteen shows on the air. Some of them were just movies, broken up into a million commercial interruptions like the Art Fern character that Johnny Carson does on *The Tonight Show.* Then there was a show called *Strictly for the Girls.* I think it was the first morning show in the country. Up to then—at least in Philly—television didn't light up until afternoon. We went on after a fifteen-minute news show that started at nine o'clock. The guy who did the news was Jack Whittaker, a crony of mine who has become quite large in the CBS sports picture.

The best way to describe *Strictly for the Girls* is to say it was sort of a TV version of Don McNeill's *Breakfast Club* radio show that came out of Chicago and one called *Breakfast in Hollywood* that Tom Brenneman did.

We had a deal with Horn and Hardart, the automat people, to pass out free doughnuts and their sensational coffee to everyone who came to our show.

The java played a part in the production of the show. Sherman Billingsley, famous host and owner of the equally famous Stork Club in New York, also had a talk show on TV at that time. It was in the evening and it was the essence of class. It opened on a glass of champagne beside an engraved place card bearing the name of the show. We copied that opening. Only instead of the champagne, we used a mug of coffee and a simple little sign saying "Strictly for the Girls."

To show you how little audience participation shows have changed over the years, we used to have about two hundred people in the audience, ranging from our daily regulars to mothers with infants and fathers who were out of work. Some of our regulars—we even had an early version of Miss Miller, who used to attend all performances of *The Tonight Show*—actually made a modest living out of the prizes they picked up from time to time on *Strictly for the Girls.*

The show included, besides me, a guy named Chris Keegan, who later worked with me on a very successful circus show I did called *The Big Top,* a couple of singers, and a combo. All, standard equipment for such a show. We had a set not unlike the *Sesame Street* set, with a street scene, an interview area, and a store in which I did my commercials. I wrote and produced the show and one of the regular features I enjoyed was a weekly round-table discussion I had with three preschool kids. We called it the Big Three Conference. Just seeing me with those little tykes looked funny. I'd ask them profound questions like, "When should a girl marry?" I'd get back answers like, "Next year," or "Not till I get bigger."

I'd also do the audience bit with standard questions like, "Do you know what you have in your bag?" Then I'd have to look through it to see how correct they were. One lady had a beautiful little pearl-handled revolver. I just gave her a prize and said nothing about the artillery.

CBS was watching the *Strictly for the Girls* experiment very carefully. Charles Vanda, then creative director of WCAU, and Don Thornburg, who ran the station for CBS, brought a mob of CBS brass to Philly to catch the show and meet me and evaluate the possibility of putting it on the network. My meeting with them led to the greatest anticlimax of my life.

But first . . . a message of importance about the other thirteen shows I did. One of these was a cooking show called *Aunt Molly and Ed.* George Burns would say, "I played Molly." Actually, I no more played Molly than the show was like the usual run of boring, homemaker type of trivia with handy hints like how to clean out your husband's pockets with a vacuum cleaner and pick up enough spare change to buy a Mexican divorce.

Molly was an older woman. I was supposed to be her nephew. Writers described me as "mischievous." I never could believe that a man my size could be called that. In fact I was never able to believe that Molly could have such an old, king-sized nephew.

I guess it was my casual approach to the things she was doing so seriously, like showing the world how to make apple pandowdy, that gave the show what appeal it seemed to have.

Then I had a very masculine show on Sunday about the men who went down *under* the sea in ships, *The Silent Service*. But my biggest and best thing in Philadelphia was Charlie Vanda's circus show, *The Big Top*. I played the clown. But that wasn't the way it was planned.

Vanda, now living in Vegas, one of the giants of radio and early TV, came to Philadelphia when his friend Don Thornburg came from Los Angeles to take command of WCAU for CBS. Charles never thought "little" and he didn't break his rule with *The Big Top*.

As he conceived it, I was to be a ringmaster, drawing on my earlier experience with circuses. But Jack Sterling was hot on radio in New York and they had a commitment to give him a shot on television. So everything got switched around and Jack became the ringmaster. It was a big disappointment to me. I'd already invested in a red coat, a top hat, and a whip.

Charlie didn't know what to do. Finally he asked, "What would you think about being a clown?"

Clowning was a branch of show business I'd never considered. Perhaps the only one. Now, as I was trying to build up the name and face of Ed McMahon I'm offered the anonymity of a Joey. But the more I thought about it, the more the challenge interested me. Could I be a clown?

I was flamboyant but not in a clownish way. I wasn't into pratfalls although I had taken a couple of pies in the face. In those days it was almost impossible to do TV without the pie-in-the-face routine. Pies made a star of Soupy Sales, who managed to get the biggest names in Hollywood to take a mess of custard in the kisser. The theory was that it made them look human.

Working with me on *The Big Top* was Chris Keegan, one of those clever, creative people you run into once in a while in show business who are more interested in having fun than in finding success. He was very malleable, had a wild, crazy sense of humor, and together we worked out a clown act in which I played straight for him.

I wore a bald wig with just a fringe of bright red hair, a pair of wire specs to hold on a nose that lit up, big black eyebrows, and a painted-on, sort of Emmett Kelly-type beard around big, fat, white lips. If that doesn't sound like a straight man's makeup, get a load of the wardrobe.

I wore an emerald-green satin opera cape with scarlet lapels, oversized black and white checkered pants, many sizes too big and held up by very fancy suspenders. And just so I wouldn't look too mousy, not go entirely unnoticed, I wore different colored shoes on each foot . . . with great big toes sticking out.

Dressed like this I tried to do what I thought W. C. Fields would do as a clown, bigger than life and seemingly, but not really, clumsy. I was the one who caused everything to happen to the poor misbegotten soul that Keegan played. Everything happened to him. If I did something to knock over a pile of bricks, they'd fall on him.

In show business there's a lot of Yiddish bandied around so you get to learn it. And Yiddish offers the perfect definition of my relation to Chris Keegan. I was the *schlemiel.* He was the *schlimazel.*

As it turned out *The Big Top* was my first network show. And I didn't vanish into the anonymity of a clown. Both Chris and I used our own names. And it became quite a publicity item around Philly that Ed McMahon, the suave host of so many WCAU shows, was also the clown in *The Big Top.*

The show opened on my bald head on which it said, THE BIG TOP. As I raised my head and faced the camera, my big red nose lit up and said, HELLO. As planned, the nose was to say CBS but I guess Mr. Paley or someone felt that a bulbous putty-nose wasn't exactly the corporate image the network wanted to project.

We were on every Saturday, sponsored by Sealtest, and we were very big with the kids. I was very happy. I was very busy.

Besides all the shows, I was knocking out about fifty commercial spots a week, really rolling. Mine was one of the first faces to appear on the cover of *TV Digest*, which later went nationwide as *TV Guide*.

Our little two-bedroom apartment at Drexelbrook had become a three-bedroom town house, with a front door and a back door and a play yard for Claudia. We were spending our money as fast as it came in. Sometimes faster. And we'd made a group of great friends including the promoter and owner of Drexelbrook, Dan Kelly. Because I was sort of a local celeb, Mr. Kelly used to invite me to his parties and we became very good friends. It was an explosive and exciting time for me.

Then the real explosion came. There was a big conference meeting in Philadelphia. They talked to me about doing *Strictly for the Girls* regionally and *The Big Top* nationally from New York. They asked me when I could move.

I was close to tears. I said, "Gentlemen, this is the greatest thing that has yet happened to me and I don't want you to think that I'm not grateful for your confidence. But please read this." I laid a brown envelope on the table. On the corner of the envelope it said, "United States Marine Corps." The message inside told why I was close to tears.

K-E-DOUBLE-L-Y

After my father, I think the man who influenced my life more than any other was Mr. Dan Kelly of Philadelphia.

If Dad showed me where to go, Dan Kelly showed me how to get there. He was, to a large degree, the architect of my present life-style.

He was, as you must have guessed, my senior by maybe fifteen to twenty years. He's dead now. And I'm sure he died with no regrets becaused he lived with zest. He had class. Panache. He knew the difference between work and play and the importance of each. This was one of the first things I learned from him. It's a very important lesson for an ambitious young man to learn.

Dan had two kinds of days. He'd say, "Ed, today's a day for work." That was it. We worked. But when he said, "Today's a day for play," not a word about business was spoken the whole day long. But between these two there was an important compromise. He never lost sight of the importance of what he called TCB—Take Care of Business. Only after TCB could there be a day of play.

He'd made a bundle in real estate in the depression days. He negotiated the sale of Hialeah Race Track for an enormous finder's fee. He was a speculator, a builder, a horse owner, a very wealthy man, and above all a wonderful friend.

Dan had a happy little habit that the operating personnel of all hotels, nightclubs, and restaurants appreciated greatly and reacted to with sudden determination. Upon arriving, he'd slip the captain of a nightclub a folded hundred-dollar bill as if

211

it were a quarter. I suppose to him it was the equivalent of that. But not to the captain. As a result, when he arrived anywhere, the whole place turned to face him.

Let me elaborate on that. In appreciation of the fact that I had successfully launched a club for him in his Drexelbrook operation, Dan took me and my partner, George Beebe, an old Catholic U. pal I brought up to help me, on a four-day, all-expenses-paid junket to the Key Biscayne Hotel—just twenty minutes from downtown Miami. Dan discovered Key Biscayne long before Rebozo or Nixon ever laid eyes on the place. He'd been going there for years. He owned about thirty-five acres which he planned to develop into a high-rise apartment, hotel, and condominium project. It became a reality only after he died.

One night on this junket he was marshaling a party of about fourteen friends and political associates around Miami. After dropping in at several spots we finally headed for Copa City, where Harry James was playing in the lounge, and Sammy Davis, Jr., still part of the Will Maston Trio, was supporting Jimmy Durante in the main room.

Dan and party were enjoying themselves to the music of Harry James and didn't want to leave. But he did want to catch Durante and Davis. So, when the word got around that Dan Kelly was going to wait for the last Harry James set before coming in to see the big show, they held that show for forty-five minutes. When we walked in we were ushered to a table front and center.

In spite of the fact that he was partially crippled by arthritis and had terrible stomach problems, he never let his illnesses interfere with his good times. Actually he was trapped between his two physical problems. He took cortisone for the arthritis. This made him a bleeder, so they couldn't operate on his stomach. Maybe it was because of these illnesses that he kept on the go-go-go all the time trying to squeeze as much life as possible into the time he had left.

One night Dan decided he wanted to wind up the evening at a certain spot to hear a girl play the accordion.

By the time we got there she had finished her act, packed up, and was leaving. Seeing this, Dan said, quietly, "I'm sorry. I guess we're too late." No suggestion that she come back and run through a few more numbers. Nothing. It was she who suggested doing that. "Just let me see if I can catch the trio," she said and scurried off to do that.

They all came back and the lady closed with "Angel Eyes," which was the number Dan had heard she did so well, the number he'd come to hear. Before she left Dan handed me some money, about $150, and said, "Take care of everything, Ed. Give her a hundred."

"Jeez, Dan! For just three numbers?"

"Well, you take care of it. Do what you think's right."

I gave her $50, saying, "Dan Kelly wants you to have this." I split the other $50 among the trio and gave Dan back what was left.

Dan would trust you with anything as long as he felt you were honest with him. If he ever heard that someone handed out his cash without saying it was from Dan Kelly, tacitly making the recipient think it was from the guy who was handing it out, that guy was finished forever with Mr. Kelly.

He'd occasionally give me $100 to put on a horse's nose. Now I knew that those $100 windows were cased not only by the IRS but by guys who didn't want only a part of your take, they wanted all of it. So after I bought the ticket, I made damn sure nobody accidentally bumped into me and happened to slip his hand in my pocket as he did so. He'd have found another hand there, mine. I kept that $100 ticket clutched in my fist so tight that when I handed it to Dan it was as limp as a bundle of wet wash.

I was fascinated by the fact that no matter how Dan Kelly seemed to be throwing money around, he always made sure that it hit the target. He didn't like to be taken. No matter how large the party, or how long it lasted, Dan never paid a check without glancing at it. In that glance he could tell whether it was his check or somebody else's, because he always had a clear idea of who was drinking what: martinis, Scotch, bourbon, champagne, vodka, bloodies. If, for instance, a couple of grasshoppers showed up on a check, he knew danged well it wasn't his. It was impossible to do the old check-switching routine on Brother Dan because of this.

Let me try to explain the old check-switching routine. Say you have a check coming for around $60. Another table has one for $80. They hand you the $80 check. Unless you're careful, you'll pay it. If you catch the switch, "Sorry! Mistake!"

Then they give your $60 check to some table that only owes $40 and so the checks get juggled with the house always the winner.

One evening about midnight, four cars of us drove up to a room called The Post and Paddock. Someone said they called it that because the steaks came from the paddock by parcel post. Not true—the steaks were first-class.

I got out of the car, walked in, and said, "I've got Dan Kelly and a party of twelve for dinner."

The maître d' put his hand to his head and said, "Oh, God! We sent the kitchen staff home about twenty minutes ago. Who eats dinner at midnight?"

"In Spain," I said, "everybody does."

"But this is Florida."

"Okay," I said, "I'll go out and tell Dan we'll go—"

"Wait! Don't do that! We'll get 'em back. Come in."

So we all went in and ordered a round of drinks while the management sent out taxis to pick up their kitchen staff, none of whom lived nearby.

The dinner worked out great and Dan never knew what had happened. I didn't tell him because he wouldn't have appreciated breaking into people's leisure time. But before we left I said, "Dan, if you don't mind I'll take care of the kitchen help because they were scheduled to go off at midnight and they stayed on just to take care of us."

"Fine," Dan said, "take care of them. Take *good* care of them. Give them a lot because what they do is hard work."

So I went back and said, "Dan Kelly would like you to have

this.'' I laid $50 on the chef and went right on down the line through the salad lady and the saucier, everybody, and each was told that Dan Kelly wanted them to know his appreciation.

If I have given the impression that Dan Kelly spent his money rather selfishly, only to buy himself special attention, I want to correct that. During the course of an evening, or a working day, if a waitress should happen to say something about ''my little boy'' (many waitresses, I've found, are married ladies whose husbands have stiffed them) the next time Dan saw her he'd ask about her kid. I was with him when one of these people told him her son needed an operation.

Next morning early Dan was on the phone giving his secretary instructions to ''check on Ruthie's son. Find out what the operation is, how much it will cost and follow through.''

Frank Sinatra's the same way. He'll read in the paper that some child needs expensive, special medical care and he sees that it's taken care of, most generally anonymously. Same with Kelly.

I was always amazed at the length of his working days. He'd be at the track right after sunup to watch his ponies work out. The Vanderbilts and the Whitneys would wander over and they'd discuss how the nags were doing. Then he'd go back to the office and put in a full day's work before most guys who'd been up as late as he had the night before could pry up their eyelids.

It was all part of his dedication to TCB—Taking Care of Business. He seemed to feel that the business of making money—and that's all he did, he didn't manufacture anything—was deeply connected with the business of living, of caring about people.

Little things were very big with him. When I was running the club for him at Drexelbrook, he'd walk through the room occasionally and pick up a glass here and there and later he'd say, casually, ''By the way, I found some glasses on the tables that never should have been there. TCB.'' And when Dan took care of business like that, you'd better be prepared to tell

him, "We know about that, Dan, and it's been corrected."
And it better have been corrected because Dan checked back.

His mother lived alone in an apartment at Drexelbrook. He
would go out of his way to drive past her window every morning. He'd honk the horn, knowing she was there watching for
him. Then he'd drive on.

There are all kinds of ways of telling your mother you care,
beyond gifts and financial aid. That personal little fly-by and
honk on the horn meant more to Mrs. Kelly than all the flowers and other attentions he lavished on her. It was something
no one else did for any mother she knew.

I learned a great deal about living and about people from
Dan Kelly. And if, someday, just one person respects and ad-
mires me as much as I did him, I'll feel that I've been hand-
somely rewarded by life.

BAD NEWS AT LACOOCHEY

A few weeks before CBS offered me two network shows to originate from New York, I had picked up and taken off on a quick vacation and to visit Alyce's folks and show them Claudia and Michael.

There was nothing ahead but sun and slumber and, possibly, a dram or two of tonic toward evening to ease the pain of seeing another sun go down. This is a pain brought on by the realization that every sundown you watch brings you closer to your own. When you begin having morbid thoughts like that, you need a vacation.

When you begin to fidget, the vacation's over. I began to fidget after about forty-eight hours. I found I couldn't "let the rest of the world go by." So I bought a Philadelphia *Inquirer* to catch up on the days I'd missed.

I wonder why it is that bad news always hits your eye first? The item that caught my eye said that Ted Williams had been called back by the Marines for active service in Korea. This told me which way the wind was blowing. Ted's career in the Corps, and mine, had been more or less parallel. We'd been called about the same time, gone to training about the same time, and gotten our wings about the same time. This gave me a gut feeling that if Ted's number was up, could I be far behind? In the Marines, as in all the services, everything goes by the numbers.

The first thing I did was hide the paper so Alyce wouldn't see it, although I don't think there was a chance in the world that she would have made any connection between Ted and me.

I must say, however, it was enough to make a guy wonder who was running things and how. Just when everything was going so well in Philadelphia, and New York loomed on tomorrow's skyline, I had to pull the Queen of Spades.

I had no doubt that, at least for the time being, my career was over. So I sweated out my two week's vacation and then left Alyce with her folks in LaCoochey, Florida, while I went back to work. The first thing I did when I got in the house—I didn't even take off my coat—was to shuffle through the mail for one of those brown manila envelopes with "United States Marine Corps" printed in the upper-left-hand corner. I found a couple.

I opened them in the order of their postmarks and couldn't believe my eyes when they turned out to be just the usual routine communications any reserve officer received. One of them referred to an earlier letter that offered me a captaincy.

I was happy as a clam. No orders. My luck was holding. Alyce came back from Florida. Life returned to the hectic normal.

Then one evening I came home with the usual cheery greeting, "Any mail?"

"There was something from the Marine Corps," my wife said, "but it's nothing."

I know there must have been panic in my voice as I asked, "Where is it?"

"I threw it away," she said. Then came the real panic.

"Where? Where?"

Next thing I knew I was rummaging through a trash bin. After a few furious moments I found it.

What she had passed over as nothing was this: "You are ordered to report to the Willow Grove Naval Air Station at ten hundred hours on 16 July, for duty involving flying. Have all civilian affairs in order. Be in uniform. Bring no civilian clothing and be prepared to transfer."

It could only mean that I was headed for some flying in Korea. Uncle Sam was about to make another collection on the thousands of dollars he'd invested to teach me to operate airplanes. It was quite a hit in the head.

Aside from the badly timed interruption to my career, there was the problem of scaling down our life-style from the serious money I was making in TV to the comparatively negligible salary of a first lieutenant in the Marine Corps. My first step was to accept the captaincy immediately, but that didn't even come close to solving the problem.

We had two kids, Claudia and Michael (who was just an infant), and when you're as hedonistic as I am you don't save. You spend. And on top of that, there was Mother. She had a serious heart condition and I didn't want to upset her.

During World War II every time there was a plane crash, she was sure I was in it. Apparently she had no confidence at all in my flying skill.

Dad and I made elaborate plans, he to withhold and me to try to curtail all publicity that might have slipped through about me being in the service again.

Mother watched every show I was on. So I had to be very careful that no one on any of these let anything slip.

When I told Dan Kelly about it, all he said was, "Don't worry. We'll have an apartment waiting for you when you come back." I was glad to hear that I *would* come back and that the place would be waiting.

The final thing I had to do was to go down to Atlantic City, where my folks were living, tell Mother about going back into service and say good-bye. Then Dad called and told me that Mother was feeling so good, why fool around with good-byes when I came down, and he'd tell her later. That was okay with me. Dad was boss.

Funny thing though, I don't know what happened but when I got to Atlantic City, Dad had already told her. She was terribly upset. The only way I could comfort her was to tell her that I was going to Willow Grove, not far from Philadelphia, which meant to her that I could live at home, be near the kids, and commute to the base. Somehow, to her, that made everything safe.

I was only at Willow Grove six weeks when I was transferred to Miami, where they were forming the Third Marine Air Wing and I was to be its PIO. That was a hunk of luck. In World War II I didn't have a "secondary military occupational specialty." Being on all those TV shows had given me a new use to the Corps. I became a Public Information Officer.

We packed the convertible full of the stuff you need when traveling with two kids, one a baby, turned the rest of our gear over to the Marines to hold till we knew where to ship it, and headed for Miami via LaCoochey, Florida, so Alyce could be with her family.

I don't think I'd finished the first beer after we arrived when Alyce's mother said, "There's someone from the Red Cross to see you at the front door, Ed." Instantly I knew why. My mother had died.

It could only have been caused by the shock of my going back into the service. I thought about this a lot on the plane going north for the funeral and wondered how many mothers are actually war casualties, casualties of a war their sons survive.

A POLICE ACTION—
WITH CLUBS

To me chorea was a disease I, somehow, associated with dogs. Then that stinking war broke out—that curtain raiser to another disaster in Vietnam—and I found myself in a place called Korea, with a "k." With thousands of men who didn't know why they were there.

In WWII there was a reason named Hitler. Robert Taylor was a Navy flying instructor. Douglas Fairbanks, Jr., was in the Navy. Jimmy Stewart and Clark Gable were bomber pilots. The biggest name in Korea was me, which really made it a low-budget war.

I quickly found out why I was in PIO and morale work. A lot of both was necessary among the men, as it was in Vietnam later, but in Nam it didn't work.

My orders to join the Third Marine Air Wing said I should be prepared for flying duty. That was great news. I hadn't flown anything but a barstool in six or seven years.

For a while it looked as though I'd never leave Florida. They kept me busy running dances and parties and MC-ing shows. I started a local TV show and things were beginning to look good again—all but the paycheck.

And then I was ordered to ship out and I was on my way to Korea to save their Seoul. True, I was a PIO and a pilot. But what they gave me to fly looked like one of "those crates" that Basil Rathbone wouldn't send a kid up in when he was commander of an RAF base in all the old World War I movies. They were Cessna 180's—little, light, fabric-wing jobs that we flew low over enemy lines to spot their artillery positions.

Aloft in those little machines, right over the nasties, we were sitting targets for anything they had to shoot at us, from handguns to antiaircraft pieces.

It was a very necessary part of the kind of war we found ourselves fighting on the kind of terrain we *found* ourselves. And it was necessary that I *do* it. I looked around for a good way to fill up my nonflying hours. I finally decided that a good way for a guy in the service to get some control of his own destiny was, somehow, to get control of the food and booze. So I volunteered for a job of mess officer. My friends thought I'd gone bananas. But I knew the guy who had the job didn't want it, rarely showed up for it, so you can imagine what kind of food got served.

The first thing I did was to stick my neck way out by giving an order to the mess sergeant that we were going to have the men come up and order their eggs the way they wanted them—over easy, sunnyside up, any way at all.

"Can't be done," the sergeant told me.

"It's going to be done, Sergeant. That's an order."

"But, sir, the men will be standing in line too long."

"They're standing in line anyway, a minute or two longer to get their eggs cooked the way they like them will be worth it."

I was right. It worked great. The men began eating breakfast again instead of just eating a Hershey bar.

Realizing that man does not live by bread alone, I also tried to do something for their spirits. I fixed up the mess hall, put in some decent lighting, toned down the olive drabness with some white trim, and when I was finished, while it didn't look like "21," it was clean and pleasant. I even had vases of flowers on the tables. And the men liked it. I'm beginning to sound like your favorite interior decorator. Don't be fooled. In the service you do what you have to do. I got little Korean kids to pick the flowers for me and I'd pay them off in sticks of gum that I bought at the PX for a nickel a pack. They sold it on the black market at a dime a stick. They also accepted candy bars and cigarettes with the same reluctance a lush shows for a fifth of Seagrams 7.

The morale immediately picked up so much I was given permission to go on with my plans, which included a trip to Japan to get a french-fry machine. When I brought that back and began offering french-fries, peas, and steak the way you like it, we almost had the war won—at least in our sector.

In my spare time from all this housekeeping I was still flying missions in that little nylon puddle-jumper, and sometimes it got very hairy. I flew twenty-three missions without a drink. Now, you know, that's not me. But I wanted to be sure I knew what I was doing up there. And if I was slated to go a little higher I didn't want to stand before the Lord with a breath you could hang an M2 on.

But enough is enough. One evening I grabbed a fifth of V.O. and took my little tin canteen cup and sat at one of the broken-down tables in our despicable officers' club that was entirely lit by one 200-watt bulb and I let myself get smashed.

I think a lot of big, important projects are started by men too drunk to realize that what they're trying to do can't be done. So they do it. I looked around at our tacky "officers' club." Like the mess hall I'd fixed up for the men, it was a dirty old hospital tent with as much charm as the floor of a garbage truck. What was good enough for the men should also be possible for the officers. So I stood up and made a big statement. "I'm going to make a real officers' club out of this joint. All I need is a little help. So I'm going to pass the hat." The "help" came to around $600. This and a special leave to Tokyo turned a tent into an officers' club that looked like a branch of Trader Vic's—with a casino, some slots, and a bar that featured fifteen-cent drinks. You couldn't afford to stay sober. There was just one problem—ice. This was bad for our martini business. You have to be a real martini lover to drink them warm. You learn, however. The first one is murder. The second . . . well . . . it isn't bad. Then the third . . . wow . . . sensational. The fourth no one ever remembers.

There were three of us who jointly held the warm martini

drinking record. Seventeen. I challenge anyone to drink seventeen warm martinis. I know I wouldn't try it—twenty years later. I just got over the hangover last Tuesday.

When the word got around about the officers' club, the noncoms asked me to do the same thing for them. Casino, bar, and all. I catered to quite a bunch of people. And every evening I made my orders come true. I really was flying in Korea.

SHOW ME THE WAY TO GO HOME

When the war in Korea wound down, I became the Flying Dutchman of the Yellow Sea. Porpoises, as they swam by me, lying there on a GI air mattress, would give me what I took to be a greeting. As they looped past me through the water they'd wiggle their tails. So I wiggled mine in return.

What gave me time to indulge myself in the joys of sun, sand, and the gentle swells of the Yellow Sea were my working hours. By virtue of my communications background I finally found myself in charge of an armed forces radio station. It was in a rear echelon and was called Mercury. Since I was the boss, I elected to handle the night shift. I'd be on the air from midnight till six A. M. for the insomniacs who got that way lying awake, grinding their teeth waiting for their orders to ship out for home.

The days I spent on the raft anchored just off the beach, with some reading matter, a bit of cheese, some crackers, and enough beer needed to wash down the stuff, resulted in a real all-American tan. I looked so beautiful I could have passed for Murph the Surf.

This tan, along with a diet of my own devising which slimmed me down to a hundred and eighty-five, gave me the physical image everyone has of the typical Marine fighter pilot. As I write this I have managed to get myself back down to a hundred and ninety in an effort to recapture the image of a second banana on a desk-and-sofa show.

I was happy that while in Korea I had the chance to improve the eating and recreational facilities for my squadron. I was delighted to have been allowed to play around with a radio station. I enjoyed the R & R time in Tokyo. But the best thing I did was to write a letter. It was based on the known facts that the Korean action ended in July and I was scheduled to stick around until late in December. So I spent a lot of time and thought drafting this letter to the effect that I thought my usefulness in that part of the world had been reduced almost to zero. For this reason I thought I ought to be released earlier than December in order to go home and resume plying my trade.

This, I pointed out, was acting in and producing television shows, and it was a seasonal business. All the new television shows got started in September. It was true then. Sometimes they ended in October, but September was when they started.

I explained that if I didn't get home before September I'd miss out on a whole new season of shows and would probably have to wait the better part of a year before I could find work. It was a very touching document.

It was promptly stamped "Disapproved" by my squadron leader and by the commander of the First Marine Air Wing. It was stamped "Disapproved" right up the ladder of command till someone must have picked up the wrong stamp and it was approved. There is only an outside chance that someone actually recognized that I had a problem greater than the Navy's need for me in Korea.

My orders came back including the line, "This man must be within the continental limits of the United States by September 1."

Now, instead of being disapproved, my action became a big deal. I had priorities. Generals were being bumped off planes because I was carrying this order.

It doesn't sound like such a big deal now. You went by prop plane and you took it in easy jumps.

From Korea to Tokyo. From Tokyo to Guam. From Natchez to Mobile. Wherever the four winds blow.

I got to Treasure Island about the twenty-sixth of August. It took a couple of days to shuffle my papers, so I just made it. And what a welcome awaited me in San Francisco!

HOME THE WARRIOR FROM THE FRAY

One of the talents I was born with, inherited no doubt from my father, was the ability to meet the right people at the right time and make friends. One of those right people was Colonel Andrew Gear, who was stationed in Tokyo in command of the Second Battalion, Fifth Regiment.

I knew the colonel in Washington and he'd helped me get my assignment as PIO with the Third Marine Wing. I secretly suspect that in some way he had something to do with getting my request for early separation honored. So on my way home, when I arrived in Tokyo, I got in touch with him. It was beautiful.

He entertained me in a way I'd never enjoyed before. He'd been a newspaperman. He was a special writer for *The Saturday Evening Post*. He was an official of the Overseas Press Club. Doors opened as if by magic wherever we went. My advice to all captains is, be entertained by influential colonels. It beats the bus.

But all good things have to end, and Colonel Gear finally poured me on my plane for home. Tucked safely away in the pocket of my tunic was a letter from him giving me entré and the hospitality of San Francisco's Bohemian Club for the duration of my stay. This is one of the country's, possibly the world's, most exclusive clubs. To get in you must have four letters after your name—R-I-C-H. The Angel Gabriel couldn't get in unless they needed him to play in the band. To give you an idea, when I stepped into a cab in San Francisco and said to the driver, "Bohemian Club, please," he turned around and said, "Wow! Who the hell are you?"

Almost apologetically I told the driver, "I'm not a member. A friend just asked me to be his guest."

"You sure know how to pick your friends!"

I thanked him and overtipped him. How could I do less?

When I walked into the club about a half a dozen doormen and bellhops rushed to me asking, "Can we help you, Captain?" But they said it in that tone of voice that told me they thought I was in the wrong building.

"Yes, I think you can," I said. "I have a note here from Colonel Gear." I handed it to the head doorman.

"Colonel Gear, sir?" he said, beaming. Everything changed. "How is Colonel Andrew? Step right this way, Captain." And off we went to my room. It was enormous. After raising the shade, lighting the lights, and doing all the other things necessary to "open" a room, he asked, "Will the captain be staying in tonight?"

"No," I said, "the captain will be going *out* tonight."

"Very good, sir. If the captain will leave his uniform on the bed when he goes in to shower, I'll freshen it up a bit for him."

The captain did that.

It was between eight and nine in the evening. By ten I figured I could be putting myself around a great big delicious San Francisco dinner. Instead of a shower, I let myself luxuriate for a while in the great big tub in the enormous bathroom. When I came out, there on the bed was my uniform.

Instead of just brushing it down he'd had it carefully pressed. This meant that he'd taken off all the buttons, the ribbons, the wings, the insignia, medallions, and all the other paraphernalia you're allowed to hang on your clothes in the service. He had shined them up, pressed the tunic and pants, and put the whole outfit back together again—correctly. Not only that. The Marine cordovan shoes had been shined brightly enough to blind a drill instructor.

I put on all my refurbished finery and started out on the town, but nothing could top the reception I'd gotten at the Bohemian Club. Not that I didn't enjoy myself. I found where

Dave Brubeck was playing and when I tooled into the club it was about four A.M.

After a great night, who do you think was waiting for me? Right! He wanted to make sure I had everything I needed and that I got to bed okay. When he was sure all was well with me, he said, "I'll awaken the captain for brunch."

"No, thank you," I said. "The captain is going to sleep all day tomorrow."

"I must insist that the captain get up for brunch."

This was a problem I wanted no part of, yet the man had been so wonderful there was no way I could beg off from his precious brunch.

But I tried. "I probably won't be hungry," I said.

"Brunch," said my friend, "is one of our specialties and the captain just mustn't miss it." He fussed around the room for a minute and then said, "I'll awaken the captain in ample time." I heard the door close.

The way I felt I didn't think he'd be able to wake me at all. It was my plan to sleep three or four days.

In what seemed like only a few minutes I was awake. My uniform was all laid out for me, pressed again. He got me all gussied up and we toddled downstairs for brunch. As an eating man, I am proud to tell you that I never would have forgiven myself if I'd missed it.

The gods on high Olympus were camping out with wienies and sloppy joes compared to what I saw on the buffet table. Talk about nectar and ambrosia—who needed it?

There were three chefs, no waiting, slicing roast beef, turkey, saddle of lamb, and ham. Each had its own special trimming. The hors d'oeuvre table was so pretty you hated to touch it. But I forced myself. To be brief, I went for the works. And I'm happy to say my appetite was equal to the challenge.

As I sat enjoying the elegant grub my den father came over and said softly, "I see the captain is enjoying himself."

The answer to that was obvious. "What's the special occasion?"

"No special occasion, Captain. We have this brunch every day here at the Bohemian Club."

I smiled and wondered where I got the idea that Bohemians were some sort of casual, carefree, Greenwich Villagey people. I could have been forced to spend a lot more time at that club. But I had to get back to Treasure Island and get my separation papers processed. I wanted to be back with my wife and kids by Labor Day.

So back on Treasure Island I put in a call for Florida. While I was waiting for it to come through—you had to take your turn in line—I thought back about a similar call I'd put through a month or so before in Tokyo to find out if a baby, who turned out to be named Linda, had made an appearance.

I could never forget that call. I had to get special leave to fly to Japan to make it. I'd left special instructions with the Red Cross people to let me know the minute the news came through, if I'd had a baby. They found me all right when the news was bad. But I wasn't hearing from them on the topic of babies. I talked it over with my CO and he mocked up a mission that would send me to Tokyo so I could make the call.

When I got there I found that every serviceman in Korea was there to call home. The wait was between twenty-four and forty-eight hours. Then I knew why the CO gave me three days. So I set up a command post in the bar of the Imperial Hotel and waited for my name to be called to take my turn at the overseas phone.

Twenty-seven hours later I got word that I was up next. It was about one in the morning their time when I put my call through to Bushnell Hospital in Florida. Finally I got the night-duty nurse. Someday I'll run into that woman. When I do, I'll have a few things to tell her that will starch her uniform.

She took my long-distance call from Tokyo for Mrs. McMahon, and said, "Mrs. McMahon is asleep now and can't be disturbed." Then she hung up. She didn't ask who I was. She didn't say what idiot calls a hospital at one in the morning. She just hung up.

Now, I knew for sure that Alyce was in the hospital. I didn't know how she was or if I had a boy or a girl or either. It left me with the most horrible combination of anger and apprehension you can imagine. It also left me with another twenty-two-hour wait because I had to go back to the end of the list and start over.

On the second call a sane person answered the phone. They wheeled Alyce's bed out to the desk so she could tell me everything was fine and that we had a little girl whom we were calling Linda. At that moment I decided to write the letter asking to be back in the States for the opening of the television season.

I had no such trouble with the call from San Francisco. When Alyce answered I asked, "What are you doing Labor Day?"

Surprised and puzzled, she asked, "Who *is* this?"

"Who were you expecting to call and ask you what you were doing Labor Day? This is a man named Ed, your husband."

With that long speech she recognized my voice and screamed, "Where are you?"

"I'm in San Francisco." That raised another scream. "I'll be landing at Tampa Airport tomorrow afternoon around three-thirty if the flight's on time."

When I stepped off the plane, there she was with the two kids, Claudia and Michael. It was in the days before people schlepped tiny infants all over. So Linda was waiting at home. Michael had turned from a baby into a little boy. Claudia was going on eight and had told everyone at the airport that her daddy was coming home from Korea. People asked who her daddy was and in this way she raised quite a nice welcoming committee of strangers.

I was the first off the plane and I felt great—suntanned, down to a hundred and eighty-five. I just stood there at the door of the plane—ham that I was—the way I'd seen it done in the movies and let everybody get a good look at "the conquering hero." Big moment.

Then I ran down the steps, kissed Alyce, and took Michael in my arms. It was a touching scene until Claudia broke it up by taking my hand and saying in a loud clear voice, "Daddy, can I sleep with you tonight?"

FIVE MINUTES MORE

As fast as I could climb out of uniform and get my family packed, we left Florida and headed north. And in almost no time at all I was operating again in Philadelphia.

It felt good to be back on the Main Line, picking up where I left off, even if there wasn't much left to pick up.

In spite of the fact that the station ran a big ego-building campaign around the line, "Guess who's back! Ed McMahon! And look who's got him! WCAU!" In spite of that, the only show I had left was *The Big Top*. Charlie Vanda had promised me that when I came back my old starring role, my clown shoes and my baggy pants would be waiting for me.

As for the balance of my thirteen shows, they had been taken over by three different guys and for three different reasons they all folded. I guess thirteen was unlucky.

After all the big homecoming ballyhoo all I wound up with was *The Big Top* on Saturdays and a five-minute spot at the end of the eleven o'clock news. I called it *Five Minutes More*. The title was suggested by a pop tune of the forties written by Jule Styne and that glibbest of all lyricists, Sammy Cahn.

I find it hard to describe exactly what *Five Minutes More* was, except it was just that. The routine sheet for the eleven o'clock news ran: news, sports, weather, five minutes more. Although it didn't sound like a very big deal at the time, it was my *Five Minutes More* show that stimulated whatever latent creative juices I had running through me. It became very popular because it sent people to bed feeling good. Instead of ending with something dismal like "the entire western part of

233

Pennsylvania is under six feet of water in the worst flood of the century,'' the news ended with me doing what could now be best described as a five-minute *Tonight Show*. But with no Johnny Carson. If they'd had him they wouldn't have needed me.

Frequently I myself didn't know what I was going to do until a couple of hours before air time. But I did have a deadline for getting together any props or art work I needed. And I also had to submit some sort of script that frequently bore no relation to what went on the air.

I have to thank the Marine Corps and the time they let me head up radio station Mercury in Korea for giving me the know-how to run *Five Minutes More*. It was a TV show that had its creative roots in radio. The guy who said necessity is the mother of invention said it all.

I like radio. If I could do the NBC Monitor spots that I used to do when I lived in New York, from California, I'd love to. And I have a feeling I may close out my twilight years doing radio somewhere, maybe on my own little station. The thought came to me when I heard Lowell Thomas on *The CBS Radio Network News*. He's been on radio, I think, ever since there was such a thing. Great voice. As long as you have that and a good, working imagination, you can cut it on radio. It doesn't matter how you look.

The reason I said *Five Minutes More* was inspired by radio is because it tempted people's imaginations.

When I did a show about George Shearing, for instance, I opened with a shot of his hands and the words, ''These are the hands of George Shearing. He has never seen them.'' What we talked about were the number of so-called handicapped people who became stars in fields seemingly contradictory to their handicaps—polio victims who had become track stars, actors who overcame speech problems, things like that.

We relied on people's imaginations. There was no budget for specifics. For the hands at the piano, I used a clipping from a magazine. I collected a whole file of such clippings—what art directors call ''scrap''—for just such openings. The show ahead of me would end, ''This has been twenty-five minutes of news to this hour." And I would come on with, "And this is Ed McMahon with *Five Minutes More.*" It doesn't sound like much but it was a huge success.

It's amazing how many different things you can do in five minutes if you use a little ingenuity and imagination. For anyone who'd like to try such a show, this is what I mean.

I had a floor manager as a character. His name was John Heatherton. He was really the floor manager, not a stooge, and he was a sort of Art Carney type. I worked him into the show in lots of ways.

Once I had him walk on, wearing his headphones, and ask, "What do you want me to do with the string band that's in the lobby?"

I bawled him out for interrupting me in the middle of the show and told him never to do it again. He said, "Okay. But what do you want me to do with the string band that's in the lobby?"

I'd set something up, you see, with one of the bands that marched in the annual Philadelphia Mummers' Day Parade. I'd MC-ed a show for the Mummers' Day Parade organization and in return they'd promised to send me a band in full plumes and everything for the show.

So, for the show they would be on, I opened with the usual still picture of a Mummers' Band and, as I played a recording, I talked about the history of the parade. It was at this point that Heatherton interrupted with his announcement that there was a band in the lobby.

"Look, John," I said, "there's no band in the lobby. All I have is this eight-by-ten glossy and the recording that's being played in the booth. The whole thing's an illusion. You're in the business. How could you get so carried away?"

Then I addressed the audience, saying, "Ladies and gentlemen, I'm awfully sorry for this interruption. But it does prove how strong the imagination is. As you can see, there's no band here." At that moment the whole Mummers' Band in full costume marched across the floor in front of me.

John and I watched them march off and as I closed the show I said, "You see how you can be made to imagine things."

Once I interviewed a talking bull, using the old talking-dog-on-the-bar bit. I apologized to the audience for the fact that the animal didn't speak, saying he'd had an argument with his owner just before the show went on, at the end of which the owner walked out of the studio and the bull called after him, "If you don't come back I'll never say another word."

When Ginger Rogers came to Philadelphia I talked to her then husband, Jacques Bergerac, about having her appear on *Five Minutes More*. He said there was something in her contract that said she couldn't be seen on TV. Then, looking around for a gimmick, I asked if she could come on if only part of her were seen.

"What part did you have in mind?" Jacques asked.

If it had been happening in the sexy seventies, who knows what part I might have suggested? "Her hand," I said. And that's how we did the interview. With me holding Ginger's hand and her off-camera. As I write this, I realize I should have just shown her dancing feet.

I ran a successful money-raising campaign to save Admiral Dewey's flagship that was waiting to be scrapped in the Philadelphia Navy Yard. And I received an enormous amount of mail of approval when I ran a campaign to abolish the lyric to "Muskrat Ramble" and make it illegal to write or perform words to any Dixieland tune.

It was fun. But it wasn't enough. With nothing to do during the day but *The Big Top* on Saturdays, I became restless and started commuting to New York to find myself some work in the commercials that New York-based ad agencies were producing.

To my friend and mentor, Dan Kelly, I complained about not having enough to do, and he suggested he could end that problem for me. There was a restaurant at Drexelbrook which he said should serve only breakfast because it was definitely laying an egg. He knew about the officers' club I'd run in Korea and asked if I had any ideas. I was glad to do anything Dan suggested. I owed him one. One? Many!

THE BID IS ONE CLUB

Anyone who has ever eaten in an empty restaurant knows how depressing it can be. If it's depressing to the customer, imagine how it must be to the owner. Dan Kelly had one of those white elephants at Drexelbrook. It was a beautiful room. The food was good. But very few people came to eat it.

The apartments were beautiful. They'd won awards for all-around excellence—for construction, for ambience, and for urban-type living in country surroundings. For the most part the tenants were rising young business executives.

But all this did nothing to bring people into the restaurant. Monday, Dan said, was the only day they made money. That was the day they were closed. Sometimes they served only sixteen or seventeen dinners. He had to do better than that to cover the cost of the band they had for dancing.

Sitting around in the empty room late one night after I'd finished my five-minute show, one of us came up with the idea of actually turning the place into a club. Man is a social animal, we argued. He hates to be alone, particularly to eat alone. But civilization has dulled the fine edge of gregariousness by making us suspicious of strangers. That is why an eating club, where you are surrounded only by your peers, is such an attractive place to dine. That was our argument and that's what we decided to have, The Drexelbrook Club.

Dan's first decision was to open on the worst day in the week, Tuesday. Then things *have* to get better, he said. Then he let his Irish hang out and did the whole place over in green. Finally, the Tuesday he picked to open was the one just before St. Patrick's Day, which fell on a Thursday that year. It figured to be a one-two punch to get off to a flying start with two celebrations. Opening Night and St. Paddy's Day.

The first thing we did to ballyhoo the joint was to issue a newspaper, the Drexelbrook *News*. It came out once a week for one week. That was the week of the opening. Nobody could complain about the absence of successive issues because nobody paid anything for it. We gave it away. We had to. It had nothing in it but stuff about the forthcoming club, the facilities, and the desirability of having what amounted to a country club only a short walk from your apartment. We sent copies to all the other "eligible" families who lived in the prosperous Philadelphia suburb of Drexel Hill in which Drexelbrook was located.

The big news story on the front page was, of course, the fact that it only cost $20 to join this great club. There was another item telling how carefully members would be screened. And they were. We paid people $5 a head to investigate applicants. It reassured them. But it was a very superficial investigation. The guy would show up at an applicant's door and say, "Hello. I'm from the Drexelbrook Club. May I come in?" One of the main ideas was to find out if there was an alcoholic in the family who might cause trouble. If the home was in too much disarray, the investigator knew the applicant was some kind of slob.

Naturally we didn't investigate our friends; we knew what kind of slobs they were. We didn't turn down many applicants, but we did turn down a few.

It would be false modesty on my part to say that the spot was anything but a smash success. But you might have guessed that. If it weren't, would I have mentioned it? We opened on Tuesday to capacity. You can't do better than that. But we did. We had a sellout on Wednesday, and the ropes were up very early for the Thursday St. Patrick's Day celebration.

After the success of "the big" room, we opened up another area, with its own bar, which we called The Hunt Lounge. As the evening grew mellow, plenty of lounging and plenty of hunting went on there among the men and women of our membership, who enjoyed the whiskey piano we offered and the general "pub" atmosphere of camaraderie that should be native to the City of Brotherly Love.

Drexelbrook Club became such an "in" spot that people began coming out from Philadelphia and along the Main Line. Dan spent a lot of his time there and that helped. And on Sunday, when there was still no drinking in Philly except in private clubs, we were literally mobbed.

For the younger marrieds and all under twenty-one who weren't really drinkers or were just learning to enjoy a beer or two, we opened a candlelit game room where they could have a good time in their own way. Although the only game I ever heard of that could be played by candlelight was post office.

We didn't really know if this room would go, so at first we just masked off a small area with only a few tables. We filled those. The next night we enlarged the area and kept making it bigger and bigger till we'd used all our space.

Don't get the idea the game room didn't have games. There was shuffleboard painted on the floor. Some of the younger members used it to play hopscotch. There were a few pinball machines and, in case some intellectual showed up, a chessboard.

Pretty soon we began to draw membership from Philadelphians who preferred drinking and dancing in our pleasant atmosphere to the crummy nightclubs in town. And we began to expand in other directions. We ran theater parties. Our membership became eligible for these. We took them by bus or train to New York to see a Broadway show, as well as the shows that tried out in Philadelphia. Ours was a real party: cocktails and dinner before starting out for the theater. We even offered cruises to Bermuda, chartered a whole ship.

One of the big pluses to me was that my father became sort of the keeper of the keys to the liquor closet. It was wonderful to work with him and it was a most rewarding time of my life as well as his. He could be near me and his grandchildren and actually be working instead of being treated like an "old man."

A CRASH CHRISTENING

My son, Michael, is learning the television production business in Hollywood. I hope he stays in the business. It's been good to me. It could be good for him. As a little boy he seemed anxious to become top driver in the destruction derby.

Ten minutes after any present-opening time under the Christmas tree at the McMahon's, I felt like taking him for a ride out to the Mattel plant to point out to him that they could make 'em faster than he could break 'em. How's that for switching an old drunk joke? That's what you learn from day-by-day association with Carson.

There was also a little indication that Michael might wind up in direct competition to Jacques Cousteau. Michael, however, instead of aiming to take things out of the water, seemed more interested in putting things into it. The sea was miles from where we lived, so Michael practiced along the banks of Drexel Brook. With almost beaverish fervor he tried to dam it. Had he succeeded, Michael would have been the first beaver to save wear and tear on his teeth by damming a stream with juvenile wheel goods.

In back of our duplex at Drexelbrook there was a play yard, a grassy place, and then the land fell off sharply for about two hundred feet to the brook. It was very calm (except when Michael was there) and rustic. The view was great. You could look down the hill and see all the little red wagons, trikes, scooters, and other items of the moppet transportation system in the waters of the brook below. They came from all over the neighborhood and were rolled down there by my son. Had he not been too young to dig Edna St. Vincent Millay, he might have said it was because, "ah, my foes and oh my friends" they give a lovely splash.

This is all prelude to the duties of Daddy when he came home tired and worn from a hard day's work here and there. The first thing he had to do was climb down that two-hundred-foot embankment and retrieve, one by one, all the playthings Michael had jettisoned. This, let me tell you, is a lousy way to start an evening. It will never replace the double martini with a twist.

But Mike's interest extended beyond disposing of other kids' toys. He had a lively interest in the field of graphic arts and was continually trying out new techniques. As a modern artist might try tempera on Masonite or, possibly, Magic Marker on oilcloth, Michael went way beyond anything previously thought of. You should have seen his work with nail polish on a light-gray velvet sofa! It sure caught the eye when you walked into the room. But that was nothing to what Michael caught.

It didn't take me long to learn, from talking to other young fathers of young sons, that you need not expect to come home to such usual wifely greetings as, "Have a hard day, dear?" Or, "How about a nice cool beaker of Glenlivet, neat?" Not even, "What kept you so long?"

No. The common greeting to all homecoming suburban husbands was, "Your son! Do you know what that child did today?" At some point in each day the boy stopped being our son and became exclusively mine. The cause was, well, such things as the sandbox caper.

After the fact, I learned from the other fathers in the neighborhood that Michael's action in this matter was thoroughly normal. There was an element of machismo in it, I guess.

What happened was that he came upon a little girl quietly playing in a sandpile that he considered his turf. Realizing that extreme action must be taken, he unlimbered his little instrument and relieved himself all over the young lady. It was a dastardly thing to do, not only to the little girl, who was not equipped to retaliate in kind, but to a father who had to maintain cordial relationships with all the neighbors. How would it be if the news reached some gossip columnist that Ed McMahon, Mr. Television, had a dirty little boy for a son? It would bring up that "like father like son" cliché and be very embarrassing.

Can you imagine the self-discipline it takes to walk next door and say to the guy you play bridge with, "I'm sorry that my son wee-weed on your Chloe?" Should you have to do this at any time, carry along an item of food you're planning to flash freeze. The mother's stare will do the job.

Michael reached his peak of creative destruction the day of Linda's christening. She'd been born in July while I was in Korea. It was decided to delay the christening till I got home in September and we were settled back in Drexelbrook. By October, owing to all the preparations I had to make, we were ready. For instance, I had to work a little magic on a handsome hunk of cypress wood Alyce's father gave us to bring north. Sounds silly but it made a beautiful bar. I was proud of it.

It's great to be able to do things with your hands beside shake drinks and write checks. I'd learned plumbing from my uncles in Lowell. I'd picked up carpentry working as a carpenter's helper on a construction job at Fort Devens. Along the way I'd picked up electrical wiring, how to shingle a roof, paper a wall, lay bricks and tile. If you want a hobby that really takes your mind off your problems, take up bricklaying or stone masonry. That was the way Winston Churchill relaxed. He also used brandy. I endorse both.

I don't lay bricks anymore. It's hard to find a place to practice. Now, when I want to go off into a world of my own, I do some gourmet cooking. You get wrapped up in a complicated recipe and if you have anything else on your mind you could come up with an anchor instead of a soufflé.

But about the bar I built. I was anxious to make it look as professional as possible, not just your average run-of-the-mill home bar where if someone asks for a whiskey sour, he gets it in an old-fashioned glass.

I not only stocked all the whiskies from bourbon, rye, and Canadian to Irish and Scotch, I even had a fifth of Suntory stashed away in case some wise guy showed up to try to stump me. There were, of course, the usual gins, vodkas, rums, and brandies; there was also a complete line of aperitifs and cordials including the esoteric items like aquavit and ouzo.

As for the glasses in which to serve all this stuff, I had 'em. There was a bar in Philadelphia that I used to visit when in need of medicine. It was run by a man called Sheeny Burns. With the help of some of my friends and me, Sheeny's bar prospered and he advanced to a little classier location. To honor this vertical move, he decided to update his glassware and got a complete new set of every variety. I bought all the old ones for my bar.

Then Alyce added her touch by putting crystal urns at each end of the bar and filling them with colored water, making it look like the window of an old pharmacy. From the colored water grew philodendrons. When you could no longer say the name of the plant, the bar stopped serving you. I even consented to barstools as a concession to our female friends who liked to *sit* as they sipped their grasshoppers.

This magnificent bar, then, like everything else in the house was all set up and ready for the party to follow the christening. We were all dolled up ready to attend the event when Michael did his number. He tried to climb up onto the bar, hanging on to the edge of it. And in less time than it takes to toss off a shot, there was Michael on the floor, under the bar, lying in a sea of shattered glass. Booze was about an inch deep on the floor. The two crystal decanters of colored water had mingled their content with the green Chartreuse, the Chartreuse yellow, and the rest of the many-colored cordials. It was a sticky, ugly mess. The miracle of it was that Mike wasn't hurt. God, they say, protects drunks and children. He didn't protect Mike from me.

Needless to say, all this didn't make Alyce too happy. She just sat down, all dressed for the christening, with Linda huddled in her arms and cried. Alyce cried. Not Linda. She loved it.

I promised Alyce I'd get it all cleaned up and ready for the party. This was accomplished by one call to the Drexelbrook Club, which sent over everything that was necessary and cleaned up the mess while Linda was being given full title to her name.

When we got home everything was in shape for the party and, if I say so myself, it was the best christening I ever attended. What's more I didn't lose a penny from all the damage. Michael is still paying off on the glassware and liquor. At the rate he's going, with interest, he should be out of debt by the turn of the century.

THE BATTLE FOR NEW YORK

While I had my own shows in Philly, New York was what I wanted. I wanted a show on a network. I also wanted some of the commercial loot that was dispensed by the casting departments of Mad. Ave.

But getting one of those jobs was an incredible routine. It could take six months for a sponsor to decide if he wanted you to sell his precious product. Everybody must case you, the ad agency people, the product's advertising department people, then all the top brass and then their wives.

To give you an idea. I was chosen as spokesman for Cheer. It took weeks, starting with the first audition, which featured a cast of 180 men. How'd you like to have been the fella who had to hear each one of those poor guys and weed out the impossibles?

At an audition like that if you get on late in the day you haven't a chance. Everyone's too exhausted. If you come too early, you may not make it because they haven't heard enough people to give them an idea of what they want. You try to get on about tenth or twelfth. If you have anything at all, you'll be called back for the quarter finals.

I made the semifinals, about twenty possibles. They said I sounded competitive. In business that's the name of the game so I became one of the two finalists. It gets rougher and rougher on the nerves because you never know what quality they're judging you on. You may not part your hair right or you have too much of it or they don't like the length of your collar points or you remind a vice-president's wife of someone she doesn't like.

At one audition involving a number of people who shall be nameless because I'm still in the business, before an actor could open his mouth to read line one, he heard, "Thank you. That'll do. You're not the type."

"Maybe if you told me what type you were looking for—"

"Forget it. We need a knight in shining armor."

Realizing he'd lost the job, and with nothing to lose, he said, "For Chrissake! Why didn't you tell me? I'd have showed up in my new, double-breasted coat of mail."

It was funny but he never got another call to audition for that sponsor. So no matter what ridiculous nonsense came your way, you kept your cool, smiled, and thanked them for their consideration.

In most cases "them" were the people in the casting departments of the big advertising agencies. When I was making the rounds I went from JWT to Y&R to B&B, to BBD&O, to SSC&B, and if I missed my Pennsylvania train back to Philly, I took the B&O.

Some of the people in these casting departments were overwhelmed with their own importance. Occasionally you'd find a lady like Evelyn Peirce [sic] at J. Walter Thompson. She was friendly. She got me jobs. And she was the only person in the business who knew I lived in Philadelphia. I'd get into town in the morning with five dollars' worth of dimes in my briefcase, pick a comfortable phone booth, and start making my calls. I got to know the best phone booths in town, the way New York salesmen come to know the best places to go to the toilet in an emergency.

The Hotel Barclay on the East Side had the largest and most comfortable booths. And it was near most of the large agencies.

In Penn Station, where I came in every morning, the phone company had a big installation with a lot of operators. You'd tell them the number, give them the money, and they'd tell you what booth your call was coming in on. I think they were only supposed to place long-distance calls but if you were nice to them and they got to know you they put through a local call and it sounded as if you had an office placing calls for you. Actually my office was in my pocket and the overhead was those dimes in my briefcase.

Every morning I'd be on the eight o'clock out of 30th Street. When you're on a train regularly like that the crew gets to know you. They not only knew me as a steady rider but, having seen me on their sets, they considered me to be some kind of celebrity. That was okay as far as the crew was concerned. But when the regular riders started to bug me about their sister who could play the toreador song from *Carmen* on two spoons while dancing the fandango, it got tiresome.

I finally worked out a way to duck all this by getting myself a regular seat in the front car where all the steady commuters traveled with their bridge games and their gin games. I had my three newspapers. These guys all smoked big, heavy cigars and it was tough on a guy like me who doesn't smoke. But I put up with it for the privacy it gave me.

Most of these men were "rag merchants" like the cigar-smoking character Jack Lemmon played in *Save the Tiger*. It seemed silly to me that these clothing men should live in Philadelphia and have their offices in New York. Of course, what I was doing didn't seem silly. That was different.

Later I would learn that commuting from Westchester to New York would have been worse for them. They'd have had to make the long trek across town from Grand Central to the garment district. From Philadelphia, they came in at Penn Station and were right in the middle of it.

I'd get myself copies of the New York *Times*, the Philadelphia *Inquirer*, and the New York *Daily News*, a cup of black coffee and a doughnut, and that was my trip to Penn Station. I arrived well up on the news, ready for my round of advertising agencies, auditions, and any conversation that all this activity might lead to.

On the way home, there was a bar. It was a four-martini trip to 30th Street Station. In almost no time it got through to me that that wasn't the way to travel. I had a late-evening TV show and I had to be fresh for it. Four martinis on the train meant you needed a couple more by the time you reached the house, then a little wine with dinner, and this, combined with the exertions and hardships of the day, left you drowsy.

So I switched from sipping to studying. I began reading the classics I'd been receiving every month from the Heritage Book Club. Suddenly they not only looked good on the shelf, they were getting into my head.

Adding it all up, the newspapers in the morning, the books at night, I put in about four and a half hours a day reading. It didn't hurt me a bit. It's why, I think, sometimes on *The Tonight Show* I find myself coming up with some piece of information that a panelist or Johnny is groping for.

Right after dinner when I got home I'd take off all my clothes and put on my pajamas and take a nap. To freshen up for my late TV show I didn't just throw myself on the couch and doze off. By undressing and putting on sleeping clothes as if for the night, I was following the advice Lyndon Johnson once gave me about sleeping. He said, "You've got to tell your body what you're doing."

Sometimes I'd only sleep fifteen or twenty minutes, but I'd wake up refreshed for the show I did at one in the morning. It was not unlike Tom Snyder's program *Tomorrow*, which comes on after *The Tonight Show*. It's possible that by the time this book hits the stalls, *Tomorrow* will have become *Yesterday*.

What I had was called *McMahon and Company*. It could not have been too bad because it went on right after Jack Paar.

We'd be on a half an hour or forty-five minutes or until we ran out of guests and material. We drew a lot of these from the shows that were breaking in in Philadelphia. And that's how Phyllis Newman was born as a perennial talk show guest. Her laugh, now as well known nationally as the chimes of the

Good Humor man, was first heard when she made her TV debut on *McMahon and Company.*

McMahon and Company and all the shows I did in Philadelphia after I returned from Korea were really only to finance my attack on the New York market. It actually got me one show, the television version of a one-time radio hit called *Bride & Groom.* Robert Page, who was scheduled to do the show, decided to move to California and I got his job. Maybe Bob knew something. Between the time I auditioned and they told me I had the job, the show was canceled. Nevertheless I did it for six weeks to fulfill the contract. It had to be a failure.

On radio they could say, "We take you now to the wedding of Sally Ditheroe and Peter Nehelmy in the beautiful, gemlike little Chapel in the Pines." And the listener would picture two ideally matched people in an ideal setting and it would all come off as very romantic. But on television you had to show a crummy little chapel-type set with back lighting behind an imitation stained-glass window, and as for the bride and groom, if you didn't care very much about them when you heard their names, you lost interest completely when you heard, "But first this word from Drano." That's actually the way it was.

I didn't let this discourage me. I hung in there and every month I got my attack on New York more organized. I had a filing system, a handful of 3 x 5 cards each with a name, sponsor, possible leads, and little notes like "Call back in April." "Wants a man with moustache," in case I ever grew one. Sometimes the cards helped. Sometimes they sunk me.

I will never forget going into New York one morning with my hopes higher than usual because I had shuffled my cards and dealt myself a hand of six very hot prospects. I got off the train, almost ran to my special phone place in Penn Station, and as I called the numbers, one after the other went sour on me. I was so disgusted I walked right downstairs and got back on the same train I'd gotten off, watched the crew flip the seats to face toward Philadelphia, and rode home.

I estimate that the first year of Operation Manhattan cost

me about ten grand. Then all of a sudden commercials started coming and things began paying off. I kept my Philadelphia shows and was able to get myself a nice new house in Gulph Mills, a suburb of Philadelphia. The same guy who thought up the spelling for Philadelphia must have done the same for Gulph Mills.

THE WELL

One night on the show after the monologue, Johnny began to kid me about my various extra-*Tonight Show* activities both in and out of show business. As he exaggerated them out of all reason and I tried to play them down, he said, "Well, with all those other projects going for you, I suppose you'll be leaving us soon. What do you need all this for?"

God or some guardian angel must have been paying attention and slipped me the answer in whatever secret way God or a guardian angel has and I heard myself saying, "My friend, my mother always said to me, 'Edward, never get too far from the well.' And this, my friend, is the well." Everything I do stems from my fifteen-year relationship with Johnny Carson.

When Dick Clark hit a hot one with his teen-ager show, *American Band Stand,* one of the smash hits of early daytime TV, he happened to be my next-door neighbor at Drexelbrook. This was the most exciting thing in the world to my daughter Claudia. It was a show that "made" stars like Chubby Checkers and Paul Anka and everyone in Claudia's age group considered it to be the most important cultural event of the twentieth century.

One afternoon I heard her talking on the phone to a girl-friend she'd said good-bye to only five minutes before. She was chattering about the one she called "our groovy neighbor" and finally let go with, "Just imagine! My bedroom wall is right next to his bedroom wall." That's the way sex was in those days, when Doris Day and Rock Hudson in *Pillow Talk*

251

got their jollies by taking a bath together . . . in different bathrooms . . . with their feet against a common wall. You don't find that kind of stuff in the *Kama Sutra.*

There must have been many others beside Claudia, however, who considered Clark to be pretty heavy, a straw in the winds of social change and grass-roots culture, and one of them was none other than the incomparable Edward R. Murrow. He chose to do one of his famous *Person to Person* broadcasts about Dick Clark.

For those too young to recall this show, it opened with Ed Murrow seated in a TV control room looking at a bank of monitors showing various shots of his subject in his home as Ed interviewed him by remote control from CBS. This meant that the whole area around our building was a tangle of wires and equipment needed for such an operation. The kids and the grown-ups, too, were having a ball.

Dan Kelly, who always had his Irish eyes on the alert for a good reason to throw a party, particularly if it would mean publicity for his Drexelbrook operation, decided that Dick Clark and all the TV technicians and bigwigs on hand from New York were a good reason. The resulting party was just heating up when Dan came to me and said, "Don't you think we ought to put on some kind of a show for these folks?"

The next thing I knew I was standing on a platform, saying into the microphone in front of me, "Good evening, ladies and gentlemen. Dan Kelly, our host, felt this evening wouldn't be complete without something in the way of entertainment . . . and if there's anything in the way of entertainment right now, I command it to move aside and let the show begin."

I didn't know exactly where I was going or what I was doing, but other radio and TV people lived in Drexelbrook—a guy and a girl who sang, a fellow who played the piano on weekends at the club, some pro and some semipro talent— and by calling on these people and asking everybody to sing along with me and drown me out a good time was had by all. It was not only a pretty good Mickey Rooney-type show—

"Come on, gang, we can save the old farm by putting on a big show in the barn"—it was also what Dan wanted, a big plug for Drexelbrook.

When it was all over, Chuck Reeves, Dick Clark's TV producer, came over to me and said, "You handled that great. I know they must have tossed it into your lap without any preparation. Do you plan to stay here in Philly or do you have eyes for New York?"

"All the eyes I have are pointed toward New York," I said.

"Well, I'll keep you in mind."

You hear that a lot when you're in show biz. The trouble is you usually get lost in the crowd of other people he is "keeping in his mind." But Chuck kept his word. He happened to know the man who was producing a show called *Who Do You Trust?*, which Johnny Carson had taken over from Edgar Bergen when it was called *Do You Trust Your Wife?*

So it came to Chuck's attention that Bill Nimo, who was Johnny's announcer on the show, was leaving because he had a show of his own. What Johnny wanted, his producer Art Stark told Chuck, was someone who could be more than just an announcer. He wanted a guy who could be sort of a foil. So Chuck told Art about the way I'd put together that ad lib party at Drexelbrook and Art said, "Get him in here and we'll take a look at him."

The next thing that happened was that Chuck couldn't find my telephone number. He called information in Philadelphia to get it and was told that there was no phone listed in the name of Ed McMahon. This was part of a status thing that reaches its peak in Hollywood. You tell people you do it to protect yourself from freaks and weirdos, but all you're doing is showing off because it costs more to have an unlisted phone. Nobody has ever been able to explain why.

The next thing Chuck did was call Dick Clark, who had come in late from work in New York, and wake him up. "Hey, Dick," he said, "go next door and tell Ed to call me right back. There may be a spot for him with Johnny Carson on *Who Do You Trust.*"

So Dick, in a fog (and a bathrobe), went next door to ring my bell. He'd forgotten that while he was in New York we'd moved away from Drexelbrook and into our new house in Gulph Mills.

Dick called Chuck back to say we'd moved and he didn't know my new number but he'd call when he found out what it was. To make a long story short, when Dick asked information for the number of Ed McMahon and got the same answer Chuck had gotten, Dick had presence of mind enough to ask if there was any listing for any McMahon and found out they had one for Claudia. Bingo!

So Dick called Claudia and got my number. He got it from me because I was home in the same house. And he told me to call Chuck back. It all sounds like something in one of those Disney-type family movies where everybody is sweet and thoughtful and trying to do the right thing to help out a neighbor. But it worked out.

The next morning in New York I went to Chuck's office and he took me to meet Art Stark. Art and I sat around and talked for a while about this and that and, finally, he stood up and said, "Let's go over to see Johnny."

So we strolled across town to the Little Theater on 44th Street. Art went into the office to talk to Carson and after a few moments came out and said, "Johnny wants to see you."

When I walked in, Johnny didn't look as if he were dying to see me. He was standing with his back to the door, staring out the window at the Shubert Theater across the street where a couple of workmen on a scaffold were putting letters up on the marquee. I walked over and stood beside him and helped him watch. It was a good guessing game, like watching someone piece together a jigsaw puzzle. We both stood there fascinated and impatient to see how it would turn out. Finally the two guys finished and we could read: JUDY HOLLIDAY IN BELLS ARE RINGING.

"What have you been doing?" Johnny asked, getting right to the point, skilled interviewer that he was.

I told him as we both continued to stare out at the now completed marquee sign. I talked fast to get it all in and it didn't take long.

Johnny is a very frugal man about time, about friends, about everything. He said, "Good to meet you, Ed," shook my hand, and I was out of the office. The whole meeting was about as exciting as watching a traffic light change.

Outside, Art took me downstairs to the theater where they were rehearsing and told me to hang around for a while. Pretty soon Johnny came down. They put me on camera with him, we talked about nothing for two minutes, and then it was, "Thanks, Ed, we'll get in touch with you," which is a version of the old familiar "Don't call us, we'll call you" routine, which was not new to me.

On the train going back to Philadelphia I let my mind linger on how nice it would be to tie up with a rising young star like Carson. We could grow together. It was a pleasant dream but it grew dimmer and dimmer as weeks went by and I heard nothing from Reeves or Stark or Carson or anybody.

Finally I put the whole episode entirely out of my mind and arranged to join a charter flight that one of the products I was doing a commercial for was offering as a premium. It was a hard contest. When I called you on the phone and asked your name and address, if you answered correctly, you were in contention. The rest was pure lottery.

I got our passports, shots, made all the arrangements, and then found that I'm standing there with two tickets and a wife who didn't really want to go. She wasn't too crazy about flying and we'd just moved into the new house and, finally, after kicking it around we decided it would be a great trip for Claudia.

Now I had to arrange for her passport and the whole routine and while I was doing it I was talking myself out of going. I had an awful argument with myself that wanted to go and myself that had a premonition it wasn't the right thing to do.

The day before we were to leave I got a call from Art Stark, who asked, "When are you going to be in New York?"

"Tomorrow."

"What time?"

"Ten in the morning."

"See me."

That killed the European junket. I was sorry for Claudia having to miss it. But she really didn't seem to care much. The trip would have meant missing two Dick Clark shows.

I didn't really read my three papers on the train into New York the next morning. I couldn't help blowing a few mental bubbles on what it would be like to be on a network show out of New York. All these bubbles burst as my talk with Stark progressed. We were having one of those nowhere chats that generally occur only at cocktail parties between two people who have never met before. There was no "Glad to have you aboard, Ed," or any such cliché, just small talk about my family and where I lived. I was aching to ask him who got the job with Johnny but I thought that might sound a little pushy or maybe even resentful.

Finally, out of the blue, Art asked, "Are you planning to move to New York?"

"I don't think so," I said.

"I thought maybe you'd want to."

"Why?"

"Well, I thought it might be tough for you, doing the show."

Now I'm beginning to catch on but I don't want to rush into a disappointment.

"What show?"

"Our show. You start Monday."

"*Next* Monday?"

"For Chrissake, didn't anybody tell you?"

I felt sick. All I could think of was what would have happened if I'd gone on that trip and blown the whole *Who Do You Trust* show. When things like that happen, it makes you believe there must be someone you can trust.

THE MAKING OF A MYTH

Nobody's ever going to make me believe that jive about thirteen being unlucky. It was October 13, 1958, that Johnny and I started together on *Who Do You Trust.*

I was just the announcer, the guy who opened the show, read the commercials, and brought out the questions that Johnny asked the contestants. Pretty soon he began making remarks about my size. "Here comes Big Ed." Then he started that bit of mythology about my drinking. To defend myself I'd drop in a zinger every once in a while. Gradually our relationship, both professional and personal, began to develop.

On Fridays we used to do two shows, a live one at three thirty in the afternoon, and at seven we taped a show for the following Monday. This gave everybody a three-day weekend. Between those two shows Johnny and I got into the habit of strolling next door to Sardi's little bar for a couple of relaxers which we felt we needed before doing the second show. We only had about two hours. How much can you drink in two hours, especially if you're talking business?

The trouble was that Johnny, as he's said many times on the air, isn't the world's greatest drinking man. Give him three shots and he gets very frisky. And sometimes when we'd come back to tape the Monday show, tongues got tangled and things got said that had to be bleeped.

And so the drinking jokes and the cracks about my size got heavier and heavier. There was so much kidding around that we sometimes lost track of the show entirely.

Sometimes as I started to read the opening of the show,

Johnny would stroll over and set my script on fire. This was always a big hit with the studio audience although it couldn't be seen by the viewers because the camera was on the opening visuals.

So while the studio audience howled with delight and the rest of the world wondered why, the studio fireman stood by in case I became a towering inferno. It was my great test by fire, to read all the sponsors' names and credits before the script I was holding became a handful of ashes.

Naturally, after the show was over, Johnny and I would have to unwind. That called for a few more at Sardi's. Then in the TGIF (Thank God It's Friday) mood, we'd wander around the town to find out what goodies other saloons were serving—and to whom.

I enjoyed that sort of recreation and I proved to be a good companion for Johnny because celebrities run into a lot of flack from drunken wise guys who don't see, for instance, what Carson has that they don't. You know, "What's hard about just talking to people?"

Occasionally I'd have to put my size between John and his hecklers or make a quick decision that the place we were in was a good one to leave.

No matter how John and I had met, however, we'd have developed a rapport, a sense of bonhomie and camaraderie. Being colleagues in show business didn't slow up this mellowing process. We liked each other's sense of humor and we believed in the same things and the same values.

Then came the reward of success. Almost immediately after I joined Johnny I was being offered enough new work, just in Philadelphia, to keep me busy about eighteen hours a day if I'd taken it all. A lot of people suddenly became friendly. It's a nice feeling. It was overwhelming and reminded me of a joke George Burns and Gracie Allen used to do. George would say, "Tonight, Gracie, we're going to a very important dinner the Chamber of Commerce is giving for the mayor."

And Gracie said, "Well, that's life. They give the mayor a dinner and there's my poor brother."

"What," George asked, "has your brother got to do with this?"

"He needs a dinner."

It's true. When you no longer need help, everyone is thrusting it on you.

When Johnny was finally selected to succeed Jack Paar on *The Tonight Show,* after four years of *Who Do You Trust,* NBC went through all the agonies symptomatic of a large organization, selecting who should sit beside him and, as it were, be his Hugh Downs, read the commercials, and make himself generally useful around the place.

There was a lot of dickering between the people of the peacock and Mr. Carson.

I'm told Johnny suggested, "Why not give me Ed McMahon because I know how he works."

Everybody agreed to try it and see how it would go. I have a suspicion that there are still some souls floating around Radio City who don't think the combination is going to last. And I agree. I think they should go right on putting me to the test.

Comes October 1, 1962, sitting around a table in Fort Lauderdale, Florida, and the producer, the director, the writers, the star, are all trying to figure out exactly what kind of show the Carson version of *The Tonight Show* should be. I was there only because I was half of the regular cast, but I didn't have anything to say about what the format should be. I did, however, enjoy being in Florida because there always came a point when all the conference tables turned into golden coaches and we went to the ball. After a few futile days they all talked themselves out and we all came home.

On the plane back to New York I said to Johnny, "How do you see my role in this show? What's my stance? How do I fit in? What function do you envision me as performing?"

He said, "Ed, if you mean, what are you going to do, let me put it to you this way. I don't even know what I'm going to do. So let's just play it by ear and see what happens." We've been doing that ever since.

At first I considered moving to New York. But I loved the

house in Gulph Mills, and since my New York connections had stimulated my Philadelphia popularity, I decided to take advantage of both and commute. I did that a total of seven years between New York and Philadelphia, doing *Who Do You Trust* and *The Tonight Show*.

It was the latter that forced me to change my pattern. I used to leave for New York every afternoon on the Congressional Limited. That was one of the classiest and most prestigious trains that ever rolled the rails. It still exists. But in name only.

It had a beautiful club car full of high-powered politicians, Du Ponts, Morgans, and Rockefellers but what I liked most about it was that it was the first train to have telephone connections with the stationary world. I used to love to call people and tell them I was calling from the Congressional Limited. It made each of us feel important.

Thinking it over, I'm sure it was only that my house was there that kept me from moving from Philadelphia. I'd spent a fortune on it and I loved it. It was the first one I ever owned and had everything in it I ever wanted, even a sunken bathtub. When you come home feeling sunk, I want to tell you there's nothing like having a bathtub to fit your mood.

That sounds like the start of a course in how to overcome fatigue. But that's not my main method. I think you know what it is.

SOMETHING ABOUT GUSSIE

"Hey, Ed! Look! We're drinking your suds."

I say, "Thanks! It's not mine. It's yours. I wish it were mine."

Then there are the really nosy, who ask me, confidentially, how big a piece of Budweiser I own. Interesting, how people who see you on TV have no hesitancy whatsoever about asking you probing questions they probably wouldn't dare ask their father or brother.

But I answer them. I tell them I own as much of Anheuser-Busch as I do of Alpo. They think I'm kidding. But it's true. It's also true that both of them are among the longest, continuous sponsors of *The Tonight Show*.

Budweiser liked me for a lot of reasons. Maybe four or five sixpacks. They must have figured the image of a genteel drinker couldn't hurt them. But I don't know why Alpo likes me. I never touch the stuff.

The first indication I had that Budweiser wanted to go steady was when I was approached by two guys from the D'Arcy Advertising agency, Jack Macheca, who was account supervisor on the Budweiser account, and Harry Chessley, the head man. They suggested we have dinner at 21. I have never been known to turn down a good meal. It looked like one of those "go-out-with-the-client" operations which I was beginning to get quite a bit of.

It turned out I was in the hands of some pretty fair drinkers, particularly Chessley. I'd rate Macheca about 4.8 on the Richter scale. But Chessley was up in the 7.1 bracket. As we became more and more "together" these two guys "let it slip" that Budweiser hadn't had a regular radio and television spokesman since Nelson Case handled the job back on the old Ken Murray TV show in the very early days of TV.

When they got right down to the bottom line, the whole point of the dinner was to ask me if I'd consider being their boy. They needn't have sprung for the dinner. I'd have grabbed the job for a Big Mac and a shake.

It was the kind of association I'd been looking for and had lost when Liggett & Myers asked me to be their voice. When they found out that I didn't smoke, the deal soured very fast. There was nothing appealing to them about the possibility of some gossip columnist like Ed Sullivan finding out L&M had a guy recommending their mildness, their flavor, and their smoothness who couldn't possibly know what he was talking about. I had to agree.

Obviously no such problem was present with Budweiser. As luck and my good taste would have it, it actually was my beer, whenever I had a choice. So things worked out. The two D'Arcy guys went back to Budweiser and before long I became related by contract to the Clydesdales.

That was a long time before this writing and it turned out to be a pretty good thing. And not only from a financial point of view. You get a lot of personal satisfaction out of being connected with a successful operation.

Beyond the pleasure of having guys hail me as "Mr. Budweiser," it's been a real pleasure to develop a very friendly relationship with the company that goes beyond business. Gussie Busch has entertained me in his home. When he entertains it's not like the old days when someone would say "drop over for a couple of beers and we'll send out for fried chicken or Chinese."

When you're invited to Grant Farm outside of St. Louis, where Augustus A. Busch, Jr., lives in the grand manner (in a *very* grand manor), it could spoil you for any other kind of living and entertainment you've known in the past. It may be the only farm in the United States where you can go out and milk a buffalo. If, on the other hand, your taste runs to giraffes, you can borrow a short ladder and try to milk one of them. Grant Farm has on its 280 acres every animal indigenous to North America and a few from other parts of the world. Riding around on the little tram they have for tourists is like getting personally acquainted with a lot of beasts you've always wanted to know. The farm is open to the public. It's a great get-together of people and animals complete with beer and pretzels with pop and cookies for the kids.

Grant Farm got its name because on it stands the log cabin in which Ulysses S. Grant lived for a few years just prior to the outbreak of the Civil War. But believe me, Gussie's home is not a cabin. It's a baronial pile with rooms big enough to subdivide into three-room, New York-type apartments.

The first time we visited Grant Farm was for a very formal dinner, and we were the guests of honor. There were only fourteen at table, a small group compared to the usual king-size Busch bash. But in spite of the exotic nature of the place and its lavishness, the personal warmth of the people gave me a feeling that I was doing this because I'd sort of been adopted as one of the family.

This started when I was down at The Homestead with a group of Budweiser sales executives who had been flown there in the company plane. When Gussie heard I was with them he invited me to Grant Farm for the Hunt Ball, an annual society event that he was chairman of that year.

The powers that be asked a place in St. Louis that rents formal clothes to stay open till I got to town so they could fit me with tails and accessories because all my stuff was home. You don't generally carry white tie and tails to business conventions unless you're in the ambassador business.

The festivities started at the big house. I was immediately directed into the living room.

The room was all decorated for the Christmas season and in the middle of everything stood Gussie Busch, resplendent in a hunting-red swallowtail, surrounded by seven little Busches—maybe they should be called shrubs—and their mother all in red and green Christmasy outfits. I greeted them all very formally and Gussie shook my hand and gave me an "Hello, Ed."

The reception line moved on and I wandered over to the bar where I made a command decision *not* to have martinis. As I'm having my more conservative Canadian on the rocks, I hear a voice behind me saying, "What did you call me?"

I turned and it was Gussie. "When you come into my home," he said, "I call you Ed."

"That's right, sir."

"Then what's this Mr. Busch stuff?" He didn't really say "stuff." He used a little saltier word. "You just call me Gussie. Understand?"

The next thing I knew we were in what he called Daddy's Room. Loaded with more trophies, this was where Gussie Senior retreated to for privacy or to entertain "some of the boys," a spot Gussie Junior seldom saw during his childhood.

It was a magnificent room, with two huge fieldstone fireplaces lighting it with conviviality.

Gussie took my arm, saying, "Over here, Ed." He led me to the bar and said, "We're going to have martinis." So I joined the boss in a silver bullet. We enjoyed a couple more before he took my arm again and we went to the limousine that was to take us to where the Hunt Ball was actually being held. It was only about a quarter of a mile away but halfway there we stopped at a little cottage, a guest house. There was a bar with everything all set up and Gussie announced, "We're going to have one more silver bullet before the ball." And that just about made it a ball.

But don't get the idea that Gussie doesn't work. One morning I got a hurry-up call to fly to St. Louis at once to shoot some film with the latest member of the Clydesdale family. The colt was about four days old and they wanted to catch it in the early-morning light as it tried walking on its spindly legs.

I flew in the night before and showed up at the stables at seven A.M. There was Gussie. He'd had breakfast, checked everything out around the farm, and was ready to supervise the shooting and then go on to a day's work at the brewery. I thought to myself, here's a man who lives like a playboy but works like a horse.

Naturally, being Mr. Budweiser entails a certain amount of exclusivity. I can't work for any product that is even remotely competitive. And I wouldn't want to. But I've been approached.

Steve Lawrence and some other friends of mine were putting together a line of liquor products and wanted my name on the board of directors. I had to turn them down. Then there was a company that wanted to create a line of cocktail mixes called Ed McMahon Club. I nixed that, too. I think I'm a little chilly to those ready-mix cocktail concoctions. So, if you don't mind, I'm still sticking to beer and mixing my own from scratch.

I FLEW WITH AN ANGEL

The Blue Angels is a Naval Aviation Drill team, six fighter pilots, one of whom is always (by courtesy) a Marine. No, Virginia, the Marine is not always the first to land.

Inevitably, no matter how skilled the Blue Angel pilots become, in flying their tight formations that make observers on the ground gasp with admiration, something occasionally goes wrong and there are accidents. But the discipline must be maintained. Not Navy discipline, I mean the "get back on the horse" discipline that keeps a fallen rider from becoming afraid of horses. The Flying Wallendas, the circus world's greatest aerial act, has had several serious accidents. But they continue to "fly."

It was in 1972, after one of the Blue Angel's fatalities, that I was invited to fly with them. There were at least three reasons why. (1) I was on the air all the time and could be expected to talk about the Angels and my experience with them; (2) I would create some morale-building within the Naval Air Arm, which was something it badly needed after the accident; (3) If an old and slightly overweight Marine could fly with the Angels, it must be fairly safe. And, if that turned out to be wrong I was 100 percent expendable.

With all this running through my mind, one sunny February morning I flew from Los Angeles down to El Centro, only about fifty miles away, to have a try at being an angel. I figured it might be the closest I'd ever come to being the real thing, even if I was actually only a surrogate angel, meaning I was not technically involved in the operation of the plane.

It was kind of a thrill to contemplate. Having done more than casual flying, I was now being privileged to participate in a maneuver about as casual as the USC Marching Band doing halftime formations at about 700 miles per hour.

I was to occupy the seat usually held down by the rear operator. And I could hardly wait to meet the incredible young men I'd watched maneuvering wingtip to wingtip, performing feats of flying that many pilots couldn't do solo, with the sky all to themselves.

To become a member of the Blue Angels, for openers you have to be recommended as the best flier in your squadron. From all these recommendations they then select three new guys. Three go out and three new ones come in with the commanding officer's tours of duty overlapping. He and five other pilots are the team. Then there's a seventh, or narrator, pilot. He calls the show so the people watching on the ground can understand what's going on up in the clouds and how difficult and dangerous it is.

When I arrived in my little one-engine civilian plane, the whole team was lined up to greet me and, because as a full colonel, I outranked any officer there, they gave me the biggest salute you ever saw.

As I returned the salute they all said, "Good morning, Colonel."

I said, "Good morning, Blue Angels," and that was the end of the formalities. We all relaxed and I asked, "Where's the Marine?" I had to ask because they were all in the same team uniform and the only way to tell was by the emblem on the cap, which I couldn't see.

"Here, sir," said a young lieutenant named Mike Murphy as he stepped forward. He was the picture Norman Rockwell would have painted if he'd been asked to do a portrait of the typical Marine Fighter pilot. Tragically, he and the guy I was assigned to fly with, Skip Umstead, were killed in an accident.

It's almost impossible that anyone hasn't seen the Blue Angels in action either on the big screen, the TV screen or in real life. But seeing them can give you no idea what it's like to fly with them. It's as much like taking a jumbo jet from LA to New York as taking an afternoon snooze is like being shot out of a cannon.

I was quickly suited-up with the others, taken to a short briefing, and straight out to where the planes were lined up waiting for us. I climbed into the back seat behind the pilot and found a note from the crew chief that said, *The crew of 5 welcomes Colonel Ed. Have a good day.* I read it and prayed I would. The pilot then gave me a briefing on the ejection apparatus. It's your only way out if anything happens.

If there's trouble on takeoff, the pilot has to eject you because he's the only one who knows there's trouble. You're shot about 500 feet in the air so you'll have falling room. As it is, I'm told, you hit pretty hard. But you live. One of the crew chiefs I met that day is the one who told me. His pilot ejected him but didn't make it himself. Something like that could happen to me, I knew, and the thought didn't please me one damn bit.

After you're airborne you handle the ejection job yourself. You just press an innocent little button that says EJECT. It might work electrically or if the electric system is gone it works explosively. But the hitchhiker, the passenger, can't make any independent decision. He's not permitted to touch that eject button till the pilot tells him. But for a guy like me, who chose to take a chance and land a crippled plane instead of heading it for the Everglades and getting out, the eject button held no charm whatsoever.

As a gag (I hoped), before we took off the crew chief handed the final coup de grace to my risibilities by presenting me with two plastic bags. "I know you won't need these, Colonel," he said, "but just in case I'll tuck them in here for you." Psychologically that wiped me out.

When I first started flying I was worried, like everyone else, about the danger of air sickness. Then one of the pilots told me to take a lemon with me and keep it handy. If I felt air sickness coming on I should take a bite of it. "The sudden shock of the bitterness," he said, "will counteract the air sickness."

I thanked him, put the lemon in my pocket, and went aloft. I was having a great time doing chandelles and slow rolls and feeling fine when I casually put my hand in my pocket and felt the lemon. Instantly I became deathly sick. Those bags brought that long-forgotten lemon incident back to mind and it bothered me. I was about to fly with some hot pilots who respected me. I even outranked them and the one thing I wanted to do was measure up to their standards in every way.

So I thanked the guy for the bags and smiled. He slammed down the canopy and *bam!*—we're off along the runway. Then, *bam-bam!*—we're going straight up. That was a climb. The power of the plane was incredible. The force with which you leave the ground is unbelievable.

Almost before our wheels were off the ground we were into a slow roll and climbing to ten thousand feet. Then, all in formation, we started doing delta rolls and a whole library of aerial acrobatics, all in formation and by the numbers. My heart started to pound and I looked down and saw I was drawing four G's without a pressure suit.

Normally everyone wears a G suit so that as the G's pull, the pressure comes in to automatically keep the blood from leaving the brain. And we had G suits on. But, guess what?— they weren't plugged in. The regular Angels don't use the suits because their bodies have become so used to pulling G's they don't really need them. They'd forgotten one little detail. I wasn't used to it.

Luckily I remembered from my early pilot training that by screaming as hard as I could I could keep the blood in my head. If I didn't do this, I'd black out. I didn't want to do that. It was too good a show to miss. So every time I felt myself starting to pull G's, I began screaming as hard as I could. The force kept my stomach muscles taut and as we pulled out I could feel the crushing weight against my body. When you're pulling four G's that's four times your own weight. But I pulled out of it and everything was fine. Then came the big thrill.

Our four planes, doing stunts, wingtip to wingtip at 700 miles an hour, pulled into two groups, banked around, and seemed to be flying right at each other. Then one pair flipped upside down and they passed about fifty feet apart, vertically. It's a kind of aerial chicken and as hairy as any game you want to play.

When it was over I heard the skipper of the outfit saying to my pilot, "Hey, Skip, how's your hitchhiker?"

Skip said to me, "Ed—er, Colonel, sir. Do you want to talk to the skipper? Just press the button by your left foot."

I pressed it and said, "Marines hang in there."

He laughed and it was a big thrill. But a bigger kick came when we landed. You have to realize that everything the team did was done by the numbers and on command from takeoff, through drills and into the landing pattern and taxiing and until we all climbed out. The last thing, of course, would be opening the canopy. So I started to look feverishly for the button that would do this. When I found one that said CANOPY OPENER, I figured I'd found it. So as we came to a halt at the chocks and I heard the command, "Open canopies . . . now!" I pushed the button and lo . . . mine came up with all the rest.

That really broke everybody up and while they were still laughing I stood up and handed the crew chief the two plastic bags he'd given me and told him, "You know what you can do with these." And they gave me a picture of the Angels over the Statue of Liberty. It now hangs in my office and is inscribed, TO COL ED, ONE OF US .

GREEN WATER

After Korea my PR work on behalf of the Marine Corps caused me occasionally to run into WW II ace and Medal of Honor Winner Joe Foss before, during and after he was Governor of South Dakota. The most memorable time was when I was asked to MC a dinner in Washington for all the Medal of Honor winners. From then on Joe and I became friends. With Wally Schirra we became partners in a company formed to produce films promoting ecological awareness.

In passing, it's interesting that although I took an interest in ecological problems, I'd never seen a place that was totally unspoiled by the hand of man until I took my children for a raft trip down the Colorado River. It was Wally Schirra who arranged it. He put me in touch with a man named Wayne Erickson, Wally's partner at that time in a Colorado River rafting operation. I knew Wally wouldn't be involved with anyone if he weren't the best. So I contacted Erickson and a trip was arranged for my three children and me. Jeffrey at that time was eleven, Linda was nineteen, and Michael was twenty-one. Claudia, my oldest daughter, couldn't join us because at the time she was heavily involved doing drug rehabilitation work in New York City.

The trip was the right thing at the right time for all of us. I'd seen pictures of Robert Kennedy on a raft trip and it looked like something I'd enjoy. But I never dreamed that I'd actually put a trip like that together because I don't spend a lot of time indulging my whims. I don't take vacations, very little

271

time off. This is not because of any Puritan work ethic. It just happens to be the kind of cat I am.

Anyway I suggested the raft trip, if they were interested, and the idea hit them very hard.

I did have second thoughts about the trip. The day before I signed on, Dinah Shore invited me to a special showing of the great Burt Reynolds film about white water in the wilderness, *Deliveranee*. We went to Warner Brothrs to see the film. Then we went to Dinah's for dinner. She's a great cook. I spent the rest of the night wondering if I should cancel the trip. Did I want to subject my children to such possible dangers? But the true me prevailed.

The trip started at a little town called Green River. Then we drove about two hours through some of Utah's most beautiful country to where our rafts were waiting. There in the silence of that untouched country I looked around and said to myself, "What am I doing here?" It was a strange place for a guy who lives at the pace I live—getting on and off jets, rushing to speaking engagements, doing a nightclub act and a five-day TV show at the same time in different cities, the bustle of the TV studios. It was all too quiet.

To give you an idea of what I mean, when I'm doing my act in Las Vegas as well as *The Tonight Show* in Los Angeles, I get off the air in Burbank at about seven o'clock. A car takes me to a Lear jet waiting at the air field in Burbank. We're in the air at seven twenty. If everything goes right, I'm out of the plane and into a waiting cab in Vegas at seven fifty-five. At eight-ten I walk out onstage and say to the audience, "Now here's something I've always wanted to do and at last I have my chance." Then I take the same stance they see every evening on *The Tonight Show* and I say, "And now . . . heeeere's Ed!"

I'm off-stage about eight forty with nothing to do but rest until the twelve o'clock show. Do I rest? No. I circulate. I see my friends and cronies, maybe even play a quick benefit and, of course, have something to eat. After the twelve o'clock show life in Vegas is just beginning to perk up so I have to get a piece of the action. I don't mean the gambling. I mean catching all the great acts that work the lounges after the big showrooms have closed.

A few hours' sleep follow and I reverse the whole routine, back to a full day of business in Los Angeles and then to NBC for *The Tonight Show*. Against that background, standing under a clear blue sky by a quiet river with only eight people around and a pile of camping equipment to load onto a raft felt . . . well, as the kids say, a little weird.

In contrast to me stands Wayne Erickson, a real salt-of-the-north-country type. You can easily visualize Wayne sitting outside a cabin whittling to keep busy while his beard grows. He hadn't shaved in several days and he was wearing an old cowboy hat that looked as if it had survived at least three or four old cowboys. In his belt was a knife. Nothing special about it, but we learned that the knife and the hat were the two pieces without which he'd never make a river trip.

It gave you a tremendous feeling of confidence just to look at him. He made you feel that no matter what emergency came up, he could handle it; no matter what went wrong, he could fix it. You knew he knew as much about what was good to eat as Euell Gibbon, who at that time had not yet become a household word. I even felt that if the necessity arose, Wayne could perform an appendectomy. He struck me as the kind of man I'd gladly trust myself and my children to, out there beyond the call of help.

Radio wouldn't work 1,500 feet down in the canyon. And the idea of spelling out the word HELP on the ground for a passing plane to see turned out to be just plain silly. It would have been next to impossible to make letters big enough in the available space and during the whole five days we were rafting down the river we only saw three planes.

You couldn't even go back where you came from. There was no way. Besides, where we came from was nothing. The only sign of life we saw was an occasional deer. But life had been there.

At one point we all got out to give a little of our best archaeological attention to some Indian ruins—homes, granaries, everything for living—built right into the vertical wall of the canyon as if by some aboriginal condominium contractor. Over two thousand years of life lay bare for us to look at.

We could clearly define where man had leveled off the land to grow his corn. It was leveling that had obviously been done by man, not nature. The geological strata were spread across the face of the canyon walls as if by some ancient Peter Max. You looked at this and then made yourself stop and think about the fact that the river you were floating on once flowed at the very top of those canyon walls and slowly, relentlessly, cut itself down hundreds of feet. Just as the stopwatch on my wrist measures time—my time—in seconds and minutes, those canyon walls measured time in centuries and eons.

Even though we were with Erickson, his two river-hip daughters, and his two incredible boatmen, I felt very isolated and close to my children for the first time in my life. It was a good feeling.

For the first few days the Green River flowed gently between its high, colorful walls and I remembered a fragment of a song my dad used to sing:

> We were sailing down the old Green River
> On the good ship *Rock 'n' Rye,*
> Hadn't gone very far
> When we came to a bar . . .

That's all I remember of it. We'd fall over the side and play in the water. We all wore life jackets, of course, and we had some wonderful water fights. This all started because one of the Erickson girls asked her father what kind of a guy I was. Could they, for instance, throw water on me? Wayne, being a man of direct action, told her there was no way of knowing till they tried it. So she did. That was the ice breaker. Just as the raft was idling into the river the first morning with me in my khaki Frank Buck outfit complete with pith helmet and hard climbing boots for any shore trips we might make, the Erickson girls hit me smack in the kisser with a pailful of water—

cold, cold water. That was the beginning of a water war that lasted up to two hours, got the trip started on the right note, and continued intermittently as long as we were in calm water.

The people in one raft would try to maneuver so they could get a good shot at the people in the other. Then there'd be an armistice. You'd quietly doze or tell stories and suddenly, bang! The war was on again.

The water was cold but the sun was so hot you welcomed the dousing. And the water fights did a beautiful thing. They created a camaraderie. There was no generation gap. We were like children at play in the wilderness without a worry in the world. If you want the definition of a perfect vacation, that's it.

Finally, the Green River flowed into the Colorado, which is the one with the rapids and the excitement. It's a strange confluence, almost as if the two rivers were reluctant to join each other. For at least half a mile after they have come together you can still distinguish them flowing, as it were, side by side, the green of the Colorado and the tan of the sand-filled Green.

There was no pollution, just sand. Scoop up a cupful, let it stand for a minute, and it's clear as crystal—beautiful, sparkling, drinking water with a little beach at the bottom of your cup. But we didn't have to drink that cool, clear, delicious, river water if we didn't want to. When the trip was in the planning stage I was asked what kind of booze I wanted to take along. So we had with us a huge supply of of Budweiser. It's the only way to rough it. This was all consumed in the five days. Everybody drank it, the four adults and the five offspring, because it was hot on the river under the pure unfiltered rays of the sun, funneling right down on us through the canyon.

The kids got a great shot of me floating down the river in a life jacket quietly enjoying my can of Bud. At night we had red wine which Wayne had thoughtfully brought along in case we happened to run into an oentologist.

This recital of the alcoholic beverages we had along with us reminds me of the two snowbound hunters holed up in a cabin and out of supplies. Finally they drew lots to see who would risk the elements to bring back food and help. After several days away the guy who lost came back driving a dogsled piled high with cases of whiskey. On top of the load was one loaf of bread. When his partner saw this he was furious. "What," he screamed, "do we need with all that bread?"

Every evening after dinner we'd fish for catfish, great big ones, keep them alive on a string overnight, and have them for breakfast. Wayne had a tricky way of filleting them that looked as simple as a cardshark riffling a deck. Then he fried them in such a way that Brillat-Savarin would have gladly autographed every piece. I'm no fish fancier but as far as I was concerned that fish for breakfast was not only the only meal in town, it was better than most folks in town were eating.

Right after breakfast, before we shoved off, the storage lockers had to be loaded. They're large, portable, sealable lockers in which all the stores were packed.

All the kids worked. It was Jeffrey's job to unload the wagon at nightfall. At home I couldn't get him to unload the trunk of the car. But unloading the wagon was something else. Out of it would come all the cooking equipment, Coleman stoves, pots, pans, pails, shovels, sleeping bags, fishing gear, the wine, and the scotch.

That was a surprise that Wayne brought along as a treat for me . . . and himself. I really didn't want to have any of the hard stuff, but Wayne said, "Let me tell you something, Ed. I know you don't want to do a lot of drinking on this trip. It's for recreation, for your kids, and for your health. But I brought a little Scotch because you'll find that after dinner it'll get you in just the right condition to sleep on the sand. Those two"—he pointed to the boatmen—"and the kids, they can sleep anywhere. But two big guys like us can find sleeping on the sand a little rough when we've grown accustomed to king-size custom-built mattresses." He was right.

We'd have our two Scotches, sipping them slowly as we

sang songs. One of the Erickson girls played the guitar. And one night I delivered myself of about an hour of poetry I'd memorized over the years—everything from *The Shooting of Dan McGrew* to A. E. Housman. By nine thirty we were all ready to hit the sack and cork off. It's wonderful how two good Scotches can add just enough goose down to the lining of a sleeping bag to make sand the softest of surfaces.

We'd shove off the next morning, after our catfish breakfast, at about six. And it was our routine on departure that made me understand what is really meant by being ecologically conscious. We left nothing behind. When we took the tops off our Bud cans, we put them back in the empty cans. Those who smoked cigarettes pinched them out and put them in their pockets till at the end of the evening meal, all the refuse of the day, including the garbage, went into the big bin it had come out of. All cans were crushed. All bottles were broken into tiny bits. All paper was folded and stowed. When we left a spot, all we left behind was our footprints. The rule was that nature must be left just as we found it. If someone had only thought of that rule two hundred years ago, the entire earth, its water, and the sky above it would not be polluted today. But, then, we'd be living in tepees.

We buried nothing. We took everything that wasn't biodegradable away with us. Scraps of food and burnt wood we could leave. They would again become part of the soil and enrich it. For safety you take your fire apart and throw the embers into the river. The charcoal will purify it. And, as all the stuff you're taking back to civilization with you piles up, you begin to think that you're taking back more than you brought out.

I was trying to be cool about this one night before crawling into my sleeping bag. We had no tents. If it rained you put a piece of plastic over your face. If it rained very hard, you got very wet. I was just sitting there staring into the fire and sort of half watching one of the boatmen tossing stones into the river. It obviously wasn't just idle stone tossing. As he threw them he seemed to grow furious. Finally I said to Wayne,

"You're going to think I'm stupid, but why is he so intense about throwing those rocks in the river?"

"One of the parties ahead of us," Wayne said, "built a fire in a circle of rocks. When they put the fire out, they left the circle. It looked manmade. He doesn't like that look around here." I asked a silly question and I got a sensible answer.

We'd start scouting for a nice sandy place to make camp and when we found one, we'd pull the boats up and after unloading we'd all go for a nice cleansing swim even though we'd been in and out of the water all day. Only I had a washing problem; I kept losing my soap because I didn't think to bring the kind that floats. Soap, toothpaste, and brush were about all you carried. You didn't need more. You didn't get dirty. But you sure got messy.

On the fourth morning we began to approach the rapids. That was the day we met the only other human beings we saw on the whole trip. It was another party going downstream and we lay back and let them play through. It was as if we all felt a kind of resentment that they had intruded on our river. And it gave me an idea of how the Indians must have felt when they first saw strangers in their territory.

WHITE WATER

When you go rafting down the Colorado, the first half of the trip is calm, all fun and games. Then you hit the rapids and it's all controlled danger. At least they tell you the danger is controlled. The question is, how effective can the control over danger really be?

About two weeks before we went down the river a lady who had made five previous raft trips was killed. At one point in the rapids there's a drop of about forty feet. Her raft tipped over and she was caught under it. The point had been reached where "controlled danger" got out of control and tragedy was the result. It's flirting around this point that makes people ride on roller coasters, surf, ski, and do all the other things that are safe until some failure of man or machine.

Of course it might have been the lady's own fault. Skilled drivers have more accidents than learners. It is possible that being so familiar with the ride, she didn't take all the precautions a neophyte is taught to take. It's as simple as being too casual and confident to buckle your seat belt.

The first thing you have to do before you hit the rapids is make sure that everything movable in your raft is battened down so that if you flip over, nothing will be lost. It won't get wet because the Army medical supplies are all packed in waterproof cases of their own and the rest of the goods are packed in waterproof ammunition cases.

You do all this work of securing while your boatmen walk along the water's edge for fifteen minutes to half an hour and watch the water, noting any new conformation of the river that may be causing any changes. They study and analyze every little swirl and eddy. A rock that was visible the last time they went through may be submerged and more dangerous because unseen.

Where the water is white and churny they know there's a concealed rock to look out for. Where it's dark green and heavy-looking there's deep water, a sudden drop. The ever-changing bed and banks of the river make navigation tricky. The men must decide from which side they will enter the rapids, at which tree they will have to make a sudden cut between boulders. They have to memorize a hundred little topographical details that will keep us tourists from getting sunk in a maelstrom of white water. That is how the danger is "controlled."

Luckily you don't have much time to worry about all this, or even think about it, when you're shooting the rapids. You're too busy bailing. The raft is constantly taking water over the side and it's important to keep it as light as possible so that it is more easily manageable.

So our little party went twisting and turning through the boiling water, confident that our boatmen would see us through safely, convinced it was all as safe as a big Disneyland ride.

I was thinking about this as the foamy water sloshed over the side of the raft faster than I could bail it out when I heard a sudden noise like the sound of Willie Mays snapping a bat or Namath snapping a knee.

At that same moment our boatman fell forward and the piece of oar he'd been holding got away from him and hit me in the middle of the back. The pressure of the water had broken his oar. The raft was out of control.

There were two spare oars lashed side by side right at my feet in case of an emergency. I figured that's what we had. I reached over to release one of the oars and heard, "Look out, Ed!"

My reactions are pretty fast, but I never pulled back quicker. As I did, his knife came down on the rope right where my hand had been. There wasn't time to untie it. If I'd been a split second slower, I might never again have been able to play the zither.

When we reached the calm at the bottom of the rapids, we hung around waiting for the other half of the oar to surface. When it did, we fished it out and it now hangs on the wall of Jeff's room—Chief Broken Oar.

Before the trip ended we had a fascinating interlude exploring about a mile or so into the canyon to see the cabin where Butch Cassidy was said to have holed up. That was not only long before Paul Newman ever heard of him; it was years before anybody ever heard of Paul Newman. It was a shipshape little pad with a dining table that lifted up against the wall the way the tables do on your average, run-of-the-mill, thirty-foot cabin cruiser, proving that nothing is really new. But the most important feature of the cabin was its location. No one could approach from any direction without being seen.

It was quite a thrill to stand in the middle of history, to look at part of a legend of the old West, and realize how much better the film made it look than it really was. What made it even more exciting was the belief everyone held that somewhere around that shack Butch had buried a lot of loot. Fortunately the place is well off the beaten tourist trail or it would look like a gopher's practice course.

I find I've forgotten to mention the one thing that blew the minds of everyone in our party. The stars. The perfectly clear air and the absence of all artificial light brought millions of stars right down on our heads and I kept humming Kurt Weill's great song, with the haunting refrain, ". . . and you're lost in the stars." And we were lucky enough to see a phenomenon that John Denver had told me about, a shower of meteorites that made Fourth of July at Dodger Stadium look like a rainy evening in the backyard with a handful of damp sparklers.

Finally we came to the end of our trip and changed from our big, circular rafts to the greatest little rubber motor launch you ever saw. It was resplendent with a striped *fin de siècle* awning and chugged us along merrily to a thriving little metropolis called Height's Landing, where a plane I had chartered was supposed to meet us.

As we were chugging along I asked the kids what they wanted to do with the four remaining days of our vacation. They voted for the absolute antithesis of what we'd had—Las Vegas. I said it was okay if they thought they could afford it.

Then I told them that as soon as we got to Height's Landing I'd phone Caesar's Palace and make arrangements. I had a pal named Mike in the massage room there. So I promised the boys we'd all have steam baths, Russian massages with tannic leaves, and a rubdown. "It's going to be sensational," I said. "We'll be clean."

Funny thing about that was that we weren't dirty, not city dirty. We were covered with real dirt, not grime; with soil, not filth. But we looked dirty. And those of us who shaved needed one. We also needed a new pair of glasses for Mike. I'd lost a pair of sunglasses while rummaging around in the water for my lost soap. I found those. Mike lost his forty-dollar, favorite, needed-for-seeing, prescription-granny-glasses in a water fight. They were our only violation of the ecology of the river. The glass might eventually get ground back into sand. As for the frames, I don't know. I like to think of one of those big river catfish, looking like Charlie the Tuna, in a pair of granny rims.

The moment I said I'd call Caesar's Palace as soon as we landed, the man who was running our launch said, "You can't call Vegas from Height's Landing."

Years of being a straight man taught me to say, "Why can't I call Vegas from Height's Landing?"

And years of listening to formula jokes makes you know that his answer was, "Because there's no phone in Height's Landing."

But it was no problem. The plane was there. It flew us over beautiful, man-made Lake Powell, which looked bigger to me than Lake Mead, and landed us at a place called Page. It not only had a telephone, but hundreds of people with houseboats. I think I'll go back there sometime and rent one of them, just cruise the lake, and do a little quiet fishing and maybe some thinking.

That's something I've been postponing too long. I mean the fishing.

THE CHRISTMAS PARTY

Our arrival at Caesar's Palace was a study in contrast.

Here was this supermagnificent, consciously rococo, hyper-elegant hostelry. Entering it were four people who looked like rejects from a Skid Row mission. But I topped anything seen in Vegas since Howard Hughes packed his sneakers and left town. I was wearing an earth-splotched pith helmet, a khaki safari suit that looked as if it had been ironed in a sandbox, and a nice thick stubble on my chin. The ensemble was given added flair by a shirttail hanging out in back.

Caesar's Palace encourages people to "come as you are," but we took advantage. However, it was acceptable because we came well-heeled. The moment we hit the Vegas Airport I put a quarter in a slot machine and said to Jeff, "This is for you." Mike put in his own quarter. He got nothing. Jeff, on the other hand, simultaneously became a millionaire playboy and a confirmed gambler. He picked up $21.50 and an idea that he would make slot machines his way of life. Fortunately, before we left Vegas I was able to change his mind. I told him about the guy who drove there in a $12,000 Cadillac and went home in a $95,000 bus.

At the desk as we entered I said to the guy, "Can we clean up before I register?"

"You're already registered, Ed."

So I tipped the bellman, gave Linda the key to her room, and told her to go shower, fluff up, and buy herself any new clothes she needed. Then the two boys and I went for the works with Mike the masseur. While we were enjoying the sauna and the whole bit, we had our clothes cleaned and pressed and as soon as we got them back we went out and bought new ones that were more appropriate.

By evening our little party was ready to do the Strip. We went to see Sammy Davis and Steve and Edie and when the evening was all over, Michael said he wished we were back in Colorado on the river. Maybe it was the river trip that influenced him to go to the University of Colorado. Although that is about as silly as saying being born in the Catholic Church forced me to go into the bingo business.

Caesar's Palace, as the name implies, is a glorification of ancient Rome—if you accept the premise that Rome *was* built in a day out of plastic, neon, glass, and just enough velvet to make it seem trashy. It's a big put-on. It's fun. The bastard-ized baroque of the decor is as big an escape from the life-style of the people who go there as Avalon, New Jersey, is like modern Rome.

We walked into our suite and practically needed snowshoes to get across the living room to the bedrooms. That carpet just wouldn't quit. It wasn't satisfied with being on the floor. It climbed right up the walls. All I can tell you about the furni-ture is that the legs on the desk looked like a lady's. The beds were not just king-size. They were the size of the king's polo field but with canopies.

The kids looked around and laughed, thinking of their nights under the stars. I did the same and said, "This is where we're holding the Christmas party." I immediately called the office and reserved that suite for August 26 and the Christmas party was actually held on that date.

Most people might not quite understand a Christmas party held on August 26. But they're not the kind that get invited to my Christmas party. This is hard to explain. But I'll try.

The idea must have been part of my inheritance from my fa-ther's desire and ability to make something out of nothing. August as a month is a good, big, hot nothing. Dad was a great believer in the no-birthday party. Excitement to him was an unexpected happening, and he brought this to people wherever he went.

When I was a little boy and Mother and Father were separated, it used to be the thrill of my life to visit my dad at the Hotel Victoria in New York. Only if you can remember what a kick a kid gets out of staying in a hotel can you realize how I enjoyed those visits to my father. Just being in a hotel wasn't all of it, either. Every day was some sort of party. "Today," he would say, "is the birthday of that great President, Alexander Polk. We must celebrate." Or he'd say to me, "Today is your half-birthday. Where do you want to go?" Once I remember we celebrated the two hundred and fifty-fifth day after Christmas. Maybe that's what planted the germ of the off-season Christmas party in my mind.

I try to do the same thing. Not long ago Jeff had been sick but it was his time to visit me. I wanted to cheer him up. Sick or well, restaurants are not a big thrill to him. I don't think any kid really likes them. I was on a diet. All I could have was clear soup and salad. But I still wanted to make that meal memorable. You may not believe what I did was anything much, but it flipped Jeff.

We went to a fancy place and when I asked him what he wanted he just said, "Oh, I don't know." So I said I'd order for him. What happened was that I'd gone out and had a Big Mac and a thick shake delivered to the restaurant. The waiter came in with a platter under a silver bell, lifted it, and *voilà*, the Big Mac. It was a gas. No pun intended.

It was the surprise that got him.

This urge for the unexpected and the feeling that his birthday was the best excuse for any party, coupled with the conviction that the date of his birth was selected arbitrarily, made me focus on the notion that there should be a party for those—and only those—you love and admire, those with whom you are in thorough harmony. That's peace and that's the spirit of Christmas. I like to think that the birth of the idea was sheer inspiration. It happened at a party in a New York restaurant. I've racked my brain to think of the place or even place some of the people. All I know is that we were having a ball.

When you get a good group going, by about two or three in the morning, when they lose all their inhibitions, they can become an awful pain in the neck and that goes right on down to the people who are serving them. But there was a waitress who never lost her cool. Her smile stayed bright. She never made a wrong move or said the wrong thing. She was wonderful.

She was the kind of waitress I'd want to be if I ever became one—the best. I don't care who you are, you're a success if you're the very, very best at what you do. As far as I'm concerned, one of the main elements of being good at anything, particularly at just being a human being, is being polite.

Driving down the Garden State Parkway from New York to my home in Avalon, New Jersey, you go through a million—maybe more—toll gates. Unless I was very late for an appointment—something I rarely am—I made it a point to drive through the gate where there was a person instead of just tossing my dough into the basket on the automatic lane. This gave me a chance to say, "Good evening," "Thank you," or whatever to the guy or gal who was taking the toll. This gave me some reassurance that the world had not yet been entirely taken over by machines. But sometimes it startled them or they thought I was nuts.

This little thoughtfulness taught me by my Grandmother Katie has turned out to be very good public relations for me. Those toll gate attendants see hundreds of people every day and hardly give them a glance. Pretty soon, however, I began hearing, "Morning, Mr. McMahon," or "Hello, Ed." It was gratifying to me and, I think, to them, and it certainly made the day a little better. It represented a moment of selfless friendliness in a crowded, pushy city. It's like the concept of light one little candle.

So it was the unflappable politeness and friendliness of that harassed waitress that impressed me very deeply. As I left her gratuity and the party started to break up, I said to someone, "She's coming to the Christmas party." It was only after I said it that I figured out what it meant. Since then, little by little, saying that someone is coming to the Christmas party has become, for me, a way of indicating my acceptance of that person into my circle of those I feel are simpático. The great author and essayist Christopher Morley called such people kinsprits. Among them the feeling persists that it's better to give than to receive. It has something Oriental about it. When I was on leave in Japan, I learned that in a Japanese home you dared not admire anything. If you did, your host would present you with it. It came to you the next day with a little note saying, "You enjoyed this so much we will enjoy it more knowing you are enjoying it."

So, among my Christmas party friends, if you say, "I like your tie," it's off and it's yours. This is beautiful. On the other hand it could ruin a friendship. One evening one of my friends said to another, "That's a swell tie." But the guy with the tie couldn't take it off and give it away because the person who had given it to him was also at the party and he didn't want to devalue the gift in the eyes of the giver, cause misunderstanding and unhappiness. So you learn.

If you're out to get stuff free, it's a cinch. I once casually commented on what a great shirt a guy was wearing. Next day a messenger showed up with seven of them. They didn't have any exactly like the one I admired so I was instructed to pick one from among the seven. I did and the next day I got a half a dozen of them. To me that is the exemplification of the sheer joy of giving, the main qualification for admission to the Christmas party. Of course, it works in reverse. When someone is rude, uncouth, unpunctual, "He is definitely not coming to the Christmas party." The expression has come to be known by my pals, as "one of Ed's cracks." Many of them unconsciously use the lines themselves. One evening at a party at LaCosta, I was wandering, glass in hand, through the various areas of the hotel and a starlet stopped me and asked, "Where are you going?"

"Wherever this glass leads me," I said.

She laughed and said, "That's the same thing Monroe Sachson always says." Then I laughed. Monroe, who's produced all the films I've been in, got the line from me.

There's a kind of braggartly thing I do that was started by Frank Sinatra one evening at Caesar's Palace. I was asked to introduce him, which I did, and then I went back to my table and sat down. As far as I was concerned that was the end of it. But it was only the beginning. After about his third number Frank said, "I'd like to dedicate my show tonight to Ed McMahon because Ed's in town."

I now have a sign that says that, given to me by a pal, hanging on the wall of my office. When I travel, I have a telephone book cover that I give to hotel operators, that says on it, "Ed's in town." It amuses them. It works well for me because I now have pals and cronies all over the country and I like to check in with them, hook up with them, and go out to dinner and have a party and it all ties in when the operator calls and tells them, "Ed's in town."

Then there's "Hi-yo." People are always asking me about that. Where did I get it? What does it mean? And how do you do it? The answer is always, I don't know.

It must come from my youthful fascination with Western movies. Like John Wayne's "All right, move 'em up. Move 'em out," it's a signal to get going. It's a cattle call or something and I dredged it out of my memory one night when it looked as if *The Tonight Show* didn't have a very responsive audience. I was trying to "move 'em out," create a little excitement, and I said, "Hi-yo." It caught on.

I get it now wherever I go and people are always asking me how I do it. There's a little glottal check in your throat that comes after the "Hi" and before the "yo." And there are a lot of *O*'s. I don't really know how to explain it. But I enjoy doing it and I'm glad it caught on. And it seems that instead of fading in popularity, it's getting stronger.

Like all Irishmen, I love words. Once when a woman friend of the family was feeling very distressed, very down and out of it—if the world didn't come to an end she was going to kill herself—I heard myself consoling her by saying, "If you believe in God and remember that each little snowflake is different, you'll realize, only then, that if he can take the time to make each snowflake different, how much he must care about you." Now, honestly, I don't know if I read that, heard my Grandmother Katie say it, or what. Maybe God took time off from the snowflakes to give me a good line. I like to think I made it up. In any case, I put in with Anatole France, who said, "When quoting someone never give the source. Those who are smart will know who you're quoting, and it won't make any difference to the rest."

Now I use the snowflake quotation as a little plaque, a sort of permanent Christmas card I give to some people.

Having wandered all over trying to say what I want to say about the Christmas party, I guess what I actually mean is that it has nothing at all to do with anything but a human feeling that transcends all differences in religion, that has to do with being pleasant, polite, and considerate, with smiling a lot and just with making other people feel good. It has to do with love and friendship and wanting to give a part of yourself to somebody else. It has to do with sharing.

Anyway, that's it. August 26, 1972, we held our first Christmas party in Las Vegas. Friends flew in from all over the country. I cooked a turkey. I'm not bad at that. I add applesauce and marmalade and half a bottle of brandy to the dressing. Then I cook the bird all night long in a slow oven. When you wake up in the morning, what an aroma fills the air—roast turkey laced with booze.

I got the hotel to lend us all their stored-away Christmas decorations. We fixed up the suite with a tree and lights and everything. We had a piano player knocking out carols and the party went on till five in the morning. Many of the guests took off and continued it elsewhere. Since then every Christmas party we have held has been better than the one before. But to me, none has surpassed the first. (A little philosophy there.)

It will never again be held in Vegas. Even though the first one was there and it was a big success, there are too many diversions. People wander off. The lure of the crap tables and the roulette wheels is magnetic. On the other hand, people working in town also wander in. On balance, I think, it's easier to keep the party together in spirit, as a unit, in less electric surroundings.

For instance, there was Christmas in August, in my home in Florida on the Gulf of Mexico. A three-day party with barbecues on the beach. The only hard problem was getting enough ice, so we told everybody, "Bring your own ice—we'll furnish the booze."

GET A LOAD OF A QUAINT CAT!

I know of only two Avalons. One is on Santa Catalina Island—"beside the sea," as the song says. The "sea" is the Pacific Ocean. There, the song goes on to tell us, some guy found his love.

My Avalon is in New Jersey, and it's also beside the sea. But the "sea" is the Atlantic Ocean. I, too, found a lot of love in Avalon.

It's a tiny community down at the southern end of the state, only fourteen miles above Cape May, which is as far south as you can go and stay in New Jersey, if that's what you want to do.

As we'd do it on *The Tonight Show:*

"How far south is it?"

"It's so far south that the mail carriers wear repossessed Confederate uniforms."

Cape May in its day was the Nice of North America. It was the "in" social spot for Philadelphia high society to summer just as Newport was for the *haut monde* of Boston and New York at the *fin de siècle.* When you write about gentry you use high-class language.

Five Presidents had their summer White House in Cape May. It wasn't too far from Washington and there was no such thing as Air Force One.

There's a project to restore Cape May to its Victorian elegance. It shouldn't be too hard. It never got very far away from it. The J. C. Penney store will become "the drapers,"

the drugstore, an "apothecary," the A&P, the "greengro-
cer." And as things are shaping up, the Exxon Station may
turn into the "feed store."

Although it's a full fourteen miles north of Cape May, Avalon, too, has managed to fight off the march of progress to
some extent. This is in contrast to the fact that it had a woman
mayor for fifty years. Possibly it was too small for a man to
bother with, a crack that should earn me my diploma as a male
chauvinist pig.

Lucky thing about this lack of forward movement, now
when the Old World charm is being rediscovered, Avalon is
still a controllable situation. It will be relatively easy to maintain its early character. Motels and hotels are now restricted
to one area, apartments and condominiums to another, leaving the rest of the town for one-family residences. That's
where I have the home I love. When you come to see me,
drive directly to Cape May Court House, turn toward Stone
Harbor, and drive north till you see me sitting on the veranda.

Actually, Avalon is at the corner of Townsend Inlet and the
Atlantic Ocean on what is virtually an island that's bounded
on the inland side by marshes and waterways. My home is
among the sand dunes on what is officially called Seven Mile
Beach. It used to have a boardwalk but the sea carried it away
years ago and no one ever bothered to put it back. What for?
This has left the beach pristine clean and unspoiled. You can
take it as official that it's one of the most beautiful stretches of
untouched seashore in North America with the possible exception of the dramatic, rock-studded black strand in Oregon.

Every so often this stretch of shoreline is attacked by some
of the most ferocious storms the Atlantic can whip up. Many
a ship has foundered off Cape May. But my house is in no
danger. It nestles safely behind its own sand dunes. The years
have proven that there is no bulkhead, no rock jetty, no concrete wall, not even those piles of jacklike objects that the
Japanese use to hold back the sea . . . there is nothing better
against the ocean than sand dunes. They seem to absorb the

shock of the water. When the storm is over, they're still there. Living among them gives you a good secure feeling that many people living in beach houses can't share.

The secret may be in the bayberries that grow on the dunes. They, too, cannot be swept away by the fury of the storm. Very hardy, those bayberries. I'll bet if you dropped one of them on the moon, it would grow.

The bayberries attract the purple martins. They're birds. They're birds that are bayberry freaks. Each year they fly for miles, all the way from somewhere in South America, to gorge themselves on bayberries. They arrive at just the right time, during the few days of the year when the bayberries are ripe and juicy. That's when the whole town of Avalon becomes purple. The martins pick and eat the berries, squeezing the purple juice all over town. But that's not why they call them purple martins. They are purple birds, very pretty, about the size of sparrows, and I find them fascinating. It isn't that I'm a bird-watcher. I'm just intrigued by the life-style of these little creatures. I hope someday someone solves the riddle of how all migratory animals know when it's time to leave a place and go to another and how they navigate.

How do they know exactly what day to shove off from South America to hit Cape May, New Jersey, when the bayberries are ready? That also happens to be when the mosquitoes swarm up from the marshes. The purple martins also love mosquitoes. This is what makes the bird so welcome in Avalon. They eat mosquitoes. If you can get some purple martins to live around your house, they'll keep the mosquitoes from eating you. New Jersey, you know, is famous for having mosquitoes the size of pterodactyls, able to devour a horse.

Besides their healthy appetites for mosquitoes fattened by the blood of Jersey burghers, these unique little birds have a very urban way of living. Unlike other members of the feathered community, with the possible exception of angels, they eschew single-dwelling accommodations. No nests for them. Put up a one-bird house and the martins won't move in. So to coax the birds to come and protect you from the insects, you buy a birdhouse that's four or five stories high, a multiple dwelling. I've seen some as high as thirty or forty stories. High-rise birdhouses.

I've tried to get these critters that devour between two and five thousand mosquitoes a day to occupy a condominium on my property. No luck. I've never been around long enough to let my Irish charm work on them. It's a blow to the ego. Perhaps it's just that I don't look like a mosquito. That premise I'll accept.

Unless you've lived in Avalon you can't believe how heavy the sky is with those little nippers when the wind is from the marshes. The martins sit on the telephone wires and just pick them off as they fly by like kids tossing ju-jubes into their mouths. Then they go home to their apartments and sleep it off.

If you can get a community of martins to live on your premises, you're set. They come back every year unless you're careless enough to let some other bird move into their place while they're gone. No sublets for them. They seem to know what it does to your furniture and nice things. So the moment they leave, you have to cover your martin house.

I find all this interesting. It is part of the uncomplicatedness of Avalon. It's nice to drive down the street and have the cop at the corner say, "Hello, Ed," instead of, "Up against the wall!" What's more, he'll tell you where your kids are and it won't call for bail. One's in the drugstore having a malt, the other's picking up a bob or two pumping gas. It's the country town atmosphere that I find to be a refuge from my much too mobile life. And it comes as a surprise to me, as I write this, that I dig quaintness. I feel I'm too big for that. I mean too big physically.

I keep the house in Avalon open all year. Just turn the key, walk in, light the lights. No storm shutters to take down or anything. I had it built solidly and there it stands ready, heat or air conditioning working, phones connected. With my schedule I never know when I'm going to have a weekend or a four-day holiday to go there and unwind. And everyone in my family has a key and is free to go there anytime. They all love it. Claudia, Michael, and Linda have lived there from time to time, and Alyce has stayed there with Jeff.

About fifty families from Philly, families we know fairly well, have summer homes in Avalon. We know their children's names, where they went to school, whom they married. So checking in at the Avalon house becomes a sort of catching-up time for all of us, and no matter who's there, there's always a series of parties.

I have a house in Florida. I had an apartment till I got burned out. But I'll set up another, and there's always that place in Avalon. Like your firstborn, although I know it shouldn't be that way, that house is special. That place way down south in Jersey holds a great big piece of my heart.

BRING ON THE CLOWNS

When Timex approached me about doing a circus special in Europe that would keep me over there about two weeks, I naturally had to talk it over with Johnny. He had to okay my absence and arrangements had to be made as to who would stand in for me and who would pick up the tab.

"They probably picked me," I told Johnny, "because they remember *The Big Top* show I did in Philadelphia."

"Who's the sponsor?" he asked.

"Timex. It's to be called *Timex Presents the All-Star Circus.*"

"And you're to MC it?"

"Be the ringmaster."

"That's all?"

"And do my old clown act."

"That's all?"

"And read the commercials."

"What became of John Cameron Swayze?"

"I don't know."

"Well, be careful."

"Why?"

"Don't let them get you involved in one of those Timex torture tests."

"In what way?"

"They might want to strap a watch on your elbow and send you out on the town."

And so it came to pass that I went on a fast tour of Europe, opening in Copenhagen. The circus we used as background and locale was the famous Benneweis Circus. It's named after the Benneweis family that had a wonderful trained-horse act and finally established this permanent, year-round circus in Copenhagen. They do two shows a day in an arena specially built for their kind of show.

There's a huge center ring with a proscenium at one end for entrance and exits. Seats rise all around but, oddly enough, the effect is less that of being in a circus than being at the opera. Of course, the smell is different.

I guess they actually could do opera there. It would be ideal for Wagner's *Ring*. I'm sure anyone who has ever made one of those bone-breaking, muscle-straining, sleep-robbing, mind-boggling seven-day tours of Europe must remember it, near the Tivoli. It's a tourist must. If it's the circus, it's Copenhagen.

It felt great to put on the old *Big Top* clown makeup and wardrobe and get in there with those wonderful European clowns. They're the best in the world, descendants of generations of clowns. I felt it was quite a compliment when they accepted me as one of them. Clowns are really a very special segment of humanity, dedicated men, and I love them. They saw I knew how to react, handle the seltzer in the face and take pratfalls. I was even to remind those old pros of some clown bits they'd forgotten, ones that I'd picked up in America.

I made my entrance with two midget clowns pulling at me and knocking me down, which was something like Gulliver with the Lilliputians. I worked with them for two regular shows a day for four days of rehearsal and then we shot the TV show on Saturday.

To the people in the audience the tall clown with the midgets was just another clown. But Copenhagen is always full of tourists so there were always a lot of Americans in the audience. It generally got a gasp, a big laugh, and a good hand when they finally revealed my identity and announced my name when the clown bit was finished. Then I went into the regular ringmaster's outfit and did the other portions of the TV show.

It wasn't easy. I'd forgotten how physical clowning is, running with those big foolish shoes and baggy pants and taking pratfalls. By the time the gig was over I was a wreck.

I was in Copenhagen long enough to fall in love with the city. It's so clean you can't believe it. Absolutely spotless. At least that's the way it was when I was there. Terrible things happen to cities. Take New York, for instance. Around those Sabrett hot dog wagons in New York the trash is literally in drifts; ice cream wrappers, paper napkins, soft drink cans, Popsicle sticks, little pieces of frankfurter rolls. Nearby is an empty trash can.

In Copenhagen, too, they have vending carts. They're bigger and more numerous than the ones in New York and the area around them is spotless. That's because there's an ordinance making the vendor responsible for policing the area around his stand and the ordinance is enforced by inspectors who come around every hour or so. The fines are heavy and a guy could lose his license. The only place in America that I can think of that's as clean as Copenhagen is Disneyland and for the same reason. Instead of cleaning up every so often they keep cleaning up all the time.

The air's a lot better there, too, because they ride bikes to work instead of driving Thunderbirds and Cadillacs. There are hundreds of bikes that seem to be stacked up at random in front of every building. None of them are locked. The last time I was in New York I saw a bike secured to a lamppost with a chain that could moor a tanker. What's more, the front wheel had been taken off. Apparently the guy couldn't carry his whole bike upstairs so he took half of it. Or maybe someone came along and couldn't get the bike loose so he just stole the front wheel. It's awful.

Maybe thrift, which we Americans are just beginning to realize we ought to find out about, has something to do with civic cleanliness. Also pride that comes with purpose. I got into a cab in Copenhagen and was astonished to note that it was a Mercedes-Benz. That's pretty classy for a cab. Then I noticed all the cabs were Mercedeses.

When I asked the driver how they could afford such an investment he said, "I buy one cab. It's for life. So I buy one that will last." That's not our way of thinking; not even when we buy such an important thing as a home.

As for the fabulous food in Denmark, get me started on that and I begin to salivate. I am convinced that a man who can diet in Denmark is a deity.

Then there's a little town called London. Like Copenhagen, the citizens also speak English, only sometimes the Danes are a little easier to understand.

To me New York has always been the excitement capital of the world, but you can't knock London. It has everything. There's gambling, if that's your bag, great theater, opera, ballet, fine music, wonderful shops, sensational places to eat and, to top it all, they're polite. To a guy like me, that's important. There's an air of elegance. You can still step into a London cab wearing your gray topper on Derby Day. I think I could live in London and be happy.

Maybe I could be happy anywhere the creature comforts are good and the ambience pleasant. Someday I must go to Paris, if only because one of my kinsmen, Comte Marie Edme Maurice de MacMahon, Marshal of France and Second President of the Third Republic, had a couple of Paris streets named after him. So many people have sent me snapshots of these streets that I have to see and walk in them.

Rome was where I found the warmth of humanity. The Romans make you feel that the reason Rome was not built in a day was because they wanted to get it just right for you. The years are in command. There are no streets named McMahon. But it's wonderful to stroll through history in a pair of brand-new Gucci loafers. It's the only way to go.

I must say I was disappointed in the catacombs which I'd heard so much about. But since I don't expect to wind up in them, what do I care?

I understand the Colosseum has been closed to tourists. When I was there, that gathering place for the Caesars and their salads and slaves and violin-playing emperors who raised the fire insurance rates, was nothing but a convention hall for old cats and whores.

There's a special kind of entertainment in Rome that goes on day and night. It always has an audience. It's free. It's exciting. It's funny. And it's all over town. It's watching the fight between two Roman drivers who have bumped their Fiats into each other but without doing any noticeable damage to either car. They scream. They gesture. They malign each other's ancestry and tell each other where to go and rot.

When they are joined by two Roman motorcycle cops the excitement grows. There is every reason to believe they're all going to murder one another. Then, all of a sudden, the two drivers get back in their cars. The two cops get back on their bikes. They all drive off. Next show around the corner in five minutes.

How could I help loving Rome? I was the guest of the head of the Italian Senate, Senator Torki. He entertained us royally, took us to the most marvelous restaurants. To paraphrase Mrs. Nixon's classic comment on the food in Peking, they have the best Italian food I've ever eaten in Rome.

And let me lay a hot tip on you chocolate lovers. You have never tasted chocolate anywhere in the world until you have had tartufo al cioccolato at Tre Scalini in the Piazza Navona. What a spot! How can you help loving a city where they close some of the streets and plazas so the restaurants can put out more tables where people can sit and eat and drink instead of dodging Ferraris?

Then came Capri. We drove south to Naples in a rented car. I found the city dirty and disappointing. Naples you can have. And to make things worse we missed the regularly scheduled hydrofoil for Capri. The ones they have there are bigger than any I've seen in the States. They go scooting across deep blue water like Greyhound buses on stilts. They have two decks, a buffet and bar, and they're the only way to get to Capri except by helicopter.

The idea of spending the night in Naples didn't thrill me so I scouted around the docks till I dug up the captain of a hydrofoil. For a few bucks more we had our own private transportation to Capri.

Capri must be the only place left in the world where you can get someone to carry your bags. Getting our gear off the boat and into a cab was a piece of cake. But the cab only takes you halfway to the hotel. The rest of the way you walk. They let you out in a huge parking lot full of enormous men. If they looked enormous to me, you better believe they're big. They're the guys who carry your goods the rest of the way up the hill to the hotel. Their performance is sensational. I don't care how much baggage you have, they handle it. They pile it on their backs, they take it under their arms, they carry it in their hands, and up they go. And walking with a heavy load on that cobblestone incline isn't easy. It's such a sensational act that you find yourself admiring their performance instead of the exceptionally pretty women who seem to be Capri's principal import.

What a time I had there! Everyplace I walked, and that's the only way you can get anyplace, I ran into people I knew. Could anything be more out of context than Ed Sullivan staring out at the little fishing boats with their colorful sails on the bright blue sea and saying, "What a show!" I said so, too, but by this time I'd given up admiring the porters and was looking at the long-legged, suntanned, bikinied beauties.

With my gregarious nature, I got along fine. The first café I walked into I found myself talking to a gal named Kathe Green, who recognized me. She is the daughter of Johnny Green, the American musician, conductor, and composer. Kathe was with a guy, she had a guitar, so we all did a little singing and had a jug of wine—but really a jug. The wine comes in a crockery liter. After a while the guitarist who works the spot came over and joined us. The party grew with the music. It was beautiful. A British lady who was closing her shop across the way joined our party and before long we were all planning a trip to the Blue Grotto, where I did a little scuba diving. Marvelous.

The next morning we all gathered again at the same café. We picked up a couple of other convivial souls and the party started all over again. Someone spoke of a restaurant that you could only get to by boat, so we hired one and went there. But the most interesting thing about that adventure was the guy who owned the boat.

Everybody called him Johnny American. I called him Johnny Hackensack because he told us that was his hometown. He was our skipper. It was so rough Johnny couldn't tie the boat up at the dock, so he let us each off, very carefully, then took the boat out about a hundred yards, threw down an anchor, and swam ashore to join us.

The restaurant was at the top of a mountain and, except for a thatched roof to protect you from the sun, it was all out in the open. I sat there with a glass of wine, enjoying myself, when a guy came up and asked me, "How's Pinky?"

Pinky, who is now married and has a family, was my secretary for several years. The guy who spoke to me knew her and, it turned out, we had mutual friends. Right then and there I decided the fella who said, "It's a small world" might have thought of it at the top of a mountain on the little Isle of Capri—a beautiful spot and a beautiful song.

GREEK TO ME

From my earliest classes in ancient history, I have come to be fascinated by what has been called the Golden Age of Greece, when Aristophanes, Plato, Aristotle, Socrates, Euripides, Euclid, and that bunch broke the code on science, poetry, mathematics, philosophy, literature, rhetoric, drama, architecture, and law. Everything we enjoy today I see as having been built on the basic blocks they gave us.

These were the men I admired, not the warriors of the world but the thinkers, and I related to them so strongly that I felt I'd been part of that scene if there is such a thing as reincarnation. Get a load of me strolling the streets of Athens with Aristophanes discussing his latest hit, *The Frogs*. For years I wanted to go to Athens, to stand there in the Parthenon and for a moment of dreams and inspiration feel myself a part of that great era.

But the great era I was part of saw the twilight of the Golden Age of radio and the dawning of television and I was so busy helping it dawn that I didn't have time to make the Athens scene. I'm a determined man, however, so when I saw my Hellenic dreams growing dimmer and dimmer, I found a surrogate to go to Athens as my ambassador. How did I know then that some years later Timex would do a circus show in Europe and I'd get to see Athens myself?

So when my daughter Claudia graduated from Syracuse University, I handed her a little model of a Pan Am plane. And I must say she was perplexed.

Whatever gift she might have expected, that wasn't it.

She'd worked very hard for her diploma and felt she'd advanced beyond the stage of a toy airplane.

"What am I supposed to do with this?" she asked.

"Look under it," I said.

She did and found an airline ticket.

"This is to Athens. That's in Greece."

"I'm not sending you to Athens, Georgia."

"But why should I go there? What'll I *do* there?"

I was a little hurt, disappointed at the reaction. Greece, clearly, meant nothing to her. I said, "Do anything you want."

"Suppose I don't like it there?"

"Come home. But you'll never know until you go there and find out."

Along with the round-trip airline ticket I threw in a Eurailpass for about a hundred thousand miles. Finally I said, "Stop anywhere you want on the way over. Stay anywhere as long as you please. Stop anywhere on the way back. All I want in exchange is that you go to the Parthenon at midnight and have a picture taken and send it to me."

My firstborn, my daughter, bathed in moonlight at the temple dedicated to Athena. It would have been beautiful. But you're not allowed to go to the Parthenon at midnight. She did, however, send me a photo taken in the golden Greek sunlight and it was great. I treasure it. But I treasure more that this daughter, this friend of mine, reluctant to make the trip I offered her, finally did it for me and took off from Kennedy Airport in New York one night at ten o'clock, alone, for Paris. She didn't know a soul there, didn't know the language, didn't even know why she was starting in France to go to Greece.

But it worked out, as things seem to have a way of doing with the McMahons. For two days she was over there entirely on her own. Then a girlfriend from college showed up and the outcome of the story is not only that she made the trip to Greece but that a new young woman was born.

She traveled all over. Went in the rain, all alone, to pay homage to those who perished in the fiery furnaces of Dachau. With such significant side pilgrimages along the way she finally wound up in Athens. She got a job with a Greek family as a mother's helper and taught English in a Greek school.

She traveled through Asia on a bus, the kind that stops wherever it happens to be at sundown. There the passengers spend the night in sleeping bags. She had adventures on a train to Calcutta and in India ranging from attempted rape to attempted marriage. She studied with two ancient gurus, one a hundred and six and one a hundred and eight, in the shadow of the Himalayas. And she came home after ten months a very different person and one I was very proud of.

All this is background for understanding my need to fly to Athens when I was on the Isle of Capri. It was only a hoot and a holler across the Ionian Sea. How could I resist?

It's a strange feeling to come home to a place you've never known before. That's the feeling I had, however, as I drove into Athens from the airport and got my first experience of déjà vu on seeing the Acropolis. For two days I hardly did anything but stand on the balcony outside my hotel room and stare at the Parthenon, the sun glaring down on it by day, the moon bathing it in beauty by night. Finally I climbed those ancient rocks and stood where I felt I'd stood before, with a conscious feeling of belonging. The whole concept, design, construction, and placement of those classic columns form a textbook on architecture that for centuries defied the ravages of time and war. Now those columns are faced with an unending battle against pollution and the legions of the seventeen-day tourists.

Is it any wonder that one of my corporations is called Parthenon Productions, another Delphi Productions?

Naturally I journeyed to visit the seat of the Oracle at Delphi because, heretical as it may seem, I know I couldn't learn all the wisdom of the world from Johnny Carson. I refer to a headline in the Los Angeles *Times* of January 10, 1974, which said, PHILOSOPHY FROM SOCRATES TO CARSON. It referred to a book that quotes Johnny, the great philosopher, as saying,

"You can always tell when it's autumn in Hollywood. They take in the green plastic plants and put out the brown plastic plants."

It's not easy to get to Delphi from Athens. It's nestled at the base of Mt. Parnassus and the road is winding and narrow, not very safe for the Cadillac in which we were driving. It belonged to a man I met named Tommy Pappus and who, as far as I was concerned, became Mr. Greece. He had a Coca-Cola franchise and owned service stations all over town with signs saying ESSO-PAPPUS. He knew his way around and it was in his car that we went to Delphi.

It's awe-inspiring. Just knowing the years it's been there is important for openers. You could still put on plays in the amphitheater and run games in the stadium. Yet, standing where the first Pythian Games were held to honor Apollo's triumph over the python, I was amazed that they only had seats on one side of the playing field. Smart as they were, they obviously had no head for business. Why not seats on the other side? Maybe not enough people cared about the games. Maybe with all their wisdom they didn't know how to build a place to accommodate enough people to get them off the nut. So much for Greek culture.

It was Tommy Pappus, the Greek lad from Boston, who got us into the Grande Britannia Hotel, one of the great hostelries of the world. And it was Tommy who showed us modern Athens, in the grand manner.

He took us to dinner in the magnificent dining room of the Grande Britannia, a room where they did things in the truly grand manner, but not grand enough for Tommy. As we progressed through the meal, which no one had ordered (things just came), I noticed that we were being served dishes in no way like those being served to any of the other guests in the dining room. Even the plates and flatware were different.

The reason for this was that everything was being prepared for us by Pappus' chefs in the kitchens of Pappus' suburban home and being brought down, course by course, in Pappus' limousines by Pappus' chauffeurs. Why didn't he just have us to his home? It's not the Greek way. He hadn't known us long enough.

It was a great meal. Lemons the size of grapefruits from Pappus' farm, tomatoes the likes of which you've never tasted, olive oil squeezed from olives grown on the Pappus trees, slices of Greek cheese that make my mouth water just to think of, lamb prepared as I have never tasted it before or since, and a Greek wine called *resinata*. It tasted as if it came right out of an Esso-Pappus pump. The Greeks love it. And they can have it. They also have some beautiful, light white wines almost as clear as water.

One popular brand has a label which you can read the reverse side of right through the contents of the bottle. What you read, if you can read Greek, is a list of the vitamins the wine contains. I don't know why that type of wine advertising hasn't hit the U.S.A.

When I started out for Delphi early one morning, in one of the Pappus Cadillacs, I asked the chauffeur to take me someplace in the country for breakfast, some place off the beaten track. It turned out to be in a little village where they'd never seen a Cadillac and seldom seen an American. At first there was some confusion and embarrassment about what to serve. But I asked for the wine of the province and whatever else they chose to bring. This made them happy and I was home free with a brunch of cold white wine, cheese, and a Greek salad with their wonderful tomatoes.

As we were leaving, I told the host we'd be back that way in time for lunch. You have to remember that all the meals in Greece are late. Dinner doesn't come on until about eleven at night. At two or three in the morning the open-air tables around Constitution Square are crowded with Greeks talking and sipping their ouzo. Then, at seven o'clock in the morning, I'd hear rush-hour noises and it was Greeks rushing to crowd onto buses in Constitution Square. I came to the conclusion that there were two shifts of Greeks, the ouzo drinkers and the bus riders.

I told my host I favored lamb and he brought out a whole side and asked me if any cut of that would do. And when he asked me how I wanted it prepared I told him to prepare it the way he would for his daughter's wedding.

I've found that the only way to eat well anywhere in the world is to leave all your eating habits at home. Don't walk into a Greek taverna and ask for a good, thick, rare steak. That's not their bag. They'll probably bring you something that you won't like because they didn't know how to fix it.

Take what they do best and learn. In Tokyo when I did that I wound up eating raw squid. I didn't like it but I tried it. That's how I got over the finicky eating habits I had picked up in boarding school. I was more finicky than Morris the cat in the TV cat-food commercial. Now I think I know the reason. What the school was serving was catfood.

On our trip back from Delphi after the marvelous lunch that had been prepared for us and took about two hours to eat, we were presented with a bottle of ouzo to sip on the way home. May I tell you, as an established drinker, when you sip ouzo you're doing some major sipping.

That night before catching my plane for home I sat on my balcony and stared at the Acropolis with the Parthenon all lit up, sipped my ouzo, ate about a million pistachio nuts, got very sentimental, and thought that maybe the Parthenon was looking back at me—all lit up.

WHAT ELSE IS NEW?

Anybody who's on television a lot gets all kinds of offers to engage in a variety of other audience-attracting activities—benefits, market openings, beauty contests, political rallies. How else could I ever have become President of the Alumni Association of Catholic University four years in a row?

That job had me hopping all over the country making speeches. It taught me a lot about the youth of America and also about how businessmen think. It also showed me I could handle myself in front of a grapefruit as well as a microphone. I found out I could get laughs as well as money. I learned I could deliver a eulogy.

Any time Pat O'Brien decides to abdicate as the Irish Georgie Jessel, I'm ready. I not only will travel, I have jokes, stories, tuxedo and, when things get real tough, I can sing a song. I made an album and people bought it. I've been involved in the Marine Corps Scholarship Fund to send deserving offspring of deceased Marines to prep school and college. As a member of their boards of directors I've worked for the Bedside Network and the Sickle Cell Anemia Foundation. And all this has been part of an ongoing learning process that opened my eyes to the fact that I might be able to do a nightclub act, if I tried. So I tried.

It was a good try. Two weeks at the Tropicana in Vegas got me a contract for four more dates at a higher stipend. That resulted in a lot of other offers.

The nightclub operators of the world know that their peers in Vegas don't book bad acts—more than once.

310

A television personality can fill his summer hiatus—when he has one—doing summer stock. I did some of that, too, with the Kenley Players in Warren, Ohio, where I did *Wildcat* with Carmel Quinn. It was the musical that Lucille Ball starred in on Broadway. I played *Anniversary Waltz* in Paramus, New Jersey, and had the pleasure of kicking in a television tube every night. But I really can't do stock because I'm on the air all year round. This makes any run at all impossible unless the theater is within quick commuting distance of Burbank, California.

Things theatrical first got rolling for me one evening in New York when I went to see Alan King, who produced and was starring in *The Impossible Years* on Broadway. He'd been on *The Tonight Show* many times so I went backstage after the show. We chatted while he got dressed and then we went out to a few spots. Suddenly, between drinks, Alan said, "You know something, Ed, this play I'm in would be great for you."

"You know something, Alan," I said, "I was just thinking the same thing. And it's nice to hear it from you."

"I'll tell you why you're hearing it from me," he said. "I have a week commitment at the Diplomat in Miami Beach. Why don't you step into my part for that week?" And the deal was set right then and there.

I worked very hard to get up in the part and when Alan went south, I became a Broadway star, and while they have yet to put a bronze memorial plaque on the theater where I made my debut, I keep hoping.

That week in *The Impossible Years* proved to be the trigger that started a career in films that I hope to make a long and gratifying one. So I have no regrets that at the end of the run I threw a little cast party that cost me $1,200. While I realized at the time that that was the sort of party a star gave at the end of a long run, I was also aware that for me it was the longest run on Broadway I'd ever had.

The salary wasn't bad for Broadway, $1,750 a week, so I cleared $550. Well, I wouldn't say I exactly cleared it. There was my agent, my business manager, and the clothes I bought for the part. But it was also the window through which a man named Monroe Sachson, first got a glimpse of my "thespiantics."

He did not attend my performance in *The Impossible Years* of his own free will, or with any intentions of scouting talent for the picture he had in preparation. In fact, he has since told me, he fought every inch of the way against coming, demanding to know, as he was dragged into the theater, "Who the hell is Ed McMahon? What can he do? Why should I waste my time seeing him?" and a few other similarly flattering remarks. But when the show was over he came back and told me how much he enjoyed watching me work and all the other flattering things that show biz people say to each other after a performance. I thought to myself, "That was nice." Those were my very words. And I promptly forgot the whole matter because, while he didn't know anything about me when he came into the theater, I didn't know anything about him when he left.

Then one day, over a year later, much to my astonishment Monroe got in touch with me because he saw me as one of the characters in a picture he was about to produce. It dealt with a couple of young thugs terrorizing the people in a subway car late at night. It was called *The Incident* and it won several awards in the world market. I was nominated as the Best New Actor at the Mar Del Plada Film Festival (there's a first) and got critical acclaim in many places including the United States of America.

But, in spite of a good press, *The Incident* never got up a head of box office steam. It just chugged along to semiobscurity, possibly because it had racial overtones a little before the public was ready to understand that sort of thing. It even forecast events that actually happened a few years later. It caused riots in some theaters. Three years later they began rating it as a classic. It introduced a guy named Beau Bridges as well as Marty Sheehan and Tony Musante. But best of all I got a friend out of it. Monroe Sachson and I became buddies and he made a promise that everytime he did a film, I'd have a part—if I wanted it. But I get ahead of my story.

What happened was, when Monroe sent me the script for *The Incident,* I saw a part that I thought would be better for me than the one he had in mind. So I asked myself, "What should I do?" Here's a film producer offering a television announcer a dramatic part in a picture. Should I argue that I thought another part would be better for me or shut up and grab what's offered? Finally I decided that no shot was right unless I thought it was the right shot.

The part Monroe had for me, the one Mike Kellem eventually played, was that of a great big Mr. Milquetoast, emasculated by his wife, played by Jan Sterling. Maybe I would have done it okay. But the character I saw myself doing was the guy with a wife and kid who, in his every action, promised to be a Mr. Everyman. He was the one the audience expected to finish up as a hero. But just as things go in real life, this didn't happen. Mr. Everyman didn't want to get involved.

I spent a lot of time with Monroe giving him my analysis of the character, and when I was finished, he told me later, he said to himself, "This guy could become a hell of an actor. I'll let him play any part he wants."

To prove that I could handle the part I wanted, I worked very hard at it. Now every time Monroe plans a picture he offers me a job. Sometimes I can't take it because of other commitments. But I finally got to do another picture for him, a sequel to *Slaughter,* called *Slaughter's Big Rip-Off,* in which I play a heavy, a Godfather type, the head of a California syndicate.

I felt taking an off-beat part like that was inherent in the learning process, a step in the direction of the parts I've always wanted to do, the kind Paul Douglas did.

One evening on *The Tonight Show,* Garson Kanin, who wrote *Born Yesterday,* which gave Paul Douglas his start, told how Paul walked into his office and said, "I want this part."

Gar, who knew Douglas only as a radio announcer, said, "What makes you think you can handle it?"

"Because," said Douglas, "I'm the best damned actor in the country."

"Then," said Kanin, "he went on to prove it."

He then asked if I was available to play the Paul Douglas part in *Born Yesterday* for seven weeks in Kansas City and then take the show on the road and into New York.

It would have been my dream come true but I couldn't get the time off, away from *The Tonight Show* and all the other things I'm contracted to do regularly.

This is the same problem I have about making films. I have been offered jobs in a lot of them. But all producers aren't like Monroe, who is willing to shoot around me, schedule shots so they won't conflict with my other commitments. To a producer, time is money and it's tough to have to tell the director, who doesn't want to be told anything, anyway, "If we don't get this take by three o'clock we lose Ed." He's apt to say, "Let's lose Ed permanently." Only the biggest stars are given the kind of consideration Monroe has given me and I appreciate it.

Maybe I'm just a guy "who cain't say no." Maybe I should decide on one thing and do just that. Become an actor. Go on the road for a year in a show like *Guys and Dolls* or *Music Man.* Become a clown and see what would happen if I took a one-ring, European-type circus on the road through America's heartland. Possibly I should quit *The Tonight Show* and concentrate on making films. But the same thing that has gotten me into all the different facets of show business that I've tried is the same thing that keeps me on *The Tonight Show*—curiosity. What else could I do and be sure of something different happening every performance? And, actually, there's no way I could quit Johnny. The NBC contract could probably be negotiated. But there's another thing. When we first started together I told Johnny, "I'll be with you as long as you want me." So John's the one who has to make the decision. Until that time comes, I'll continue. I'm also happy that Joey Bishop, Shecky Greene, John Davidson, David Steinberg, Della Reese, Vicki Carr, Sammy Davis, McClean Stevenson, and even Jerry Lewis with all his savvy, they all tell me they look on me as a sort of defensive blocker waiting to help them get out of trouble when I see it coming. And after years of sitting there on the sofa watching for it, I've learned to see it coming quickly enough to be able to head it off most of the time.

Of course, now that Johnny's married, we don't see each other after hours as much as we used to. I once mentioned on the show that we made a date one night—just like old times—to go out on the town and have a ball. We had a nice dinner, a bottle of wine, and at nine forty-five we were both in the parking lot getting into our cars to go home. Doesn't that sound like a big night on the town?

But I'll say this, Johnny and I have the kind of friendship every man would like to share with another man, the friendship that means you always have someone to depend on.

. . . AND IN CONCLUSION

Of all the things I do, there's one thing I really love and don't have enough time for—flying.

Often when I'm in some private plane the pilot will let me fly "right-hand side"—that's the co-pilot's position. I try to keep up my minimum so that I could pass an exam anytime but I never give myself enough spare time.

Occasionally I've been flying in a commercial plane with someone who is nervous and I've bragged to give him a little courage, "If anything happened to those guys up front I could fly this aircraft." It's true, theoretically. I could probably land a 747. But I'd hate to have to try it. I'd need an awful lot of help from those cats in the tower.

Funny how telling people I could land the plane seems to calm them. Apparently the feeling is, "If this guy can do it, it can't be too tough, and if it's that easy, why am I worried?"

I've even toyed with the idea of buying my own plane but I've been talked out of it by my business manager, Lester Blank. He said, "You want a plane so you can fly more in your spare time, right?"

I said, "That's right."

He said, "What spare time?"

When the gas shortage came along he just chuckled and said, "Now what would you be doing with that plane you wanted?"

"It would make a nice planter," I said. But everybody like me should have a friend and adviser like Lester to take care of his money and keep him on the right track. Because if you do enough different things, as I do, you begin to accumulate dough. It comes in from here and there and what do you do with it?

I did some very foolish things before Lester and I hooked up. In some I was taken, in others, things didn't just work out as planned. Sometimes it was because I'm not temperamentally suited to "doing business." I find it hard to say no to people, particularly friends. And this can get you into bad financial trouble.

Also, I have no patience with incompetence when I see it. I get irritated, sarcastic—my father was great in that department—and that has gotten me into a lot of trouble. I've finally learned to bite my tongue to keep from telling off people who aren't doing things sensibly. The only trouble with that is that someday I may wind up with no tongue.

I'm extremely punctual and I expect everyone else to be. I'm constantly being forced to remind people of that ironic little saying, "It does you no good to be on time because there's never anyone there to appreciate it." When I get a call for rehearsal, for instance, and then have to hang around waiting for hours till they get to my part, I become very annoyed. I can't work. It is, at the very least, unprofessional.

People have told me that Bing Crosby was never late for a rehearsal or for an appointment. The same goes for other top people like John Wayne and Frank Sinatra. The best way to get where you're going is by being on time to catch the train, by doing things right.

If you can't do something right, find it out quickly and get someone to do it for you. Someone to help you. That's why I have Lester.

Everytime I see an oil well pumping away, I wish it were pumping for me. Just a few barrels a day is all I need. But I know, if left to my own devices, I'd own a lot of them—all dry.

Once I sunk a bundle in an outfit that was making a novelty

"fun" item. Just as we got into production, money became tight and people got to be more interested in food than fun and we went broke. No fun.

Now Lester puts me only into basic things, things on which the economy of the country rests, things that may fluctuate but never go out of style.

Professional people like doctors, dentists, architects, even businessmen need help, certainly actors and writers all want to make their money work for them. A few may be smart enough to do it alone. An ophthalmologist named Jules Stein played the violin in dance bands and built MCA. But most people need someone to give them hardnosed advice and see that they heed it.

So that's where I am as I write this. Where I'll be in the months it takes to move a manuscript out of the typewriter and into the bookstores, I have no way of knowing.

This I do know. I have never knowingly disappointed anyone who had faith in me, nor have I ever taken advantage of anyone who trusted me.

I set a course at an early age and I have pursued no other. There have been detours and side trips. Sometimes I have retreated when I thought I was advancing.

I always managed to get back on course although the actual goal has never been fully defined, but I'll know it when I reach it. I am fearful, however, that when I reach it, it may not be as glamorous and desirable as I thought it would be.

Should that happen it will be too late for anger and remorse. I plotted the course. I steered by it and I will have no one to blame but myself if I founder.

With those words, I'm happy to hold the helm steady as she goes.

EPILOGUE

The view from the bridge shows nothing but clear sailing ahead. The kids are all doing well, constantly searching for whatever will make their own lives most meaningful, sometimes running into snags along the way that require a phone call or a visit to Dad. And that's fine with me . . . I wouldn't have it any other way.

As for me, to put it in the language of today, well, I just keep on truckin'! Personal appearances and my nightclub act take up most of my spare time. But I like it that way. It's the nature of this wonderful business that I'm in that brings me to all the cities, and puts me in touch with all the people in this country that I would otherwise probably never get to know.

The most beautiful example of this is the lovely lady from Houston, Texas, Victoria Valentine, who will, this spring, become my wife.

And with Victoria at my side and as long as I'm able to push Johnny Carson out onstage in a wheelchair and keep him awake long enough to hear me say, "Heeeeere's Johnny," the future will indeed be very bright.